# Urban Systems: Strategies for Regulation

# Urban Systems:
## Strategies for Regulation

A COMPARISON OF POLICIES IN BRITAIN,
SWEDEN, AUSTRALIA, AND CANADA

L. S. BOURNE

CLARENDON PRESS · OXFORD
1975

*Oxford University Press, Ely House, London W. 1*

GLASGOW  NEW YORK  TORONTO  MELBOURNE  WELLINGTON
CAPE TOWN  IBADAN  NAIROBI  DAR ES SALAAM  LUSAKA  ADDIS ABABA
DELHI  BOMBAY  CALCUTTA  MADRAS  KARACHI  LAHORE  DACCA
KUALA LUMPUR  SINGAPORE  HONG KONG  TOKYO


CASEBOUND ISBN 0 19 874054 9
PAPERBACK  ISBN 0 19 874055 7


© OXFORD UNIVERSITY PRESS 1975

Text set in 11/12 pt. Photon Imprint, printed by photolithography, and bound in Great Britain at The Pitman Press, Bath

To My Parents

# Preface

National development planning in most western countries has been largely concerned with ameliorative problem-solving. It has been a response to rapid population and economic growth, massive social change, and to the unequal impact of technological innovations. Regional planning more specifically has traditionally attempted to influence the geographic distribution and functioning of these same phenomena, and urban planning has sought to contain the consequences they generate through direct and indirect means at the local level. The processes, the issues, and the planning response vary from country to country, and tend to shift, often dramatically, from time to time. There are now signs, however, that more consistent, comprehensive, and longer-term strategies for directing the form of national development are beginning to emerge.

This is a study of one aspect of this emerging process—the formulation of strategies for regulating urbanization at the national (and regional) level. It is a review and comparison of urban policy experience in four countries, Australia, Canada, the United Kingdom, and Sweden, and an attempt to assess the lessons that might be inferred from this experience. The unifying theme in the comparison is the concept of an urban system. This concept implies that cities in a country form an integrated system, or more appropriately a set of interlocking subsystems, through the transmission of economic impulses, the diffusion of innovations, and the movement of populations. Increasingly economic growth is articulated in and through the system of cities and this system in turn defines the scale and direction of growth in terms of flows of information, innovations, and ideas in that country. The urban system concept is used here both as a framework within which to organize and evaluate recent policy developments in each country and as a basis for identifying needs and priorities for future research and policy evolution.

The review is not intended as a detailed account of political or planning practices nor as an inventory of urban planning legislation. Such inventories are available elsewhere. Instead, it seeks to catch the principal directions of thinking in both policy and research in attempting to control urbanization and regulate its social and spatial consequences.

Emphasis is given to the particular strategies which define policy thinking and implementation. The use of the term strategy is intentional—it is meant to encompass the framework of ideas, theoretical constructs, and information which lies behind the formulation of explicit policies and decisions on their application.

The four case studies were selected with several objectives in mind. Canada, the author's home base, provides an example of fledgling attempts to influence urbanization in a young and diverse country of vast area, small population, and rapid urban growth. As such, it may offer useful insights into the problems of planning in a complex social, geographical, and political situation. Sometimes, although not frequently, newer countries such as Canada can introduce innovations more easily than societies with longer historical traditions. One of the closest parallels to Canada, in political structure, geography, and socio-economic environment, is Australia. While both countries have recently initiated a search for means to influence and redirect their national urban future, in neither case have the means and the objectives been specified. This review, then, may be timely in both contexts.

Britain and Sweden, on the other hand, represent two textbook examples of planned urban environments. Their success in containing and ordering urban growth on the local level is now well known. Yet an evaluation of their much more recent experience in national urban planning should add to existing knowledge because it is recent, but more important because it derives from a different comparative perspective and draws on different concepts. Moreover, both countries are re-examining their planning machinery in considering the appropriateness of a formal strategy for national urbanization. Only Sweden has actually adopted such a strategy, and this very recently. Both countries also offer some direct comparisons with Canada and Australia: Britain in terms of political and social structures; Sweden in terms of geographic size, the historical pattern and rapidity of urbanization, and in the wide range of alternative urban futures which are considered to be possible.

The discussions on each country are structured around the same general topics. While this is only possible and appropriate to a certain extent, as the histories, problems, and policies of each differ so widely, the benefits of some standardization of the approach to assist the comparative review are thought to outweigh the possible distortions and injustices to the uniqueness of each national situation. These topics in sequence include the following: brief comments on the social, geographical, and political background to urbanization; a review of the major urban issues, primarily those expressed at the national and regional levels; the policy response to these issues, with selective examples of policy application; and an assessment of the relative success of these policies. Finally, in each section an attempt is made to summarize the principal directions of recent thinking on the regulation of urban and spatial systems. The concluding sections draw out general lessons and pose inferences from the comparative review and then in conclusion briefly speculate on the potential for new policy innovations.

My interest in undertaking such a study developed over the last several years. During that time I was involved in research on the changing patterns and future forms of urbanization in Canada, with primary concern for urban development in the Central Canada heartland (the provinces of Ontario and Quebec). From this research derived the present emphasis on urban systems concepts both as an organizing framework for research in general and specifically as a basis on which to undertake forecasts of future patterns of urbanization and their consequences. As the study neared completion the opportunity to carry the analysis one step further in an attempt to identify national policy implications emanating from the research, became increasing apparent. To do so adequately, it seemed, necessitated a broader perspective than that based only on North American and Canadian experience. This perspective must take into consideration the parallel experiences of other western countries—either those which already had made advances in shaping national urban development patterns (such as Britain or Sweden), or those which provided a reasonably productive basis for comparison in terms of the development parallels noted above, such as between Canada, Sweden, and Australia.

This volume is a result of a year's effort in this direction. The basic materials for the study were prepared between August 1972 and September 1973 while I was on sabbatical leave from the University of Toronto and resident in Australia, Britain, and Sweden. A leave fellowship was granted for that year by the Canada Council, with additional assistance for research and travel provided by the Ministry of State for Urban Affairs (Ottawa). This support is gratefully acknowledged.

While on sabbatical leave I was in residence at two universities: Monash University in Clayton, Victoria, Australia; and at the London School of Economics and Political Science (LSE). I would like to extend my appreciation to these two institutions, and particularly to the Departments of Geography and their convenors—Professors M. I.

Logan and M. J. Wise respectively—for their hospitality, open access to departmental services and facilities, and, most important, for providing a stimulating academic environment. Excellent cartographic services were also provided by the Departments of Geography at LSE, the University of Toronto and the Clarendon Press.

In each country a number of individuals and institutions provided additional and invaluable assistance. In Australia, the Australian Institute of Urban Studies in Canberra under its Director, Derek Cartwright, was most helpful in arranging interviews in the Australian capital and throughout the Commonwealth. In Sweden, Professor Olof Wärneryd then of the Department of Geography in Göteborg University, who at that time was in residence at Nordplan in Stockholm, acted as co-ordinator for my visit. Numerous others in Sweden, including Sture Öberg, Lars Nördstrom, and Professor Torsten Hägerstrand, were most generous in terms of their time and information. In Britain, where I spent the greater part of the year, there are far too many people to mention individually, and most have had more personal expressions of my thanks. However, John Goddard deserves specific mention. His assistance was immensely important, both as a source of contacts as well as stimulating ideas. Ian Jackson in the Ministry of State for Urban Affairs in Ottawa acted in an administrative role. His encouragement and direction were most helpful. Finally, special thanks go to Bev Thompson in the Centre for Urban and Community Studies at the University of Toronto who painstakingly typed an excellent final draft.

Many friends and colleagues read and commented on all or portions of the manuscript in draft form: Brian Berry, Hans Blumenfeld, John Britton, Derek Cartwright, Derek Diamond, J. S. Dupré, R. C. Gates, John Goddard, Torsten Hägerstrand, Peter Hall, Ron Johnston, Mal Logan, Bill Michelson, Sture Öberg, D. Michael Ray, Jim Simmons, Jacob Spelt, Pat Troy, and Olof Wärneryd. In addition, reviewers of the prepublication draft provided numerous substantive suggestions for revision, and the Editorial Staff of the Clarendon Press provided encouragement and help.

As usual, I should stress that the views and opinions expressed in the text do not necessarily represent those of the supporting bodies or any of the reviewers. Although many of the reviewers' comments have been incorporated, all errors, misinterpretations, and other failings remain my responsibility alone.

The book is dedicated to my parents, for their long-standing support and interest. Closer to home, completion of the book depended most directly on assistance and inspiration from my wife Paula, and the good behaviour of our infant son David, who travelled around the world with me while I prepared the study.

Toronto,                                                                                      L.S.B.
June 1974

# Contents

# List of Figures

# List of Tables

Systems of course have been studied for centuries, but something new has been added. Until recently scientists and engineers tended to treat systems as complexes whose output could be expressed as a simple function of the outputs of the component parts. As a consequence, systems were designed from the inside out. Increasingly researchers have come to deal with systems whose output cannot be expressed as a simple function of component outputs and it has become more productive to treat them holistically and to design them from the outside in.

R. ACKOFF (1959)

# SECTION I

# Introduction

AMONG the many consequences of the rapidity of social change in post-war years has been an accelerated interest in urban problems and development policies. Some of this interest has centred on the national level of responsibility in urban affairs and on the merits of a national perspective in controlling urban growth.[1] Most major developed countries and many in the Third World have by now initiated efforts to assess the conditions of their urban body politic: to chart its growth and spread, to measure the quality of living and working environments, and to devise policies for treating the consequences of continued urbanization. In the search for solutions observers in each country have often sought insights and assistance through a comparison of their urban experiences with those of other countries. This volume is intended as a contribution to that search and to a learning process which may assist in the clarification of problems and policy alternatives.

## 1.1. THE SOCIAL CONTEXT

Several factors have converged in increasing the interest of governments, researchers, the media, and, more importantly, the general public in regulating urban growth. Public interest has been in large part a reaction to rapid change and the insecurity it brings, rather than growth *per se*, and to increasing city size and complexity. Government involvement is more belated. Quoting Rodwin's (1970) preconditions, before governments will take an active interest in any problem area, such problems must be perceived as problems and they must

---

[1] In approaching a massively complex topic such as urban growth the author has frequently found it is useful to fall back on Boulding's (1953) classic study on the principles of growth and its recent extensions (Boulding, 1970). Briefly, he differentiates three types of growth: (1) simple growth—a physical increase in the size of the system under study; (2) population growth—changes in the demographic character, that is the vertical stratification, of that system; and (3) structural growth, the internal reorganization of parts within the system and changes in the relationships between those parts. Simple growth almost inevitably implies structural growth, whereas the latter may occur without the former. This important point is often overlooked in the current debate on urban growth.

appear capable of solution by political means. On the one hand, urban problems have become more economically real, more socially visible, and certainly more politically sensitive during the post-war years. On the other hand, the relative success of some countries in shaping their urban futures has had the effect of stimulating other countries to pursue more actively solutions to their own problems. What are these problems and what have been the policy responses? Subsequent political action in the urban policy sphere must also be seen as part of a broader trend toward an awareness in capitalist countries of the need for more comprehensive social and economic planning at the national level.

Recent governmental initiatives in urban affairs in most western countries have been largely implicit and indirect, often operating through policies and programmes which are not urban in name or design. Explicit urban policies, when they have appeared, generally represent direct extensions of a long-standing government interest in two problem areas—regional economic development and urban land-use planning. Most such problems boil down to questions of distribution, that is malfunctions, or simply the non-functioning, of processes which allocate society's resources to social groups and to regions. The latter are usually associated with urban and/or regional differences in growth rates, income, employment opportunities, housing, public services, and the like. It has been extensively argued in the literature that such disparities represent a direct source of social injustice, a misallocation of national resources, a measure of structural inefficiency in the economic order, and, in some instances, pose a direct threat to national unity (Alonso, 1968b; Robinson, 1969; Jakobson and Prakash, 1971; Hansen, 1972; European Cultural Foundation, 1972; Elkins, 1973; Smith, 1973). What is surprising is not that such disparities exist, since they are to some degree inevitable, particularly during periods of rapid economic growth, but that governments and researchers were so long in recognizing their importance and so much longer in beginning to assess their implications (Brewis, 1970; Chisholm and Manners, 1971; Friedmann, 1973; Cameron and Wingo, 1973; O.E.C.D., 1973d).

Even more surprising has been the belated linking of these problems of the inequitable distribution of wealth and social opportunities to the processes of urbanization and the ways these processes shape national development (Hägerstrand, 1972; U.S. National Academy of Sciences, 1972). The argument developed throughout this book is that a comprehensive perspective on urbanization is essential to national planning. Urbanization is viewed here primarily through the national urban system and its various regional subsystems. This perspective provides one critical component in a policy framework designed to influence the structure and geographic distribution of urban development. Regulating urban systems, and shaping the consequences of redistributive mechanisms operating through those systems, is also a means of achieving greater equality in society as a whole.

## 1.2. OBJECTIVES

Although many aspects of the complex processes of urbanization and of urban development strategies could be treated in this book, the present review must be limited in scope if it is to be worthwhile. The principal objective is both descriptive and perspective. It is an attempt to define and evaluate the current state of policy, research, social thinking and attitudes on the problem of regulating urban systems in four different countries—Australia, Canada, Sweden, and the United Kingdom. How have these countries approached the question of regulating urban growth? How would the question be approached in terms of urban systems concepts? The latter objective, of course, assumes the existence of cities as urban systems—a concept to be defined in more detail later—and it implies that such systems represent an identifiable social and economic problem of national political importance. This, too, will be elaborated upon somewhat later. It is anticipated that setting each nation's experience in a comparative context will assist constructively in identifying the important lessons which each contributes to improving our understanding of urbanization and urban growth.

The second objective involves a concentration on the spatial organization of urbanization. To what degree is the current state of policy, research, and social thinking, as noted above, cognizant of the geographic ordering of the nation's economy and of the urban system? Which components of this ordering are important? And what are the spatial consequences of current trends in urban development? In assessing recent policy developments, the discussion emphasizes hierarchical, structural, and growth properties of the urban system, with a view to isolating issues deriving from existing urban forms and to identifying policy alternatives. These are not trivial questions. Few studies in the literature of economic development and economic history are spatially sensitive; and many national urban problems can be interpreted as involving questions of allocating scarce resources. Those questions which are not geographical by nature usually have substantial spatial implications. It should be stressed, however, that those spatial inequalities resulting from such processes, whether regional or urban, are a subset of the larger problem of inequalities in society as a whole and cannot therefore be completely eradicated without a more equalitarian social structure.

The present study is very much a learning process—for the reader, particularly the beginning student, as much as it was for the author—rather than a completed package. Similarly, planning for economic and social development can also be considered a continuous process of social learning, as Dunn (1971) has argued. Equally, the current debate on the formulation and implementation of national urban policies is very much a learning process in political terms. Needless to say such policies are never formulated in a vacuum. They derive from a specific social environment and are set within a political system which provide limits on, as well as directives for, social change. Given this approach, then, the present volume leaves many questions unanswered and most assertions untested. Yet it may serve to stimulate interest in devising new ways of thinking about urban problems and of setting strategies for guiding national development.

## 1.3. THE URBAN CONTEXT: FOUR CASE STUDIES

The four countries under review were selected with several criteria in mind. Initially they were chosen as case studies because they represent two sets of comparative types, each with substantive implications for each other's urban experience, and with relevance specifically to the policy needs of emerging urban nations.[2] Australia and Canada, as examples of the latter, provide intriguing parallels as 'evolving' urban systems, both set within a federal political structure, which have developed in a largely 'unregulated' environment. The latter does not mean that urbanization has been totally out of control, although some may believe that to be so. Instead, it implies that controls have tended to be specific in design, largely uncoordinated in application, and limited in strength by prevailing conservative attitudes. In both countries a national perspective on urbanization has in historical terms been con-

---

[2] Other countries, the U.S. and West Germany for instance, could have been selected on the basis of similar arguments. These two at least share a federal system of government, and thus the difficulties of achieving national action on social issues such as urban growth. The U.S. however is well represented in the contemporary literature; and in the interests of time and space an attempt to be universal would simply add to the superficiality of the discussion. The four selected here represent a unique combination for comparative purposes, and may thereby provide insights not duplicated in previous research.

spicuous by its absence. Recently, however, both countries have entered the forum of debate in assessing their respective national urban futures.

The two attributes given above as reasons for selecting Australia and Canada as examples of 'evolving' and largely 'unregulated' urban systems, are in sharp contrast to the state of affairs prevailing in Sweden and the U.K. As most readers will agree, these two countries offer text-book examples of situations in which urban growth has for some years been under some degree of formal regulation and spatial containment (Hall *et al.*, 1973, Vol. 1). Consequently both provide scope for evaluating previous policy applications. Further, Britain offers a view into the problems and policy options of older and more 'mature' urban systems.[3]

Both countries also display parallels with the urban policy context in Canada and Australia: Britain through common cultural, political, and institutional origins; and Sweden through similar size, geography, and the patterning of urban and economic development. Yet Britain and Sweden are not passive members of this review. In fact they provide as expected the bulk of the policy material used for evaluation. And both have also initiated extensive reassessments of their own elaborate planning machinery, one component of which is a formal national strategy on urbanization. Neither as yet has tested such a strategy.

## 1.4. COMPARATIVE BACKGROUND STATISTICS

The four countries differ markedly on a number of statistical scales (Table 1.1). Most differences are obvious and need no elaboration here. What does emerge in and between the lines of Table 1.1, however, is an important part of the background conditions which appear in the urban policy discussions in each country. Within these statistics lie measures of the origins and definitions of many contemporary urban problems, and of constraints on their eventual solution. Differences in economic and population size, trade, growth rates, age structures, and degrees of urban and metropolitan population concentration are clear. So are differences in economic wealth and national independence, inflation, and unemployment. Each of these bears heavily on the scope for

---

[3] The term mature is used here in reference to urban systems in a rather general sense. It suggests a situation in which the urbanization process has been a prominent force in restructuring the economic and cultural landscape for some time and in which the pattern and hierarchy of cities have essentially filled in and integrated the nation's territory and remained stable for a similarily long period. Terms such as mature and stable of course are primarily relative measures—but in this case, comparing Britain with Australia, Canada, and Sweden, they make some sense.

## TABLE 1.1

### ECONOMIC, SOCIAL, AND URBAN INDICATORS: U.K., SWEDEN, AUSTRALIA, AND CANADA

|  | U.K.[1] | Sweden | Australia | Canada |
|---|---|---|---|---|
| 1. Population 1960 (millions) | 52·6 | 7·5 | 10·2 | 17·9 |
| 1965 | 54·3 | 7·7 | 11·3 | 19·7 |
| 1971 | 55·7 | 8·1 | 12·7 | 21·6 |
| 2. % annual growth in population | | | | |
| 1960–5 | 0·65 | 0·70 | 2·00 | 1·90 |
| 1966–71 | 0·45 | 0·80 | 1·95 | 1·60 |
| 3. G.N.P.[2] 1960 (billion U.S. $ constant, 1963) | 78·90 | 14·52 | 16·77 | 34·90 |
| 1965 | 93·13 | 18·83 | 21·16 | 45·64 |
| 1971 | 105·82 | 22·86 | 28·61 | 60·04 |
| 4. % annual change in G.N.P. | | | | |
| 1960–5 | 3·4 | 5·3 | 4·8 | 5·5 |
| 1966–71 | 2·2 | 3·9 | 5·3 | 4·5 |
| 5. G.N.P. per capita, 1971 | 1,900 | 2,825 | 2,250 | 2,770 |
| 6. Industrial production index, 1971 (1963 = 100) | 126 | 153 | — | 159 |
| 7. Wages index,[3] 1971 (1963 = 100) | 172 | 195 | 156 | 168 |
| 8. % unemployment level, 1971 | 3·2 | 1·2 | 1·6 | 6·4 |
| 9. Consumer price index, 1971 (1963 = 100) | 148 | 145 | 132 | 130 |
| 10. Foreign trade index, 1971 (exports *per capita* in U.S. $) | 33·5 | 76·5 | 34·2 | 68·2 |
| 11. Crude birth rate, 1970[4] (per 1,000 population) | 17·1 | 14·3 | 20·0 | 17·7 |
| 12. % population under 15 years | 23 | 21 | 29 | 33 |
| 13. Years required to double population[5] | 140 | 88 | 37 | 41 |
| 14. Infant mortality rate[6] | 18·8 | 12·9 | 18·3 | 22·0 |
| 15. % population urban[7] | 79·5 | 69·4 | 83·1 | 76·1 |

TABLE 1.1—*continued*

| | | | | |
|---|---|---|---|---|
| 16. No. of metropolitan areas (>1 million population) | 7 | 1 | 2 | 3 |
| 17. No. of urban areas (>250,000 population) | 29 | 3 | 6 | 12 |
| 18. No. of urban areas (>100,000 population) | 100[a] | 22[b] | 10[c] | 23[d] |
| 19. % population in largest centre (urban region) | 13·3 | 17·3 | 22·8 | 12·8 |
| 20. % population in three largest centres (regions) | 15·1 | 31·4 | 47·0 | 30·1 |
| 21. Median population forecast,[8] year 2000(1) (in millions) | 64·0 | 9·5 | 21·0 | 31·2 |
| 22. % growth rate forecast 1971—2000(1) | 15·0 | 17·3 | 65·4 | 44·4 |

Notes: [1] Includes England, Scotland, Wales, and Northern Ireland.
[2] Using 1972 current exchange rates, and definitions of each country of gross national (or domestic) product.
[3] Hourly rates, manufacturing, male employees.
[4] Or latest available year.
[5] Assuming current (1966–71) growth rates continue.
[6] Deaths under one year per 1,000 live births.
[7] Definitions of threshold size of an urban centre vary widely. See Davis (1972).
[8] Crude estimates derived from Commonwealth Bureau of Roads (Australia), Centre for Urban and Community Studies, University of Toronto, and Systems Research Group (Canada), Department of the Environment (U.K.), and Ministry of Labour and Housing (Sweden).
[a] Standard Metropolitan Labour Market Area (SMLA).
[b] Regions of Co-operating Communes.
[c] Principal Urban Areas, statistical divisions.
[d] Census Metropolitan Areas (CMA) and Oshawa–Whitby.

Sources: Varied, but including OECD and United Nations publications and those of the respective urban agencies in each country.

regulating the spatial distribution of urbanization and economic growth. The challenges of the future also vary, as is evident in the scale of population forecasts—from a 15 per cent increase in the U.K. to 65 per cent in Australia—for the rest of this century, and the estimated length of time necessary to double the present population. While all of the forecasts, given very recent population trends, are likely to be exaggerations, they do suggest differences in the degree of aggregate population growth and, therefore, of future urban development, anticipated by researchers and policy-makers alike. Other and more subtle differences require other measures of urban growth. Further reference will be made to these measures in following sections, primarily in the more detailed reviews on each of the four countries.[4]

## 1.5.  INTERNATIONAL RESEARCH CONTEXT

The now essentially universal debate on controlling urban growth—at regional, national, and even international levels—has lead to almost feverish research activity. Such activity has taken two principal directions: first, to document and understand the process of urbanization *per se*; and second, to identify policy strategies to deal with its consequences. The latter has included enumerations of problems and priorities, inventories of legislative instruments available, and in some instances assessments of the consequences of previous applications of these instruments. Some studies have gone further by attempting to assess the feasibility of attaining alternative futures.

A few examples of those studies being undertaken by international organizations at the time this volume was prepared will suffice to illustrate the extensive context for comparative urban policy research. In Europe, for instance, OECD has published a major review of regional location policy in member countries (1973b) and has also recently completed another study assessing the 'Policy Instruments for Influencing the Form and Structure of Urban Development and the Location and Distribution of Urban Growth' (1973c); the Centre for Area Development Research in Japan has completed an international comparative study of the problems of megalopolis; the European Cultural Foundation (1972 and 1973) is continuing its 'Plan Europe 2000' project, including a component studying future forms of urban development; and a working party of the European Free Trade Association (EFTA, 1973) has recently released a major study entitled 'New Patterns of Settlement: A Framework for Regional Development', with the intended objective of identifying measures to avoid an over-concentration of population and employment among its member countries. The World Bank (1972) has also completed an extensive overview of world urbanization and is continuing investigations of urban growth in selected countries. Unfortunately, most of this work is being done (or has been done) in isolation (if not in competition) and therefore tends to be redundant and non-cumulative.

---

[4]  For each country a selected bibliography on national urban research and policy is provided at the end of the text. General references are also given at the end of the text.

Research groups have been equally active in North America and Australasia. In the U.S. various presidential and congressional committees have been created in recent years to report on future population distributions, and the resulting social and policy implications of urban growth (Commission on Population Growth and the American Future, 1972; U.S. Domestic Council Committee, 1972). The President is now required to report to congress every two years on the state of national urban policy (Berry, 1973a and c). In Canada, as well as in Australia, governments have commissioned a range of reports on the current state of urban development (Lithwick, 1970; Science Council, 1971), on the quality of urban environments (MacNeill, 1971), and on changing population distributions (Australia, Department of Urban and Regional Development, 1973). This study has taken considerable stimulus and information from these research efforts, particularly in extracting descriptive materials on trends in urbanization and on the historical records of policy responses to urban problems.

## 1.6. STUDY DESIGN AND ORGANIZATION

This study seeks to identify the key issues, prominent attitudes, and current directions in urban policy thinking, and then attempts to compare and evaluate recent experience in controlling urbanization in the four countries selected for study. It is not a chronicle of political events nor an inventory of the evolution of specific policy instruments. These details are available elsewhere (Rodwin, 1970; Strong, 1971; ASPO, 1971; International Colloquium, 1971; Beckman and Langdon, 1972; World Bank, 1972; EFTA, 1973; OECD, 1973c). The emphasis is on macro-level urban systems, that is, the national and regional aggregates of cities in each country, and on distributional issues both spatial and hierarchical which flow from properties of those systems.

The organization of this book follows from the learning process approach identified above. The discussion is divided into six substantive sections, building on this general introduction. The following section (II) contains a brief description of urban system properties: their definition, conceptual bases, and behaviour; as well as their possible application as a framework for research and decision-making in urban policy. A brief assessment of trends in urban development and the spatial consequences of these trends concludes Section II and sets the stage for a general overview in Section III of the types of policy responses, decision-making styles, and planning approaches employed in regulating urbanization. The body of the comparative analysis, including the four case studies, is contained in Sections IV and V. Section IV reviews the national urban planning experience of Britain (4.1) and Sweden (4.2) while Section V examines the situation in the less regulated environments of Australia (5.1) and Canada (5.2). For each of the four case studies, attention is given to the background issues involved, the public policy response, specific policy innovations, and recent directions of thinking in planning activity at the national and regional level. Section VI undertakes to summarize the predominant trends and insights apparent from the comparative review, and then proposes frameworks for matching policy needs with the urban system and for assessing the preconditions of such policies. Section VII then speculates on future directions in the regulation of national urban systems.

While the presentation of materials in the sections on each country is generally consistent, the emphasis on individual topics is often different. This in part reflects the author's differing exposure to sources of information and to aspects of the policy debates in each country, and in part it reflects the timing of the review.[5] It also documents the fact that definitions of urban issues and of the range of policy options available to governments obviously vary widely between countries and over time in each country. What is relevant to broader issues of the potential for regulating urbanization also differs in each situation. The selection of topics in each country then reflects those which contribute most to a comparative review. Even a cursory glance at the literature suggests that the same socio-political conditions do not necessarily produce the same policy responses. Even the same responses do not by definition produce the same consequences.

An additional bias will no doubt appear in the interpretations due to the author's closer familiarity with the Canadian and North American urban environment. However, where implications are drawn from the comparison in the final two sections they are primarily directed toward general strategies for regulating urbanization based on urban system concepts, and toward what lessons all countries can learn from the experience of these four case studies. The interpretations nevertheless remain highly personal.

---

[5] In the rapidly changing arena of national policy the timing of any review is critical. A first draft of this volume was completed in September 1973, with revisions through May 1974. Developments since then, of course, are omitted.

# Urban Systems: Concepts and Empirical Background

THERE are numerous ways to approach the study of urbanization. These approaches differ in terms of the level of generalization at which one initiates the analyses and in terms of the fundamental conceptualization of the urbanization process. The latter underlies any assessment of current knowledge and tends to delineate the platform for policy debate. This section briefly examines the concept of the urban system, its definition and properties, and summarizes selected aggregate characteristics of urbanization in the four countries under study.

The conceptualization of urbanization proposed here as the basis of this review is that of the urban 'system'. Simply stated, this view holds that urbanization—the demographic, economic, and geographical changes involved in the shift of population from rural to urban—is in fact a process of system growth and structural transformation.[1] The cities and urban regions of a modern industrial economy constitute a set of interrelated subsystems nesting in a complex hierarchy of increasing scale upward from individual urban areas to a national urban system. With over three-quarters of the population and economic plant now resident in urban areas it goes without saying that the social and economic life of most western nations is vested in its cities and in the way these cities operate as an integrated system.

## 2.1. DEFINING URBAN SYSTEMS

Frustrating any attempt at regulating urbanization, whatever the level, is the simple fact that an adequate understanding of how these

[1] The complex relationships between national economic development and patterns of urbanization have still not been adequately assessed. In a recent paper, Lasuén (1973) provides a useful conceptualization which attempts to take account of both sectoral agglomeration as well as spatial concentrations. One important point made in conclusion is that policies aimed at regulating national economic growth can be used to achieve urban goals and that, in turn, urban regulatory policies can be used to achieve national economic goals. The former—urbanization policies—may be, at least in theory, the easiest to apply, but in the long run, he argues, may be the least productive in terms of changing the existing geography of concentration. This is a point worthy of further research and discussion.

systems operate has not been forthcoming. It is now standard practice to emphasize, as a recent new cities' conference in Canberra concluded, that 'Any major programme directed at the redistribution of urban populations must be intimately associated with a programme of research into the nature of the urban system and the distribution of growth among its various nodes.' In the meantime, however, while waiting for this research, we must proceed with the theoretical and analytical methods and knowledge now available (Thompson, 1972; Richardson, 1973a and b). Although a detailed discussion of the blossoming urban systems literature is beyond the scope of the present volume, a brief summary of some of the key arguments on the definition and operation of these systems, specifically as they affect regulatory questions, is in order.

We do know that economic growth in any given country is increasingly articulated through the nation's set of cities (Berry, 1964, 1972a, and 1973b). This articulation has led, in advanced western economies at least, to a particular type of urban system organization. This organization may be summarized as consisting of at least three levels:

(1) *a national system* dominated by metropolitan centres and characterized by a step-like size hierarchy, with the number of centres in each level increasing with decreasing population size in a regular fashion;

(2) nested within the national system are *regional sub-systems* of cities displaying a similar but less clearly differentiated hierarchical arrangement, usually organized about a single metropolitan centre, and in which city sizes are smaller over all and drop off more quickly than in (1) above as one moves down the hierarchy;

(3) contained within these subsystems are local or *daily urban systems* representing the life space of urban residents and which develop as the influence of each centre reaches out, absorbs, and reorganizes the adjacent territory. In a small country levels (2) and (3) may be difficult to differentiate, whereas in larger countries both of these levels may show further subdivision.

These systems are not easy to illustrate graphically. They are hierarchical in terms of city size, function performed, and the types of interaction which define the role of each urban centre within the larger system. They are also organized in spatial terms. Both the spatial and hierarchical dimensions are interrelated in numerous and complex ways, not all of which can be clearly demonstrated. Following a search of the literature for maps and charts suitable in a general introduction, a

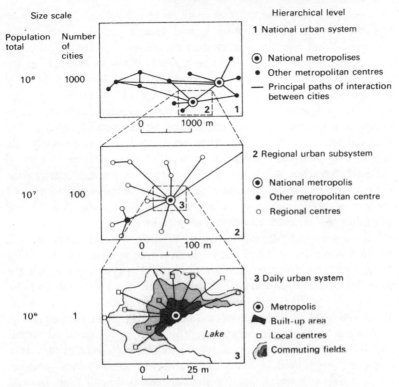

FIG. 2.1. Definitions of Urban Systems: Hierarchical and Spatial Levels (Schematic).

search which turned up illustrations either incomplete, too complicated, or unique to a given country, Figure 2.1 was drafted. It is a simple, obviously schematic, and highly generalized description of three (possible) levels of urban systems. The scales and labels are approximations, added to help clarify terminology in this volume. While the maps in Figure 2.1 are not specific to any nation, the layout of cities does bear some resemblance to the Canadian urban system.

The essence of this urban typology—and it is essentially a classification scheme—consists of all the linkages or paths of interconnection which are the functioning identities of a modern economy. Such linkages may take varying forms at different levels in the urban hierarchy. At the national level they may primarily involve economic impulses, exchanges of information and ideas, rather than actual movements of goods or people. At the regional level social service connections may dominate, or road traffic or telephone-call generation or regional hospital administration. In each case the linkages between the metropolis and regional centres may be one-way or reciprocal (two-way), and may be either direct or indirect (such as through an intermediate centre to or from the metropolis). At the local level the daily movement of commuters or shoppers or the distribution of social contacts may define the system. Over time these systems reach out to encompass ever larger proportions of the space economy and of the national territory. In so doing they have reordered the economy, life styles, and political boundaries as well as changed our images of national character. While the concern of this review is primarily with the first two levels, the important point is that all levels are interrelated aspects of the urbanization process and that policies designed to deal with this process must encompass all such levels.

The problem of defining the levels of such systems in reality still remains unresolved. While the national urban system may be easily recognized the differentiation of levels within that system is not. Nor are these levels likely to remain fixed over time. Rapid growth and the spread of urban life styles have blurred traditional boundaries between urban and rural, and even between small and large cities. Consequently, traditional attempts at boundary definitions, for individual urban regions and urban hierarchies, have been brought increasingly into question (Berry, 1968; Hall *et al.*, 1973; Simmons, 1974). Clearly no one set of definitions will suffice for all purposes, or for all time. Instead what is needed is a set of definitional constructs based on simple guidelines, each set nesting within a larger one, but capable of being extracted from that larger set. This would allow several definitions of what constitutes the levels and boundaries of the system under study to exist simultaneously. As a focus for policy the essential ingredient in this flexible approach is an over-all guiding construct which is easily understood, such as that given above, and the ability to retrieve whatever units are desired from the larger set.[2]

## 2.2. PROPERTIES OF URBAN SYSTEMS AS SOCIAL AND SPATIAL SYSTEMS

These systems have three basic dimensions: structural, spatial, and temporal. Structural refers to the hierarchial or vertical organization of

[2] One possible approach to this problem has been applied to the definition of a suitable study area for the study of urbanization in central Canada (see Bourne, MacKinnon, and Simmons, 1973; and Bourne *et al.*, 1974). In this example several definitions of urban regions were allowed to exist at the same time, but cumulating upward from the urban core through to the national urban system.

the national and regional economies which constitute a modern nation. But this organization also has a spatial expression which is, in turn, contained within the geometry of time. Unfortunately, for the analyst, all three dimensions are interrelated and the first two are continuously evolving functions of changes in each other. All too frequently we engage in studies, identify problems, and propose solutions to these problems within the narrow confines of one of these dimensions or in one sector of one dimension. We do not for instance have simply a national economy, we have a national 'space' economy (Institute of Economic Affairs, 1973), an economy which is obviously 'dynamic' in space and time. The nation's total social and political organization can be viewed in a similar perspective.

The renewed interest in geographical space in policy analysis derives from several sources, but primarily from a growing awareness of the critical contribution of spatial and environmental differences to national growth and well-being (see U.S. National Academy of Sciences, 1972). The operation of spatial allocation mechanisms in all aspects of urban life, hence the underlying causes of spatial disparities, are brought increasingly into the debate on policy problems and alternatives. Chisholm and Manners (1971), in a review of policy problems in the British economy, have suggested other generating factors in the trend to a more sensitive spatial and environmental perspective in the public sector. One is the long-term historical trend toward increased government involvement in social and economic life, and the recognition that this involvement has substantial 'spread' effects vertically through sectors of society as well as geographically across regions and cities. Another factor is the renewed interest in government reorganization—part of which is the redefinition of spatial administrative units and the reallocation of governmental responsibilities. A third factor is the question of environmental quality and the growing conviction that existing private mechanisms are insufficient or unwilling to compensate for negative externalities among urban activities and between users of urban space and environmental resources.[3]

The specific properties of an urban system which are of particular interest to questions of policy are, however, seldom explicitly identified in the literature. One of the most useful discussions of system properties in this regard is a book on social ecology by Emery and Trist (1972) subtitled

[3] While the concern with environmental quality derives largely from the local community or daily urban system level, environmental problems are increasingly seen as relevant to the planning of regional and national urban systems (see Berry and Horton, 1974).

'Contextual Appreciations of the Future in the Present'. The basis of their approach is the concept of a 'complex social system'—systems which do not submit easily to traditional methods of formal systems theory. The properties of these systems, listed below, provide a useful heuristic framework for filling out the conceptualization of what is meant by an urban system. Complex social systems may be characterized as:

(1) *adaptive* rather than mechanistic systems. That is, a given stimulus A does not automatically call forth a predetermined response B;

(2) *learning* systems, which are continually changing their centre of gravity, structure, and external linkages in a *cumulative* response to generative factors;

(3) systems which are *open* to influences deriving from their external (or contextual) environment;

(4) systems marked by extreme *interrelatedness* among the constituent parts—that is organized complexity;

(5) systems in which there is considerable *substitutability* or interchange of parts and functions.

Each of these properties has important implications when applied to the urban system context. The first two suggest that urban systems, like all social systems, are evolving in many and varied ways and that this evolution follows no simple mathematical or predictable fashion. The openness of urban systems, with their internal interdependencies, indicates that such systems must be analysed holistically and future states of development must be anticipated in relation to changes in the contextual environment. This environment may, in the urban example, consist of the national economy in aggregate, social values, or the international urban economy. Which is relevant depends on the specific purpose of each analysis. The fifth property illustrates why the detection of emerging trends in the structure of urban systems is extremely difficult and so frequently open to misinterpretation. Such trends are often masked by widespread substitution among components of the system, even though the over-all structure may appear to remain stable, which may continue until the trends are irreversibly advanced. This is one of the important arguments for continuous monitoring and research on the urbanization process.

## 2.3. REDISTRIBUTIVE MECHANISMS AND INEQUALITIES

It is relatively easy to document, as previously noted, that cities in advanced economies harbour the lion's share of national wealth and power and that these cities have become increasingly linked together in mutually adaptive systems (Urban Studies, 1972; Friedmann, 1972a and 1973). These attributes are probably most explicitly recognized and utilized in national planning in the Socialist world (Harris, 1970; Khorev and Khodzhayev, 1972). However, less is known about, hard data are more difficult to come by, and certainly policy thinking is less sensitive to the spatial ramifications of the growth and behaviour of these systems (Pred, 1973a and b; Simmons, 1974). Nevertheless, probably the simplest rationales for the approach taken here rest first on the premises that urban systems exist and that they are suitable objects of policy interest (Mesarovic and Reisman, 1972), and second on the importance of distributive mechanisms operating within the urban system and the effects of these mechanisms on growth and on inequalities in living conditions and social choice. While attempts to document the processes underlying these mechanisms (Forrester, 1969; Harvey, 1971; Wilson, 1972; Berry, 1972a, b, and c; Pred, 1973b; Lasuén, 1973; von Boventer, 1973) and to construct indices of the resulting inequalities (Hughes, 1972; Flax, 1972; Smith, 1973) have not been particularly successful to date, their increasing importance is generally not open to question. Nevertheless, there is a danger in constructing and interpreting such indices in a spatial context of overemphasizing place to place inequalities at the expense of person to person inequalities. These two patterns are not necessarily the same.[4]

Despite the lack of substantive evidence, most readers will agree that there are many distributive and redistributive mechanisms operating in modern society—capitalist and socialist—serving to allocate income, resources, goods, ideas, opportunities, and generally the elements of social well-being. Often these mechanisms are described in terms of whether they contribute to improving social equity or economic efficiency, neither, or more rarely both (Alonso, 1968a and b). Stated in this way, some of these mechanisms are considered to be more critical as potential policy problems than others. John Stuart Mill for example once argued that society has a greater responsibility for the distribution of wealth within the social order than it does for the operation of the

---

[4] The potential problem here, which Alonso (1968b) labels as a 'geographic fallacy', is not new to either research or policy, but is none the less important. The problem according to Alonso is whether equity should be directed to regions or to individuals; that is, in Winnick's (1966) terms, 'people prosperity vs place prosperity'. It is possible for the average income of a region to go down, while the incomes of every family increase. The difference is selective migration—people move, regions do not. The lesson in this debate is that spatial and aspatial policy measures must be undertaken together.

economic system as a whole (Daedalus, 1973). Of course the two responsibilities cannot be totally separated. Further, it can be argued that government has a particularly central role to play in delimiting the spatial expression of these mechanisms since political representation is territorially based and because national unity questions come into play.

The range and complexity of these distributional mechanisms has defied simple analytical evaluations. One widely debated example, that of interurban or interregional migration, may be noted briefly here. Who benefits and who suffers from such migration? Should policy encourage or discourage those movements directed toward the larger centres? That is, do we encourage people to move to where jobs are available or do we subsidize jobs to move to where people currently live? The well-being of three groups has to be considered: the migrants themselves, those people left behind, and those the migrants join in the larger centres.

Thompson (1972) has attempted schematically to represent some of the interrelationships between these three groups in the migration process (Figure 2.2), in reference to population size. Migration from rural areas (A) to small cities (B, C, and D) is argued to be in nearly everyone's best interest (in terms of real income), including those the migrants joined in the cities. On the one hand farming may become more efficient with fewer farmers to support, and on the other hand, the labour market of the receiving city should become more diversified and a larger population should improve the range and quality of urban services available to existing residents as well as to the migrants.

There is, however, a point of diminishing returns (as one moves along the graph from A to E). In the most widely publicized case, the movement from small towns (B) to the large metropolitan centres (E), Thompson argues that the migrants themselves may gain in income (well-being?), but those left behind and those already in the large cities will on balance lose. The small town will suffer because it has trouble even at its present size in providing sufficient labour opportunities and services. The big cities into which the migrants move may have little to gain from greater size but much to lose (in congestion costs, pollution, etc.). Thus, migration of this type may be of net benefit to the individual migrant but is not in the broad public interest. However the case is argued, it is clear that measures of the impact of migration must consider the welfare of all sectors of society, not just that of the participants.

Most of these mechanisms probably have their most serious and visible consequences at the local level, that is within the daily urban system

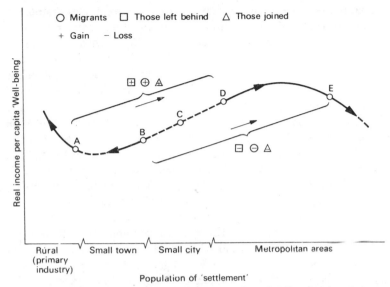

FIG. 2.2. Schematic Outline of Welfare Changes through Migration in relation to Population Size (from Thompson, 1972, 115).

and even within and between urban neighbourhoods, rather than at the national or regional level. Thus the first priority in urban policy must continue to be, as it has in the past, at the intra-urban level. The most immediate and substantial social benefits from planning, as Richardson (1972) has argued, will probably come from improvements in the spatial organization of the metropolitan system itself. Even so, what goes on at the intra-urban level is intimately interrelated to broader processes of growth and income redistribution in the nation as a whole. The above migration example is an excellent illustration. It still may be more efficient for the nation's economic system for the population to continue to concentrate in even larger urban centres. The costs of such concentration, increased congestion, traffic, service costs, and pollution, however, are borne locally. So the argument can be made both ways, and it is not clear how one defines the public interest. Nevertheless it is obvious that intra-urban growth and change cannot be fully understood independently of processes of urban and regional systems development, and that socio-economic problems at the local level cannot be effectively solved without influencing these broader processes in desired directions.

Nowhere is the operation and the impact of these redistributive mechanisms more evident and sensitive than in the complex example of poverty. Harvey (1971) and Pahl (1971), among others, have argued that in our society an individual's well-being is as much determined by where he lives as by his position in the contemporary social order. While not a new discovery, the recognition of this duality in social welfare has only recently come to play a part in the formulation of urban growth strategies (see Section 4.2 on Swedish policy). Harvey goes on to argue that research must explore and policy must attempt to regulate what he refers to as the 'fringe benefits' of the operation of the urban system. Pahl (1971) also suggests that the range in spatial inequality by region is probably greater in most western countries than is the range of inequality embedded in the occupational structure. Moreover, he suggests that the former appears to be widening more rapidly than the latter.

Whatever the relative balance in the source of inequalities, it is generally accepted that the failure to understand the redistributive mechanisms operating within the urban system inhibits, if not precludes, effective moves on the part of government to achieve greater equality in social welfare (Hockman and Paterson, 1974). A Marxist interpretation (Harvey, 1973) would of course deny that such equality is feasible within the capitalistic urban-economic system, but even if accepted this premise does not eliminate the political necessity of at least trying to reduce the differentials through direct government intervention. Even in Eastern Europe massive efforts to redistribute resources in favour of society's less fortunate have been frustrated in part by the redistributive effects of the urban system which appear to be creating new or deeper patterns of social inequality (Konrad and Szelényi, 1969).

## 2.4. GROWTH IN URBAN SYSTEMS

Growth within (rather than of) urban systems has been one of the principal factors in accentuating these redistributive mechanisms. Variations in growth among cities have been interpreted in various ways. One approach, taking the example of population distribution by city size, assumes that population growth is a stochastic random process following the law of 'proportionate effect'. That is, the relative growth of a city is a constant but random component of its present population size. Robson (1973), for example, has examined nineteenth-century urban population growth in Britain using this approach.

The population size of any given city in such frameworks is determined by its historical position (or rank) in both national and regional hierarchies, by its location with respect to the urban system as a whole, and by the size, density and occupational character of the population in the hinterland it serves. The first of these relationships is commonly expressed in terms of the logarithmically normal rank-size relationship; the latter in the formulations of central place hierarchies (Berry and Horton, 1970; Parr, 1973). While these two have recently been related mathematically (Berry, 1972b; Domanski, 1973), a comprehensive theory of size distributions has yet to emerge (Richardson, 1973a). The most likely size distribution of cities under this assumption, the lognormal rank-size, is that which achieves or tends towards an equilibrium or steady state, or what Wilson (1970) has called an 'entropy' maximizing state for the entire system, but in which individual cities may grow in a seemingly random and inconsistent fashion.

Other interpretations view growth within an urban system as a special case of the general theory of the diffusion of innovations (Pedersen, 1970; Berry, 1972b; Pred 1971 and 1973a; Brown, 1974). One such argument holds that the spatial and hierarchial variability in urban growth rates is a function of two processes: first, the 'filtering' of growth-inducing innovations down the urban-size distribution from the centres of innovation—the large metropolises—to increasingly smaller centres. Those smaller centres located in the nation's heartland receive the innovation first and then subsequently those in peripheral areas.[5] The second process is the 'spreading' of these innovations outward from each centre into its tributary area, but primarily within what has been called above the daily urban system (Figure 2.3).

Three possible explanations for this strictly hierarchical pattern have been suggested by Berry (1972b): (1) a sequential 'market-searching' process in which entrepreneurs seek new opportunities in a purposeful sequence from larger to smaller centres; (2) a 'trickle-down' process in which the larger centres spin off older and declining industries to smaller centres in pursuit of cheaper labour; and (3) an 'imitation effect' in which decision-makers in small cities follow the innovation adoptions made in the larger centres.

If one accepts these complementary notions, even in the very brief form presented here, then much of the concern over regional inequalities and urban system growth becomes a question of diffusion. The nature,

---

[5] The reasoning here is similar to that of the basic or export sector in the economic base of the city. Innovations received (or adopted) by a centre generate local impacts which stimulate growth in the non-basic sector. This growth in turn increases the probabilities of receiving (and eventually spawning) further innovations, setting in motion a cumulative process which solidifies the hierarchical differentiation of urban centres (see, for example, Robson, 1973).

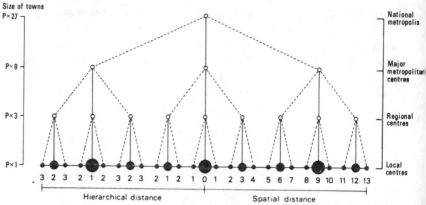

(a) Strict hierarchical diffusion, noting formal distances between towns in the size hierarchy and in spatial terms (adapted from Pederson, 1970).

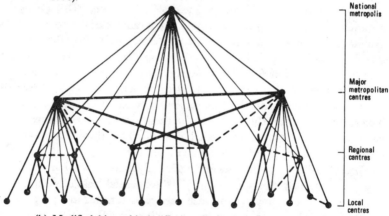

(b) Modified hierarchical diffusion, displaying numerous paths of interaction between cities of different levels (adapted from Pred and Törnqvist, 1973b).

FIG. 2.3. Two Models of Diffusion in an Urban System.

extent, and rate of diffusion between cities thus become potential policy variables, and the consequences of differential diffusion become the objects of that policy. For instance, it is held that the income-producing value or social benefit deriving from the introduction of any given innovation generally declines rapidly over time. Also, most innovations have a minimum threshold size of city necessary for adoption which, although the threshold may fall with technological change, effectively truncates the allocation of opportunities within that social system. Consequently, urban centres which are peripherally located and small will receive fewer benefits from innovations later, with relatively less economic and social impact, than the large metropolitan centres or those smaller centres located closer to the heartland of the urban system.

Pred (1973b) has recently provided a more extensive basis for interpreting urban systems growth in advanced economies in terms of interaction among cities and organizations. He argues that the most telling inadequacy of classical location theory is its neglect of information as a location factor (Isard, 1970). He then outlines a conceptual framework based on concepts of interurban information circulation and the multiplier effects of location decisions of large organizations. These two are considered to feed-back upon each other in determining the development pattern of systems of cities. The component processes of urban development in this approach may be summarized as:

(1) the generation, by the expansion of metropolitan-based activities, of non-local multiplier effects through the operation of large-scale organizations. By non-local is meant the intermetropolitan scale of interaction.

(2) the rapid diffusion of growth-inducing innovations from one large city to another, often skipping intermediate but smaller centres; and

(3) the resulting accumulation in a few large urban centres of operational decision-making functions, which in turn affects the distribution of job-providing organizational units. One important policy implication in looking at organizations in this manner, for example, is that efforts at decentralizing productive functions to periphery regions may result in a much larger growth in administrative jobs within the organization involved, jobs which increasingly are concentrated in the metropolitan cores.

This view focuses primarily on the role of major urban centres in capturing and redistributing urban growth, and is, in the words of the author, a 'big-city' model of urban system evolution. It is most relevant for our purposes here in that it emphasizes the increasing dominance of large cities, and the need for policy-oriented research to focus explicitly on the organizational structures of society, as well as the range of linkages within and between cities and the large organizations.[6]

[6] Interaction patterns within regional or daily urban systems may obviously be short-term or long-term, or anything in between, and in turn these patterns are intimately integrated with national growth and business cycles. Recently there has been considerable interest among geographers and regional scientists in the short-term fluctuations of economic growth and interaction within an urban system (see King, Casetti, and Jeffrey, 1969; Bassett and Haggett, 1971; Casetti, King, and Jeffrey, 1971; and Jeffrey, 1974, for examples). Most such analyses use variations in production or unemployment rates as surrogates for the transmission of economic impulses, and the time lags involved in urban interaction in general.

While Pred's framework has not been extensively tested (and due to its complexity may never be), the concepts are also useful here as a guide-line in identifying some of the practical problems facing policy-makers concerned with altering urban growth patterns and city-size distributions. Multiplier effects from economic growth and social change do not primarily diffuse down the urban hierarchy. Instead they are disseminated between cities of similar size, initially the large metropolitan centres, and then somewhat later filter down to smaller centres, producing a modified hierarchy of diffusion patterns (Figure 2.3b). In the case of innovations originating in smaller centres, they may move quickly up the hierarchy to the metropolitan centres and then outward across the nation, with little or no impact at the point of origin. The increasing scale, integration, and power of modern organizations (Galbraith, 1973), assure that this complex pattern of interaction dominated by large cities continues, and consequently that small centres are consistently left out.[7] From a policy viewpoint Pred concludes that government decisions on such issues as urban decentralization and regional balance must take into account the interdependence between organizations, and in particular the direction of information flows and the distribution of interurban multiplier effects, if they wish to succeed. Similarly, an urban system strategy must be cognizant of these same fundamental processes if the systems terminology is to mean anything in an applied policy sense.

## 2.5. OPTIMAL CITY SIZE AND URBAN POLICY

Another variant of the interest in urban growth and city size has been the continuing search for an 'optimal' size of city, or an optimal city-size distribution. This search has permeated much of the debate on urban policies as well as shaped the direction of basic research (Neutze, 1965; Parr, 1970; Mirrless, 1972; Richardson, 1972, 1973a and b; Mera, 1973). One rationale for this interest is obvious. As a policy issue, the specification of an optimum would provide a concrete objective and an explicit criterion for decisions in allocating scarce public resources. And it would lessen some of the political opposition to limiting the size of certain cities where it was considered necessary for other (but often undefined) reasons. In terms of research, the optimal city problem also

[7] In developing countries the effects of these processes are particularly extreme. Friedmann (1972a and b, 1973) has developed an elaborate framework, his 'general theory of polarized development', which stresses the increasing disparity between heartland and periphery in underdeveloped economies. The heartland–periphery dichotomy has also been applied to European urbanization (Kuklinski, 1972) and to North America (Ray, 1971).

forms part of a broader interest in minimizing costs while maximizing the benefits of urban growth and increased agglomeration in large centres.[8]

While there has been some success in defining optimal ranges of city population size for specific urban activities, notably deriving from general and partial equilibrium theory in economics (Isard, 1970) and applied operations research (Forrester, 1969), the goal of an optimal city remains illusory. In part this difficulty arises because more than one problem is involved. That is, an optimal size for a city is a different problem from that of an optimum for a set of cities. Similarly, while there may be optimal states for individual urban functions and services defined in terms of cost efficiency, such as in wholesaling or public transport, these cannot easily be optimized when other functions are taken into consideration. Also each optimal state will be variable depending on local conditions and geographic settings, not to mention various interest groups. Nevertheless, the question of optimal sizes is important because it crystallizes many of the issues which people think are significant to the arguments for regulating urbanization and specifically for urban decentralization. Some of these issues are summarized in the next section.

The search for optimality itself may in fact be of lower priority. Richardson (1972), for example, has concluded that it is neither a particularly useful problem nor a suitable basis for the formulation of national urban policies. He rejects the suggestion that any specific optimal state for city sizes exists because of the enormous functional complexity of contemporary urban systems noted above and the varying degrees of sectoral and regional specialization within those systems. Instead he argues that the more flexible policy objective of achieving efficiency within different city size ranges may be more practical and useful. One part of this objective might well involve the identification of a minimum size of city necessary to provide and to perform a specific mix of functions and services (Neutze, 1965; Thompson, 1965; Alonso and McGuire, 1972). This minimum would involve at least two components: an infrastructure aggregate sufficient to maintain an appropriate level of diversity in jobs and living conditions, as well as a

---

[8] The argument has its roots in the view that today's large metropolitan areas have exceeded some abstract optimal size, with optimal commonly measured in terms of an efficient return on investment in both public and private sectors. However, as Richardson (1973a) and Mera (1973) have demonstrated, there is little or no factual support for this position; and positive net benefits attributable to increased size may still be possible even for the world's largest metropolitan areas.

built-in mechanism which would ensure self-sustaining growth above a certain threshold size of city.

Much of the literature on new town planning and regional development policy has focused explicitly or implicitly on this problem of defining a minimum size of centre. Usually this minimum is measured in the narrow sense of total population and the estimates vary, depending on the purpose, from 25,000 to over 1 million. There is some agreement that in the context of cities as self-sustaining regional growth centres a minimum population of between 200,000 and 250,000 is necessary (Alonso, 1970; Hansen, 1972; Richardson, 1973b). Whatever the size range of threshold specified, any framework for regulating national or sub-national urban systems will have to consider the question of matching city size ranges, employment opportunities, and the allocation of public services, if it is to achieve more orderly and equitable growth within those systems. This matching process is now an integral part of the Swedish regional structure policy to be discussed in Section 4.2. Otherwise, the question of optimality in urban systems *per se* does not constitute a major theme in this review. It may, however, be useful for the reader to keep this question in mind in interpreting the following discussions on the patterns and consequences of urban growth in the four countries under study.

## 2.6. URBAN STRUCTURE IN THE COMPARISON COUNTRIES: SELECTED FACTS

All countries exhibit differing patterns of urbanization and varying expressions of the above system properties. The four under review here are no exception. Britain has an older, more mature, and industrially based system of cities. Australia and Canada still have components of a frontier economy, based on natural resource exploitation and exports, underlying their patterns of urbanization. As a result their urban systems are still filling out, with new cities arising to replace others in the hierarchy, and with patterns of linkages between cities remaining weak relative to external linkages. Sweden has many of these same properties, but tends to be somewhat more isolated from external pressures than Australia or Canada, or Britain for that matter.

Given these differences, and the stated emphasis on policy, few direct empirical comparisons of urbanization in the four countries are undertaken here. This would be the subject of another book. Fortunately, extensive descriptive reviews of urban development in each country already exist—for Canada (Lithwick, 1970); Australia (Rose, 1972); Britain (Hall *et al.*, 1973); and for Sweden (Ödmann and Dahlberg, 1970)—and need not be repeated here. The closest parallels in urban systems structure are between Australia and Canada, some of which have been documented elsewhere (Bourne, 1974). However, as background to subsequent sections, a selection of summary statistics is provided below.

Urban system structure can be succinctly displayed in terms of a few standard indices: the degree of urban population concentration, numbers of cities and size distributions, and growth rates. These indices are also key issues in the urban policy debate to follow. Relative to most of Western Europe none of the four countries shows an extremely high degree of metropolitan concentration (Table 2.1), although the

## TABLE 2.1

COMPARATIVE LEVELS OF URBAN POPULATION CONCENTRATION: AUSTRALIA, CANADA, SELECTED WESTERN EUROPEAN COUNTRIES, UNITED STATES, 1960/1–1970/1

| | | Proportion of Total Urban Population Living in: | | | |
|---|---|---|---|---|---|
| Country | Per cent Population Urbanized | Largest Centre | Three Largest Centres | Largest Centre | Three Largest Centres |
| | | 1960/1 | | 1970/1 | |
| AUSTRALIA | 83·1 | 24·9 | 54·5 | 24·9 | 54·4 |
| Austria | 48·8 | 53·9 | 71·7 | 51·0 | 69·4 |
| CANADA | 76·1 | 16·3 | 35·0 | 16·9 | 39·3 |
| Denmark | 77·3 | 46·2 | 64·0 | 45·7 | 67·1 |
| Finland | 63·1 | 25·0 | 33·7 | 27·6 | 43·9 |
| Norway | 57·9 | 33·1 | 50·4 | 33·1 | 50·3 |
| Portugal | — | 54·9 | 78·7 | n.a. | n.a. |
| SWEDEN | 69·4 | 27·2 | 48·3 | 28·2 | 50·7 |
| Switzerland | 49·3 | 24·3 | 46·3 | 23·2 | 55·9 |
| UNITED KINGDOM | 79·5 | 25·7 | 38·9 | 24·2 | 37·5 |
| United States | 77·2 | 10·3 | 21·5 | 9·7 | 20·8 |

Sources: European figures adapted from EFTA (1973) study; others derived from national sources.

populations of Australia and Britain are among the most highly urbanized in the world (83 and 80 per cent respectively). Specifically, the
proportion of urban population resident in the three largest
(metropolitan) centres is highest, as expected, in Australia, and lowest
in Britain. These indices, of course, depend in large part on the country's geographic size and total population as well as on the method of
delimiting urban areas. Britain differs sharply from the other three—in
both scale and complexity—containing more major centres than the
other three countries put together and a larger population in the three
dominant conurbations than in either Sweden or Australia nationally.
All four countries clearly have much higher levels of population concentration by size than the United States. Over time there seems to be little
in the way of a consistent trend except that in most of the larger countries other than Canada this particular index of concentration has
tended to decline.

Unfortunately, all such uniform indices suffer from the same limitation. Urban population concentration takes varying forms, and differing
consequences, in each country in response to a dissimilar mix of
developmental processes and constraints. In Australia, for example,
concentration is primarily a convergence of state population on the state
capital cities; in Britain it is the growth of the South-East and the
Midlands regions; in Canada it is the polarization of heartland and
periphery; and in Sweden concentration continues in southern coastal
locations. In Canada and Sweden concentration in the three largest centres as in Table 2.1 is a useful measure, although the consequences
differ, simply because each has three dominant metropolitan areas.
Some of these issues will be discussed further in the sections on each
country to follow.

Obtaining even remotely comparable population data for cities in
different countries is a difficult task. Of particular concern are the dis-
torted images that result from using political definitions of cities. The
populations of individual urban centres are listed in Table 2.2 for Britain,
Table 2.3 for Sweden, Table 2.4 for Australia, and Table 2.5 for Canada.
In all four cases, the definitional units represent some form of the
'extended' or functional urban area concept. The units are larger than
municipal cities, and all conform in varying degrees to the metropolitan
area concept (SMSA) used in the U.S. Census (Berry, 1968).
Consequently, all four definitions emphasize the economic integration
of city and outlying suburbs—largely in the form of commuting criteria
and regional labour catchment areas—in the context described above as

### TABLE 2.2

POPULATION OF METROPOLITAN LABOUR MARKET AREAS
(SMLAs), ENGLAND AND WALES, 1961–6
(over 250,000 population)

| Rank | SMLA | Populations (thousands) | | |
|------|------|------|------|------|
| | | 1961 | 1966 | % Change |
| 1 | London | 9,156·7 | 8,890·7 | −2·99 |
| 2 | Birmingham | 2,693·1 | 2,750·1 | 2·12 |
| 3 | Manchester | 2,041·7 | 2,012·7 | −1·42 |
| 4 | Liverpool | 1,480·9 | 1,450·2 | 2·08 |
| 5 | Leeds | 1,163·5 | 1,177·9 | 2·24 |
| 6 | Newcastle upon Tyne | 1,061·7 | 1,056·7 | −0·50 |
| 7 | Sheffield | 949·5 | 956·3 | 0·7 |
| 8 | Bristol | 661·2 | 694·5 | 5·1 |
| 9 | Coventry | 643·7 | 687·9 | 6·8 |
| 10 | Nottingham | 654·7 | 654·9 | 3·2 |
| 11 | Stoke | 519·1 | 523·8 | 0·9 |
| 12 | Leicester | 456·6 | 503·5 | 10·3 |
| 13 | Cardiff | 432·6 | 440·8 | 1·9 |
| 14 | Southampton | 401·8 | 432·8 | 7·7 |
| 15 | Portsmouth | 410·4 | 427·5 | 4·2 |
| 16 | Hull | 419·5 | 425·8 | 1·5 |
| 17 | Brighton | 337·8 | 342·8 | 1·5 |
| 18 | Derby | 314·5 | 324·1 | 3·1 |
| 19 | Bournemouth | 305·0 | 317·7 | 4·2 |
| 20 | Oxford | 286·9 | 310·7 | 8·3 |
| 21 | Middlesborough | 289·6 | 300·5 | 3·8 |
| 22 | Luton | 266·8 | 299·3 | 12·2 |
| 23 | Reading | 241·7 | 279·1 | 11·4 |
| 24 | Plymouth | 269·5 | 274·0 | 1·6 |
| 25 | Southend | 246·8 | 271·2 | 9·8 |
| 26 | Bolton | 249·7 | 250·8 | 0·4 |

Source: Adapted from Hall *et al.*, 1973, Vol. 1, Chap. IV.

TABLE 2.3

POPULATION OF THE MAJOR URBAN REGIONS IN SWEDEN, 1950–70
(with over 100,000 population)

| Rank | Urban Region* | Population (in thousands) | | | % Change 1960–70 | Population of Major City (in thousands) 1970 |
|------|---------------|------|------|------|--------|--------|
| | | 1950 | 1960 | 1970 | | |
| 1 | Stockholm/Södertälje | 955 | 1,122 | 1,277 | 12·6 | 973 |
| 2 | Göteborg | 419 | 511 | 603 | 18·1 | 486 |
| 3 | Malmö/Lund | 275 | 345 | 390 | 13·1 | 264 |
| 4 | Hölsingborg/Landskrona | 135 | 158 | 179 | 13·0 | 82 |
| 5 | Västerås | 87 | 117 | 148 | 27·2 | 99 |
| 6 | Örebro | 103 | 115 | 140 | 21·9 | 87 |
| 7 | Trollhättan/Vänersborg/ Uddevalla | 108 | 112 | 128 | 13·6 | 41 |
| 8 | Norrköping | 110 | 117 | 126 | 7·5 | 91 |
| 9 | Uppsala | 75 | 98 | 123 | 25·9 | 93 |
| 10 | Gävle/Sandviken | 68 | 101 | 116 | 4·0 | 65 |
| 11 | Borås | 81 | 103 | 113 | 10·1 | 73 |
| 12 | Jönköping | 57 | 96 | 112 | 17·4 | 81 |
| 13 | Linköping | 80 | 96 | 109 | 12·7 | 77 |
| 14 | Sundsvall | 66 | 88 | 100 | 15·1 | 54 |
| 15 | Eskilstuna | 70 | 82 | 100 | 22·7 | 69 |

* Refers to local labour market areas: the population within a circle of radius 30 km from the city centre.

Source: unpublished data from ERU (Expertgruppen for Regional Utredningsverksamhet), Stockholm, October 1973

**TABLE 2.4**

POPULATION OF PRINCIPAL URBAN CENTRES IN AUSTRALIA,
1961–71
(over 50,000 population)

| Rank | Urban Centre | Population (in thousands) | | | % Change |
|------|--------------|------|------|---------|----------|
| | | 1961 | 1966 | 1971(a) | 1966–71 |
| 1 | Sydney, N.S.W. | 2,183 | 2,447 | 2,725 | 11·4 |
| 2 | Melbourne, Vic. | 1,912 | 2,108 | 2,394 | 13·6 |
| 3 | Brisbane, Qld. | 622 | 714 | 818 | 14·6 |
| 4 | Adelaide, S.A. | 588 | 728 | 809 | 11·1 |
| 5 | Perth, W.A. | 420 | 500 | 642 | 28·4 |
| 6 | Newcastle, N.S.W. | 209 | 234 | 250 | 6·8 |
| 7 | Wollongong, N.S.W. | 132 | 162 | 186 | 14·8 |
| 8 | Canberra, A.C.T./N.S.W. | 56 | 92 | 156 | 69·6 |
| 9 | Hobart, Tas. | 116 | 119 | 130 | 9·2 |
| 10 | Geelong, Vic | 92 | 105 | 115 | 9·5 |
| 11 | Gold Coast, Qld./N.S.W. | 34 | 53 | 74 | 39·6 |
| 12 | Townsville, Qld. | 51 | 57 | 69 | 21·1 |
| 13 | Launceston, Tas. | 57 | 60 | 62 | 3·3 |
| 14 | Ballarat, Vic. | 55 | 56 | 59 | 5·4 |
| 15 | Toowoomba, Qld. | 50 | 52 | 58 | 11·5 |

(a) Includes Aborigines.

Source: *Population and Dwellings in Localities, Census 1961* Part v, Australian
Bureau of Statistics. *Australia—Population and Dwellings in Local
Government Areas and Urban Centres, 1971 Census,* Bulletin 6, Part 9:
Australia, Table 6; Australian Bureau of Statistics.

**TABLE 2.5**

POPULATION OF METROPOLITAN AREAS (CMAs) IN CANADA,
1961–71

| Rank | CMA | Population (in thousands) | | | % Change |
|---|---|---|---|---|---|
| | | 1961 | 1966* | 1971 | 1966–71 |
| 1 | Montreal, Que. | 2,110 | 2,571 | 2,743 | 6·7 |
| 2 | Toronto, Ont. | 1,825 | 2,290 | 2,628 | 14·8 |
| 3 | Vancouver, B.C. | 790 | 933 | 1,082 | 16·0 |
| 4 | Ottawa-Hull, Ont./Que. | 430 | 529 | 603 | 13·9 |
| 5 | Winnipeg, Man. | 476 | 509 | 540 | 6·2 |
| 6 | Hamilton, Ont. | 395 | 457 | 499 | 9·0 |
| 7 | Edmonton, Alta. | 337 | 425 | 496 | 16·4 |
| 8 | Quebec City, Que. | 358 | 437 | 481 | 10·0 |
| 9 | Calgary, Alta. | 279 | 331 | 403 | 21·6 |
| 10 | ªNiagara–St. Catharines, Ont. | 217 | 285 | 303 | 6·3 |
| 11 | London, Ont. | 181 | 254 | 286 | 12·9 |
| 12 | Windsor, Ont. | 193 | 238 | 259 | 8·5 |
| 13 | Kitchener, Ont. | 155 | 192 | 227 | 18·0 |
| 14 | Halifax, N.S. | 184 | 210 | 223 | 6·2 |
| 15 | Victoria, B.C. | 154 | 175 | 196 | 11·7 |
| 16 | Sudbury, Ont. | 111 | 137 | 155 | 16·0 |
| 17 | Regina, Sask. | 112 | 132 | 141 | 6·3 |
| 18 | ªChicoutimi–Jonquière, Que. | 105 | 133 | 134 | 0·9 |
| 19 | St. John's, Nfld. | 91 | 118 | 132 | 12·1 |
| 20 | Saskatoon, Sask. | 96 | 116 | 126 | 9·1 |
| 21 | ᵇOshawa–Whitby, Ont. | 81 | 106 | 120 | 13·0 |
| 22 | Thunder Bay, Ont. | 92 | 108 | 112 | 3·2 |
| 23 | Saint John, N.B. | 96 | 104 | 107 | 2·4 |

\* Revised and expanded 1966 Census areas based on 1971 definitions.
ª CMA created in 1971 Census; figures for preceding years are estimates.
ᵇNot officially classed as a CMA in the Census although its population exceeded
the minimum threshold of 100,000 in 1971.

Source: Statistics Canada, preliminary estimates, 1972.

the daily urban system (Berry and Horton, 1970). In Canada the corresponding area is the 'census metropolitan area' (CMA); in Australia, the census 'urban area' (excluding rural fringes); in Britain, where such statistics are not yet in common usage by the census, it is the unofficial 'standard metropolitan labour market area' (SMLA);[9] and in Sweden, the urban designation is described as 'regions of labour market accessibility'.

Such figures, given varying criteria, should be treated with caution in any international context (Davis, 1972). Yet they are the best approximations we have to the functional 'daily urban systems' which form components of the national urban system. Where cities stand isolated in predominantly rural areas of low density, changes in the location of boundaries identifying the outer limits of the metropolitan region will have little effect on statistical results or on our images of the processes of growth involved. Problems arise where the fringes of urban areas tend to coalesce, or where rural farm or non-farm densities are high, or both. Thus, the Australian and Canadian population figures, and to a lesser extent the Swedish figures (except in the lower city size ranges), are most closely compatible. Estimated urban populations for British urban areas, as expected, are more difficult to interpret and most tend to be underestimated in relative terms because of tighter definitional criteria, the abutting of one metropolitan area against another, and much higher over-all rural population densities (Clawson and Hall, 1973; Robson, 1973).

Plotting the size distribution of these centres (Figure 2.4), that is population against rank, in logarithmic terms, emphasizes one of the differences in urban system structure which has fascinated researchers for some time. All four show varying degrees of metropolitan primacy or dominance—that is the concentration of population in one or a few centres, as reflected in the steeper slope of the city size curve, although the dual primacy in both Australia and Canada is obvious (Rose, 1972; Simmons, 1974; Bourne, 1974). Britain, given its larger population, has a more uniform and continuous size distribution of centres; Sweden,

---

[9] The British SMLAs were defined by staff at Political and Economic Planning (PEP) for a study of metropolitan development in England and Wales using 1961 census data (Hall, 1971; Hall *et al.*, 1973). The SMLA consists of an urban core and an inner metropolitan ring—the latter consisting of administrative areas sending 15 per cent or more of their resident employed population to that core. The SMLA usually forms part of a larger areal unit, the Metropolitan Economic Labour Area (MELA), with the latter adding to the SMLA a second outer ring of contiguous administrative areas which send more of their resident employed population to the core of that SMLA than to any other core.

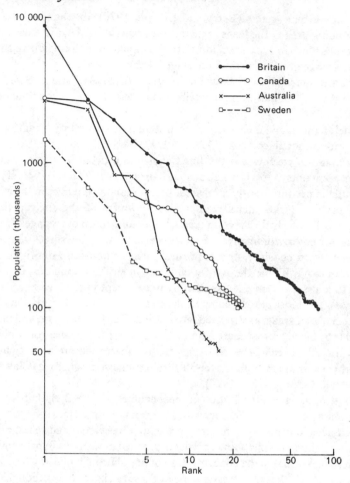

FIG. 2.4. Size Distributions, Major Urban Centres—Britain, Canada, Australia and Sweden.

aside from the three largest metropolitan areas, has an unusually equalitarian distribution; while Australia's size distribution is severely truncated below the level of the state capitals largely because of its limited population base (see Section 5.1).

While numerous authors have searched for gaps in each of these distributions—and some have read important policy implications into the existence of such gaps—there do not seem to be any general patterns in this example, nor any reason to expect that there should be. There will, of course, be gaps if the urban system contains few cities or there is a dominant primate city. Although there are no common gaps in the size distributions in Figure 2.4, there are breaks in the middle-size population range—in fact the range which researchers have frequently specified as a minimum necessary for creating growth centres capable of acting as alternatives to the dominant metropolitan centres (Hansen, 1972). These breaks occur at different population sizes in each country: in Sweden, from 200,000 to 400,000; in Australia, from 250,000 to 600,000; in Canada, from 300,000 to 450,000; and in Britain, from 350,000 to 450,000 and from 700,000 to about 1,000,000. It is interesting and perhaps disturbing to note how consistently these same crude figures emerge in the discussions on limiting metropolitan development, as well as in the new town and growth centre literature, in all four countries (Sections IV and V). Whether they mean anything in reality is quite another question.[10]

Differences in the recent growth behaviour of these systems also provide another dimension to the current urban policy debate. It is to be expected that the growth rates of individual urban areas will converge, with increasing city size, on the national growth rate, or the average growth of all cities in the urban system as a whole. In other words, the variability of urban growth is highest in the smaller city size ranges and decreases steadily upward through the size hierarchy. This empirical relationship has been widely demonstrated, as examples: for the American urban system by Thompson (1972) and Berry (1973b), for Soviet cities by Harris (1970), for British cities by Robson (1973), for Welsh towns by Carter (1972), for central Canadian cities by Barber (1972), and for both Canadian and Australian cities by the author (Bourne, 1974). The latter comparison is included here as Figure 2.5 since it illustrates the point, and given that census definitions for the two sets of cities are reasonably compatible. The possible reasons for such a regularity are numerous: larger cities represent a greater share of total national population and therefore through weight of numbers will strongly influence the average rate of growth; smaller cities are more specialized in functional make-up and are therefore more susceptible to

---

[10] If one were to argue that a continuous distribution of city sizes is to be encouraged—presumably on the basis of providing a maximum range of choice in living environments and economic opportunities—then breaks in these distributions become focal points for policy debates. The question, however, is far more complicated, and measures other than population aggregates are necessary to evaluate city-size distributions. For a summary of the issues involved see Hansen (1972), Friedmann (1972b), Alonso (1972), Hägerstrand (1972), Pred (1973b), Mera (1973), Berry (1973), Richardson (1973b), and Scott (1974).

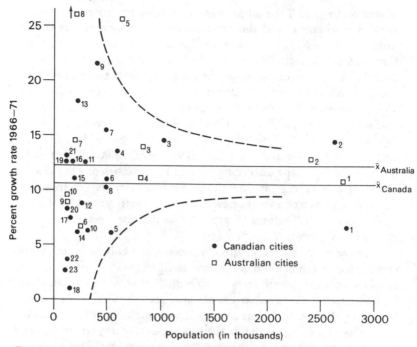

FIG. 2.5. Relationship of Growth Rate to City Size, Australian and Canadian Cities (Numbers refer to Tables 2.4 and 2.5).

irregular periods of boom and bust; and, if the diffusion process works in the manner briefly described in Section 2.4, then smaller cities will suffer from an inconsistent flow of benefits from new innovations. In any case, as Berry (1971c) notes, one important policy problem may lie in stabilizing the growth of the smaller centres.

In comparing the figures in Tables 2.2 to 2.5, one obvious contrast is the very rapid growth of the larger metropolitan centres in Sweden, Australia, and Canada (excluding Montreal in recent years), and the slow growth or even decline of populations in most of the large British conurbations.[11] The imprint of past regulatory policies on urban growth (or the lack thereof) is present in each of these trends. Overlying the issue of population concentration noted above, therefore, is the further

[11] Although a debatable point, the SMLA definitions as employed in the PEP study of urban England tend to underestimate the spatial boundaries of urban regions. Thus, some of the declines in population may simply reflect outmigration from the urban core to suburban or exurban locations outside the region as defined but still clearly within the 'daily urban field' as outlined above.

problem of excessively rapid national population growth and its impact in both urban Canada and Australia; and the possible social consequences of population decline on living conditions in the British conurbations which Eversley (1972) has effectively described. These issues will be taken up again in Sections IV and V.

The highest proportional growth rates in all four countries were recorded among two types of centres in the middle-size range: for independent or free-standing centres in favoured locations and with growing local economies (such as Edmonton, Calgary, and Ottawa; Perth and Canberra; Leicester and Southampton; and Göteborg), or smaller centres adjacent to the 'daily urban systems' of the metropolitan cores (such as Kitchener and Oshawa near Toronto; Wollongong near Sydney; Luton, Reading, and Southend near London; and Västerås and Uppsala near Stockholm). Whether these trends suggest a slowing down of population concentration in the largest centres has yet to be determined and even so it should be remembered that in terms of the impact of growth absolute numbers of people are as important as percentage changes in population.

The degree, density, and complexity of contemporary population concentration in urban Britain warrants further emphasis. It is only really apparent if one looks, as the PEP group did, at contiguous labour market areas (see Hall *et al.*, 1973). Their study identified two major urbanized regions in Britain (excluding Scotland)—London and the Midlands (Figure 2.6). Around London there are 26 contiguous SMLAs—akin to the standard metropolitan 'consolidated' statistical area employed in the U.S. Census (i.e. Chicago–Gary, New York–New Jersey). These SMLAs encompassed one-third of the total urban population in England and Wales in 1966. A second contiguous grouping, representing 40 SMLAs, covers almost all of central England including the East and West Midlands, Lancashire, and Yorkshire, and contained nearly 44 per cent of the 1966 urban population. With a few minor extensions, these two areas combined encompass 90 per cent of the urban population in England and Wales and 75 per cent of the total national population.[12] The only comparable concentration in the other three countries is in Canada around Lake Ontario (Oshawa–Toronto–Hamilton–Niagara–Kitchener, CMAs), but with 3·8 millions and

---

[12] Population figures for SMLAs for 1971 were not available at the time of writing. Also the delimitation and analysis of SMLAs at present exclude Scotland, but are being extended given 1971 Census returns to include the main Scottish urban centres. See Department of Geography (1974) for details.

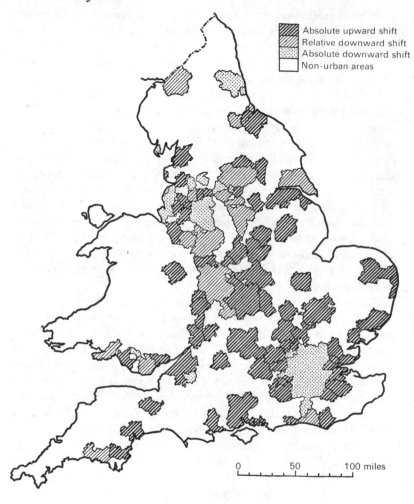

FIG. 2.6. Urban Concentration: Growth and Extent of the Conurbations (SMLAs) of England and Wales (after Hall *et al.*, 1973; and EFTA, 1973).

NOTE: Urban units are classified into three types according to percentage population change relative to the national average. 1. Per cent increase above average (absolute upward shift); 2. Per cent increase below average (relative downward shift); 3. Population decline (absolute downward shift).

less than 20 per cent of the national population total it is on a significantly smaller scale.[13] Obviously the detailed spatial geometries of the urban systems viewed in aggregate are largely unique to each country. So too are the expressions of urban problems.

One final point, and a critical property of all social systems, is the importance of external influences on economic development and urban system growth. The urban systems of Britain and Sweden differ from those of Australia and Canada in terms of the specific nature and direction of their 'openness' (or, conversely, their closedness) to external influence, but all four countries are, by international standards, far from closed systems. Such interaction may take several forms: goods movement, migration, risk capital, and trade.[14] The relative extent of foreign ownership typical of the Australian and Canadian economies (and natural resources), is unique, and it effectively limits independent national policy action, but the trend toward increasing international ownership is not unique. Sweden, as history has shown, tends to be somewhat socially insular (and in Europe, geographically isolated); consequently it has had more time and internal freedom to exercise control over its own social and urban problems. But it also is increasingly dependent on foreign trade and multi-national firms, many of which, although based in Sweden, are responsive to international economic cycles. Britain's economy is also closely linked to economic and social impulses whose origin is outside the area of direct political control. While this interdependence is characteristic of all trading nations, it is unusually strong in Britain, and it will probably increase as policies of the European Economic Community (EEC) on economic and monetary integration begin to work themselves out. The effect of the EEC on future locational planning strategies in general, and urban policies in particular in Britain (and in Sweden), may be one of the most interesting new dimensions to watch.

[13] For a discussion of this Canadian urban agglomeration, see Bourne and MacKinnon (1972) and Yeates (1974). For an assessment of future urban agglomerations in Australia—including the central New South Wales conurbation around Sydney and the Melbourne–Geelong–Westernport area—see Clarke (1970) and Rose (1971).

[14] One measure of the 'openness' of a country's economic system to external influence is the importance of foreign trade in the national economy. As a proportion of total gross national product (GNP) foreign trade is almost equally important in at least three of the countries under study. Trade accounts for 23·5 of GNP in Britain, 25·1 per cent in Sweden, and 25·3 per cent in Canada. The figure for Britain is the highest for any major nation in Europe; Canada's is the highest of the middle-size western economies; while Sweden's is the lowest (except for Spain) of the smaller European economies, many of which approach the 50 per cent mark. Generally, however, the proportion of GNP represented by trade flows decreases with increasing size of country. The U.S. figure is about 5·9 per cent, and therefore the U.S. represents a relatively closed national economic system in relation to the above four countries.

# Urban Strategies:
# Issues and Responses

---

PUBLIC policy formulation is the art of political decision-making under uncertainty. Different styles, modes, and sequences of decision-making are of course involved in and appropriate to the setting out of any public policy (Boulding, 1970). In western societies most policies tend to be ameliorative and responsive, directed towards short-term goals and the solution of past or current problems rather than to the anticipation of future needs or the creation of desired future states.

The normal sequence of events in urban policy-making also tends to be *ad hoc*: that is, ongoing processes (in and of society) lead to certain outcomes, part of which become defined as problems; some of these in turn become important social issues, which may (or may not) solicit a political response in terms of policy. Traditionally, although the particular mixture and sequence varies in each country, policy approaches to the problems generated by twentieth-century urbanization have followed this same pattern.

The present section attempts, in very brief terms, to set a context of definitions and frameworks for decision-making which may assist in ordering and interpreting the attempts of four diverse countries to regulate urbanization. How do we define urban strategies? What conceptual models exist for organizing studies of decision-making in national planning? Can these models be related to the processes of urbanization and specifically to urban systems concepts?

## 3.1. DEFINING URBAN STRATEGIES

If what is intended by an urban system strategy is explicitly and narrowly defined, then this study would have next to nothing to review. No country known to the author has as yet a formal and operational policy of urban system regulation. If on the other hand the concept is relaxed somewhat, to include any and all information with an implicit bearing on the two themes of this volume—urban systems and location policies—then virtually all of the literature in regional development and planning, transport, housing, growth poles, national physical and environmental planning, as well as aspects of public finance, become relevant. Not all can be treated adequately in one book.

Therefore, in casting a net over the enormous quantity of academic literature, government reports, and political pronouncements on urban policies and problems the catch will vary widely depending on the mesh of the net. Thus we will tread rather softly here on a middle course between these extremes; one which is selective but which maintains a unified focus around the stated themes while recognizing the obvious contribution of insights from policy fields related to these themes.

The use of the term strategies in the title of this book is central to the basic approach. It is employed to cast a wider net than would be suggested by the term policy. In common usage policy implies a plan or plans outlining a course of action to be followed by the responsible decision-making unit. In professional usage of course the theory and language of policy-making is more complex (Dye, 1972), and has its own theoretical basis and conceptual debate. The concept of strategy as used here, however, allows equal consideration to be given to questions of attitude, of political and social philosophy, of organizational procedures, as well as policy *per se*. Therefore, strategy, when divorced from its traditional military connotations, implies a value position as well as a specific plan for action. It is thus broader than, and in fact encompasses, tactics, including the design of policy instruments and legislation.[1]

How, then, do we identify national urban strategies? The intention here is to keep the frame of reference broad and flexible. First, while the focus is primarily on the national level, it is not solely a study of federal policies (Australia and Canada), or any and all central government policies (Britain and Sweden). In a federal state, a 'national' perspective on urbanization, as Swain (1972) has argued, refers to the summation and integration of regional, provincial, or state and federal policies. Second, urban strategies are those strategies designed to influence the evolving shape and character of that nation's aggregate urban structure. Such strategies in their simplest form translate into frameworks for decision-making. As noted earlier in this context, that structure will be approached and policy developments will be evaluated within the framework of urban systems concepts.

---

[1] This interpretation, for the interested reader, might be contrasted with that of Vickers (1972), in which tactics encompass strategies, and compared with that in studies of business and organizational behaviour (Ansoff, 1965).

However, this is not a review exclusively of national urban growth policies (see EFTA, 1973). This is too limited a perspective. The term is widely applied to a myriad of planning approaches, and even to single development projects, such as those described by Rodwin (1970), and therefore has an unclear meaning. Also, the term commonly refers to specific urban plans and to those planning objectives deriving from central governments rather than to the design and philosophy of regulating a dynamic process at all levels where it is appropriate to do so. A further limitation in this terminology is that the emphasis on growth *per se* may itself be too restrictive in the long term. Urbanization strategies involve essentially long-term planning horizons, when absolute population growth (in terms of the recent past) may not be as serious a problem.[2] Yet regulating changes and transformations operating through urban systems will continue to be necessary. That is, *regulation*, not remedy, in Jantsch's (1972) terms, is the key notion for long-term planning.[3]

## 3.2. FRAMEWORKS FOR DECISION-MAKING

Again, given the complex nature of social systems, the application of planning strategies in regulating urbanization can take several forms (Cooper, Eastman, Johnson, and Kortanck, 1971). In one example, Ozbekham (1969) proposed a three-level organization for planning such systems. These three include: (1) operational or tactical planning—which emphasizes short-term policies and more easily attainable targets; (2) strategic planning—which focuses on broad aims and objectives and the achievement of comprehensive and multi-faceted goals; and (3) normative planning—which seeks to shape both the means and the goals relating to the regulation of urban areas as dynamic social systems.

[2] Most western nations, for example, have seen their national (total) fertility rates drop in recent years to below what is considered the standard 'replacement level' of 2·1 births per family. The 1973 figure for the U.S. is 1·9 births per family. While zero population growth will not be achieved for some time, because of the present demographic structure and through immigration, the pressures of increased numbers of people should decline.

[3] Regulation implies control at different levels, and is a study in itself. Vickers (1973) for example, identifies a five-level hierarchy of control mechanisms applicable to social systems: (1) innate response, the lowest level, where the response is exclusively an organismic one; (2) control by rule—the type of response conditioned by simple conditions and circumstances; (3) control by purpose—a learning or heuristic process in which the result of the intended activity leads to revisions of the choices available; (4) control by norm—the matching of results and goals and the working out of conflicts; and (5) control by self-determination, in which policy-making becomes a debate on changing values and ethics and is the collective responsibility of society. Clearly, in the present study, most planning approaches would fall under types 2 through 4. Readers, however, should make their own assessment.

This framework differentiates between planning approaches principally on the basis of the treatment of goals and the time horizon employed. But that is not sufficient. As one extension, Berry (1973a) attempts to encompass the kinds of problems to which the planning process is commonly addressed and the modes of decision-making involved in that process. Four modes are suggested:

(1) *ameliorative problem-solving:* that is, planning as a reaction to past and current problems. In attempting to reduce the present consequences of these problems, the future is in effect designed by accident.

(2) *allocative trend-modifying:* again planning of this type is largely a response to existing difficulties, but in which the decision-making procedure at least tries to make the best of recent trends and available resources in achieving a future state specified beforehand.

(3) *exploitive opportunity-seeking:* planning which attempts to utilize aspects of predicted futures in order to maximize resource allocation and to minimize future problems.

(4) *normative goal-oriented:* this approach, conforming closely to Ozbekham's third level of planning strategies, works explicitly toward desired urban futures. In this context expressions of goals and values become the future states to which the system is directed.

These four modes convey a sequence, representing a progressively broader articulation of both the scope and intent of urban planning and of the degree to which change is a design rather than a happening. Few countries have attained the fourth stage in the sequence in any sector of planning at the national or local level.

## 3.3. A SIMPLE POLICY MODEL

Applying these generalizations to diverse political systems necessitates a simple framework for understanding different policy decision-making processes. Here we might conveniently fall back on one of the classic models of national economic planning. Figure 3.1 displays one such model, revised and extended for use in the present context of urban systems.

There are five basic components to the model: strategies, input variables, structural interrelationships, outputs, and feedbacks. Reading from left to right, it is suggested that strategies should serve as guide-lines within which ideas are translated into specific policy instruments for application to urban problems, and through which *a*

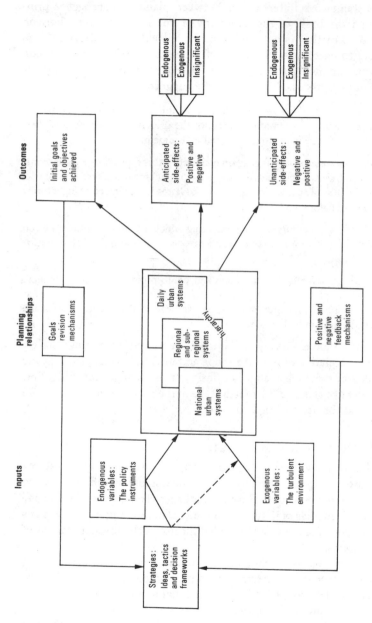

FIG. 3.1. A Schematic Design for Urban Systems Strategies.

*priori* goals for those policies are set. Input variables, the objects of policy, are of two types: internal (or endogenous) and external (or exogenous); differentiated by the point of origin of that variable relative to the system under study and, therefore, by whether the variable is susceptible to direct policy manipulation. Those variables deriving from sources outside the country—the turbulent external environment as defined by Emery and Trist (1972)—are only considered to be susceptible, if at all, to indirect policy influence (the dotted line in Figure 3.1).

The application of specific policy instruments to these variables, combined with the effects of the exogenous forces, leads to two possible outputs or outcomes: the achievement of the initial goals as postulated, and the emergence of background outcomes or side-effects. These side-effects may be differentiated by intention or design (that is, whether they were anticipated or not anticipated), by direction of impact (positive or negative benefits), by scale (significant, insignificant), and also by source location (endogenous, exogenous). In theory the planning system should allow for these varied impacts to feed-back upon the process of setting strategies and provide a mechanism for continually revising goals and evaluating past policies.

The core of the schema in Figure 3.1 is the working out of the relationships between and among policy instruments and exogenous variables. In each instance these are set within the three dimensions (structural, spatial, temporal) discussed in Section 2.2. For illustrative purposes Figure 3.1 also identifies an urban hierarchy, based on that described in Section 2.1, intended to encompass some of the relationships which the above strategies are designed to shape. The principles guiding those strategies are of course social goals and political structures.

## 3.4. POLICY RESPONSES TO URBANIZATION: BASES AND GOALS

The search for common bases and trends in urbanization, and for universal solutions to urban problems on an international scale, may easily be overemphasized. Urbanization has derived from several different processes and historically has taken different paths in various countries. Equally important, the goals and objectives of national and urban policies, and of the society from which they are drawn, differ widely (Vickers, 1973). Berry (1973a) also argues that these paths may now be diverging rather than converging, in part because of the imprint of the increasingly different decision-making modes noted above.

Although the sharpest contrasts are between Third World urbanization and that experienced in developed nations (Friedmann, 1973), even among the latter—notably between Western Europe, North America, and Eastern Europe—there are striking differences. Failure to grasp these essential contrasts has limited our awareness of the many possible forms which urban development has taken in this century and may hinder the formulation of strategies for creating new patterns of urbanization in the future. This does not mean that cross-national policy comparisons are invalid or unproductive, far from it. Rather it points to the limitations of employing a single conceptual model or philosophy in interpreting urbanization processes and the potential dangers involved in adopting uniform goals and strategies for regulating those processes.

While the specific expressions of goals vary between countries, a few basic themes seem to underlie the urban policy debate in all countries (Richardson, 1972; OECD, 1973c). Three in particular appear most prominent:

(1) The desire to reduce or at least scale down the increasingly massive social and environmental consequences of a continued concentration of population, economic opportunities, social services, and decision-making power in a few metropolitan centres.

(2) The desire to raise living standards above a minimum threshold in disadvantaged cities and regions; and as a corollary of point (1), to reduce the expanding inequalities between growing and disadvantaged regions.

(3) The maintenance of aggregate economic growth at rates commensurate with the perceived rise in social aspirations and international living standards, combined with the need to conserve scarce natural resources.

The first two goals represent an attempt to achieve a balanced distribution of welfare within the country, while ameliorating social problems at the margins: congestion in the urban cores and poverty on the national periphery. The third incorporates a distinct trade-off between the allocation of gross returns as opposed to net benefits deriving from growth, the latter taking into account environmental impact and resource conservation (Alonso, 1968b and 1970b).

Each of these goals might be further subdivided and extended, and each could and should be criticized. Economic growth has now come into open question, as evidenced by the important debates at the U.N. Urban Environment Conference in Stockholm in 1972 and the dire report of the Club of Rome on the limits to resource exploitation. Other goals are notable by their absence. The above conventional description of goals does not, for example, say anything about the distribution of political power and the relative balance of centralized and decentralized decision-making authority in urban affairs. Each of these questions bears on the operation of the policy model outlined above and its success in any given country. Who has responsibility for what?

In following sections we shall see how each of these goals, when weighted in terms of local conditions, influences the direction policy thinking has taken in each country. All three goals must be approached in concert, although this is seldom true, and some are viewed as inherently contradictory, although this need not be true. The real difficulty of course, especially in a pluralistic society, is that of achieving a consensus on social goals and of translating policy directions accordingly.

## 3.5. DISSENTING VOICES

Not surprisingly, there are many dissenting voices in the national urban policy chorus. Some researchers have questioned the urban system as a focus and instrument for urban policy (Thompson, 1972), and some have downplayed the role of urban strategies in influencing national development (Lasuén, 1973). Others have argued that in federated political states, particularly those which are capitalistic and socially pluralistic, there is no reason (and little hope) for explicit and comprehensive urban policies deriving from the national government. For example, the U.S. President's 1970 Report on National Growth (Berry, 1973a) commented that: '... it is not feasible for the highest levels of government to design policies for development that can operate successfully in all parts of the Nation' (p. 31). The rationale for this view was based on the presence of a wide degree of decentralization and local independence in urban policy decision-making in the U.S. The report went on to state: '... the Nation's growth is shaped by countless decisions made by individuals and firms seeking to fulfill their own objectives. Few of these decisions, individually, take on *national* importance. The vast majority of them have significance only within a single local jurisdiction ... Thus, it is all but certain that future problems of growth will be met at these levels ...' (p. 65).

Clearly this was a politically opportune decision for the U.S. government to take at that point in time. One might infer that the underlying strategy was to sidestep the difficult issues and political decisions involved in national urban planning, relying on support from the prevailing American social philosophy, which has been described as 'privatism'.[4] Nevertheless, there is some justification for the argument in favour of a decentralization of decision-making in urban policy—and it is common in varying degrees to all federal systems, Canada and Australia most certainly, and to centralized political systems such as Britain. The justification simply is that many decisions involved in planning or regulating urban development need not be taken at the national level, and may in fact clutter the policy stage.

The difficult problem which no one has yet mastered, is how to reorder the distribution of responsibilities to match more closely the hierarchical levels and spatial systems through which urbanization is expressed.[5] Whatever the arguments for or against a national role in urbanization within a democracy, it is certain that while national governments exist, their actions will have widespread regional and urban implications (Chisholm and Manners, 1971). The question, therefore, is not whether one government or another is involved, but rather what the responsibilities of the various levels of government are, or should be, in regulating urbanization.

The urban system concept has several advantages in such a decentralized policy-making context. One is the obvious direct link with research, a point which the Swedish experience (Section 4.2) has effectively demonstrated. Equally important, the urban systems approach has some political validity. Despite the politicians' general dislike of jargon, analytical research, and complex academic rationales, the systems approach in general, and urban systems in particular, allow for the potential integration of different aspects of the urban environment with areas of political jurisdiction and statutory responsibility. It also recognizes the continuity and increasing scale of organizations in modern societies and in mature economies. The capabilities and advantages of integrating modern systems methods and theory with public policy formulation are also now widely appreciated (Richardson, 1971). National urban systems consist of varying hierarchical aggregations of regional urban systems, and these in turn as described in the previous section consist of cities themselves defined as social and spatial systems.

---

[4] One exception to this assertion is the increasing political pressure in the U.S. for a national land-use policy, emanating largely from widespread environmental destruction. However, even in outline form the proposals are not nearly as comprehensive as those in Britain and Sweden.

[5] The hierarchical distribution of constitutional responsibilities in any country will have a great deal to do with how (and if) these regulatory strategies evolve. Interestingly, the four countries under study here have recently undertaken major reassessments and revisions of the assignment of constitutional powers at regional as well as local government levels.

For each of these systems, the processes of urbanization differ, as do the sectors and components of political responsibility.

## 3.6. THE ISSUES: AN OVERVIEW OF THE SPATIAL CONSEQUENCES OF URBANIZATION

Regulating urbanization takes on different meanings at each level in the urban hierarchy precisely because the issues and the consequences differ. Many different typologies of these issues are possible and plausible. While the details of trends and patterns are in large measure unique to each country, and therefore are left for discussion in the following sections, it is worthwhile to outline briefly a limited number of consequences of urbanization applicable to most urban systems as background for these discussions. Five types are identified here: (1) agglomeration; (2) decentralization; (3) polarization; (4) disequilibrium; and (5) externalities. Each is both spatial and hierarchical in origin and expression; and all are symptomatic of the mix of socially sensitive problems generating specific urban policy responses in each country.

Agglomeration is the broadest of the five. It encompasses the obvious concentration of a nation's economic and social resources in a few large metropolitan nodes—and within those nodes the concentration of employment in the core of the city. This global phenomenon, amply documented in nearly every country (for example: Davis, 1972; EFTA, 1973; ECF, 1973; Elkins, 1973), is a direct consequence of the trend to increasingly larger scales of industrial decision-making and organizational power in modern societies. The term agglomeration is used because of its well-known application in describing the clustering of economic activities (Mera, 1973). Little is known, however, of the balance of social costs and benefits of this process although this balance underlies much of the debate on the current urban malaise (Alonso, 1968b and 1972; OECD, 1973c; Scott, 1974).

The second effect, decentralization, is often more localized in extent. Although the term is used in widely different contexts, here it is taken to mean the movement of people, jobs, and activities primarily from the centre or core of the major metropolitan centres to outlying locations with the urban field. In this sense decentralization is a regional phenomenon, but one contained within and responsive to the above national agglomerative forces. With decentralization come the problems of urban sprawl, deterioration of the core, social imbalance, and investment insecurity: problems which are a function largely of the extent, rapidity, and internal sorting of growth processes—and thus of the agglomeration mechanism. In their study of metropolitan England, the PEP research group (Hall *et al.*, 1973) differentiated two measures of decentralization—absolute and relative—and made a similar distinction for the converse phenomenon—centralization. The latter, of course, in recent decades has been much less dominant, although it still occurs in selective employment categories.

The third effect attributed in part to the behaviour of the urban system is polarization. It is both a consequence and a sub-process consisting of extreme outcomes of both the agglomeration and decentralization processes usually working together. In one sense polarization is also a process of agglomeration, but it is commonly applied in a slightly different manner. If, for instance, we array regions, cities, or locations along a continuum measuring common social indicators of well-being and the quality of urban life—such as average income, education level, availability of services, or personal opportunities—there is evidence that in both Europe and North America the distributions are becoming increasingly bi-modal (EFTA, 1973; Economic Council of Canada, 1971; U.S. National Goals Staff, 1970; Smith, 1973). The premiss that the rich are getting richer and the poor poorer still applies.[6] Rather than converging on a national mean, many of our standard indicators of the quality of life (Wingo, 1973) suggest an increasing segregation, both hierarchically and spatially, of income, jobs, living styles, services, and economic power. This polarization is most evident between the metropolitan centres of the urban system and peripheral rural regions at the macro-level and between the central city core and suburban areas at the local level. Three brief examples of the former are included here: poverty in the U.S. (Table 3.1); household consumption patterns in Sweden (Table 3.2); and corporate concentration in Britain (Table 3.3). Selective investment, migration patterns, and public policy have tended to accelerate these extremes.[7] Note that what appears on the surface as a

[6] The debate on the issue of urban income and occupational polarization has been particularly strong in the case of very large metropolitan areas, such as London, where planning restrictions have been most widely and thoroughly enforced (see Donnison and Eversley, 1973).

[7] The fact that polarization takes different forms (and thereby has different consequences) at varying levels of the urban system implies that difficult trade-offs exist in terms of policy. This is again evident in the debate on altering city size distributions, particularly limiting the growth of the major metropolitan regions. One of the arguments Mills (1972) and others have employed for not limiting the size of large cities (at least in the U.S. context) is that the consequences will be most severely felt by the low-income rural migrant. He would, in theory, be prevented or discouraged from moving to the metropolis where, although poverty is severe, it is less severe and less permanent than in many rural areas from which such migrants are drawn. At the same time one must consider the costs borne by those who are left behind by migrants moving to the metropolitan areas.

TABLE 3.1

INCIDENCE OF URBAN AND RURAL POVERTY,
UNITED STATES, 1965

|  | Percentage of Population Classed as Poor | Index of Poverty* (U.S. = 100) |
| --- | --- | --- |
| Metropolitan Areas—total | 12·6 | 67 |
| Metropolitan suburbs | 6·7 | 33 |
| Non-metropolitan areas | 32·0 | 150 |
| Rural farm | 29·7 | 193 |
| Urban areas | 14·8 | 81 |
| Rural areas | 29·7 | 155 |

* Calculated as (% poor in sector (area)/% non-poor in sector)/(% poor in nation/% non-poor in nation).

Source: U.S. National Advisory Commission on Rural Poverty (1967).


TABLE 3.2

INDICES OF CONSUMPTION OF GOODS AND SERVICES
BY HOUSEHOLDS, BY LEVEL OF URBAN HIERARCHY, SWEDEN

| Consumer Item | Metropolitan areas* | Other city regions | Sparsely populated areas |
| --- | --- | --- | --- |
| Individual goods |  |  |  |
| 1. Food | 116 | 102 | 100 |
| 2. Clothing | 131 | 129 | 100 |
| 3. Household inventories | 125 | 133 | 100 |
| 4. Liquor and tobacco | 190 | 134 | 100 |
| 5. Housing | 168 | 148 | 100 |
| Subtotal | 137 | 123 | 100 |
| Semi-collective goods |  |  |  |
| 6. Private health and beauty | 208 | 122 | 100 |
| 7. Amusements | 163 | 144 | 100 |
| 8. Restaurants and processed foods | 223 | 161 | 100 |
| 9. Trips to other countries | 377 | 227 | 100 |
| Subtotal | 199 | 151 | 100 |

* Stockholm, Göteborg, and Malmö.

Source: Andersson (1973), 15.

**TABLE 3.3**

LOCATIONAL CONCENTRATION IN THE CONTROL OF AN ECONOMIC SYSTEM, BRITISH SAMPLE, 1970

| Region | Head Offices | | Central Services | | Divisional Head Office | | Research and Development | | Operating Units | |
|---|---|---|---|---|---|---|---|---|---|---|
| | No. | % | No. | % | No. | % | No. | % | No. | % |
| London | 40 | 58.0 | 9 | 29.0 | 58 | 28.2 | 23 | 26.7 | 180 | 10.1 |
| Rest of South-East | 11 | 15.9 | 6 | 19.4 | 28 | 13.5 | 18 | 21.0 | 327 | 18.4 |
| Subtotal | 51 | 73.9 | 15 | 48.4 | 86 | 41.7 | 41 | 47.7 | 507 | 28.5 |
| South-West | 0 | 0.0 | 0 | 0.0 | 7 | 3.4 | 4 | 4.7 | 97 | 5.4 |
| West Midlands | 6 | 8.7 | 12 | 38.7 | 53 | 25.7 | 19 | 22.1 | 264 | 14.8 |
| East Midlands | 3 | 4.3 | 0 | 0.0 | 10 | 4.7 | 8 | 9.3 | 146 | 8.2 |
| East Anglia | 1 | 1.4 | 0 | 0.0 | 2 | 1.0 | 2 | 2.3 | 54 | 3.0 |
| Yorks./Humberside | 1 | 1.4 | 0 | 0.0 | 9 | 4.4 | 2 | 2.3 | 174 | 9.8 |
| North | 1 | 1.4 | 1 | 3.2 | 3 | 1.5 | 3 | 3.5 | 68 | 3.8 |
| Wales | 1 | 1.4 | 0 | 0.0 | 5 | 2.4 | 0 | 0.0 | 62 | 3.4 |
| North-West | 3 | 4.3 | 2 | 6.5 | 20 | 9.7 | 5 | 5.8 | 286 | 16.1 |
| Scotland | 2 | 2.9 | 1 | 3.2 | 11 | 5.3 | 2 | 2.3 | 124 | 7.0 |
| Totals | 69 | | 31 | | 206 | | 86 | | 1782 | |

Source: Westaway, 1973.

simple geographic pattern becomes a complex socio-economic and political process operating within a spatial urban system.

The fourth and fifth effects are more specific in expression, but also apply at both local (within city) and national (between city) levels. Disequilibrium, an awkward term for the generation of sectoral and spatial inequalities, is not the same as polarization, although, like polarization, it is closely interrelated with concentration and decentralization. Inequalities arise because of the malfunction of the distributive mechanisms cited above (Section II) and their failure to compensate for the consequences of agglomerative, decentralization, and polarization effects. This failure comes primarily from two sources: barriers to the operation of the economic system, and deficiencies in its regulation, as well as a bias in the allocation of public goods. Polarization implies an uneven spatial distribution, yet it does not necessarily mean that this unevenness is of critical concern in political or social terms. In other words, spatial and structural variations within a society arc not by definition problems of inequalities. Their existence is probably inevitable even in societies under rigid regulation. When they become persistent, socially inhibiting, and politically sensitive, the policy reaction changes. No long list of examples is needed to illustrate these problems.

Externalities are an inseparable part of the inequality issue. While an integral consequence of urban system behaviour at all levels in the hierarchy, they tend to be most pronounced in the intra-urban use of space and in the provision of public goods on the same scale. Briefly, externalities may be defined as 'external' effects, either positive or negative in direction (Thompson, 1965). In economic terms these represent differences in the costs (benefits) borne by those populations inside and outside the system which reaps the benefits (costs) of producing and consuming whatever goods and services are in question. These differences often emerge from the public domain. In the geographer's terms these are a spill-over phenomenon in which one location transmits effects to another location, but in unequal proportions and with inadequate feedback. If not limited in this way, externalities become simply 'interactions' of all types within the urban system. They may vary in geographic extent from the influence of industrial pollution on an adjacent residential area, to the demise of a major employer in one town on the health of the service sector in an adjacent town, city, or region. Such effects, whether of public or private origin, are usually transmitted through and exaggerated by the market system.

One obvious policy consequence of this phenomenon is the attempt to 'internalize' externalities. In the public sector this might involve bringing the jurisdictional arrangement of urban space and public services into line with the spatial spread of external effects. The creation of metropolitan governments is one example. On the regional scale, externalities become even more difficult to control and to internalize in part because they tend to be less visible publicly and because their effects often straddle more rigid political jurisdictions. Not surprisingly, many of these jurisdictions owe their delimitation and historical stability to attempts to ensure that externalities are concentrated outside their respective sectors of the urban system.

There are obviously numerous other types of consequences of the rapid urbanization of the last few decades—many are spatial and many are not. There are also widely different social and cultural interpretations of these effects in different countries. The purpose of briefly illustrating their spatial expression here is to demonstrate that they are important and ubiquitous, more so than is commonly held to be the case. The following two sections turn to the discussion of urban policy developments in the four study countries—Britain, Sweden, Australia, and Canada—all of which are now seeking means to regulate and contain these consequences.

# Urban Systems under Regulation: Britain and Sweden

---

BOTH Britain and Sweden have long histories of direct government involvement in urban development. Each has evolved an elaborate array of checks and balances on the spatial distribution of population and economic growth. The design and implementation of these policies are now generally well known as they have been the subject of frequent reviews internally and by foreign observers (Rodwin, 1970; Strong, 1971; Merlin, 1971; Berry, 1973a). Often the reviews from abroad turn to points of envy, particularly when viewed from the more chaotic context of urban North America, while others may be unduly sceptical of who bears the economic and social costs of such policies. In neither case, however, is the supporting evidence as yet sufficient to give a balanced judgement.

Whatever the reader's position in the latter debate, the value of the British and Swedish experiences in a comparative context is obvious. Both have demonstrated, in quite different ways, that normative planning in certain critical social and economic sectors at the national level, and urban planning at the local and regional level, are feasible as well as beneficial within a democratic political framework. Equally important, and despite differences of opinion, they have shown that a sufficient consensus on objectives among the public, the professions, and the politicians as to the desirability of direct intervention in the market processes underlying urban development can be achieved, nurtured, and then eventually translated into policy. As such they provide excellent illustrations of specific approaches to designing urban environments; approaches which are immensely useful for other countries in deciding what they might or might not do in responding to the increasing pressures of urban growth within their own territorial boundaries.

The essence of the review in this section is not primarily on the specific instruments and plans used, but rather on the evolution of differing strategies of urban regulation. One clear argument in support of the emphasis in this study on strategies rather than policies is that translating specific policy experience from one political and environmental context to another is hazardous at best. Furthermore, the extensive literature on planning practices in Britain and Sweden allows us the option here to stress the more nebulous issues of changing attitudes and decision-making strategies, while not losing sight completely of the detailed instruments which translate these strategies into policy.

There are other reasons for selecting Sweden and Britain as comparative examples. The former exhibits many of the same geographical underpinnings of urban and economic development as those prevailing in Canada and Australia. By European standards Sweden is a large country with low population densities, and by world standards it has a high (if not the highest) standard of living and a diversified post-industrial economy. Combine these with high levels of occupational and geographical mobility, and the existence of frontier regions with resource-based economies, other parallels likely to emerge in policy debates are clear. The frontier provides much the same preoccupation with filling national 'territory' in Sweden as is found in both Canada and Australia. The obvious argument for including Britain need not be elaborated since it shares a common socio-political background with both countries. Yet because the urban systems in Britain and Sweden are so vastly different in character, scale, and complexity, the materials in this section are not directly compared as is the case in the following section on Australia and Canada. Instead this section seeks to cut across more traditional research lines to explore the various arguments put forward in each country in support of or in opposition to the introduction of locational and urban policies, but with a focus on the most recent developments and their relation to questions of urban system regulation in general.

Britain and Sweden have certain advantages over most countries in generating national strategies for controlling urbanization and its consequences, although neither has as yet done so. Both are relatively compact countries by comparison with North America; and they are more homogeneous than most in culture, value systems, aspirations, and life styles. The latter are particularly true of Sweden, and are directly reflected in the relative success of urban planning ventures. One is also struck in assessing recent developments in both countries by the extent to which both policy thinking and urban research have been locationally and environmentally sensitive. This same theme—or value position—pervades the social fabric, élite and otherwise, and is directly reflected in a widespread interest in environmental issues among the public and consequently among politicians. Further, both Britain and Sweden have an immense, highly skilled force of planning professionals and urban administrators, a manpower source which newer and historically less planning-oriented nations such as Canada and Australia do not have. Consequently, the scope for consensus on urban issues and planning priorities is wider and the ability to act on that consensus is all that much greater.

## 4.1. URBAN BRITAIN

Britain[1] is widely recognized for its experiments in urban planning, regional policy, and social welfare. The achievements are mirrored in specific legislative packages which attempt to rationalize competition among land uses; in programmes for new towns, green belts, and environmental preservation; in the regional redistribution of industry and offices, in slum clearance, and in public housing and social service systems. This array of legislation was made possible by a combination of circumstances which encouraged a consensus on purposes, and provided the means, of controlling the processes of urbanization.

This section attempts to document the evolution of strategic planning policy in Britain relating to the guidance of urban development at the national (or macro-) level. Interest focuses on two policy areas: urban planning, particularly the new towns, and spatially sensitive regional policies, rather than on the details of local (or micro-level) city planning. The latter clearly cannot be ignored here since it is largely through local channels that national policies are applied and therefore have their greatest impact. Inclusion of both urban and regional strategies is considered essential, as argued in Section I, given the concern for regulating urban systems in a spatial context.

A number of questions provide a basis for the review: why did Britain respond to urban problems in the way that it did? What are the current objectives of controls on land use (urban containment), industrial and office location, and the new town programme? Do present urban policies have a national perspective; or are they regional policies applied centrally?

Any brief review of such an extensive subject must be rather selective

---

[1] For the most part the discussion here is concerned with England, Scotland, and Wales, but with England, and the usual confusion of the terms Britain and England is likely.

and therefore superficial. Fortunately, the student of urban Britain is now well served by a rapidly expanding inventory of background literature on national urbanization trends (Cowan, 1969; Stone, 1970; Hall, 1971; Hall *et al.*, 1973) and the spatial aspects of economic development (Chisholm and Manners, 1971; Lee, 1971; Manners, 1972; Chisholm, 1972; Brown, 1972). Further, and more specific to this review, analytical research on the attributes of urban areas and their behaviour as national and regional urban systems is now growing (Moser and Scott, 1961; Bassett and Haggett, 1971; Armen, 1972; Centre for Environmental Studies, 1973; Cameron and Evans, 1973; Westaway, 1973; Goddard, 1973; Robson, 1973). Amongst the enormous literature on planning the most useful for this study were recent reviews by Cherry (1972), Cullingworth (1973a and b), Cowan *et al.* (1973), Berry (1973a), EFTA (1973), Hall *et al.* (1973), Burns (1973), and Clawson and Hall (1973).

### 4.1.1. BACKGROUND: THE SOCIAL CLIMATE AND URBANIZATION

Urban planning in most countries is primarily concerned with the physical imprint of urbanization. Only in a few countries is it also a vehicle for directing social change toward specified goals. Hall *et al.* (1973) summarized the basis of British urban policy experience in the following terms: 'The free operation of the laws of urban development, ... was to be controlled and organized to serve basic values held by certain portions of the society, and represented for the most part in the ideologies of the planning movement.' These basic values were translated into specific planning goals. 'These goals included preservation of both cities and the countryside, conservation of natural resources, the achievement of public economies, and the preference for small, compact and self-contained urban units ...'

Values in themselves reflect the prevailing social order, an order which explains much of the response to social change through urbanization documented in subsequent pages. Britain has an elitist social structure, at least relative to North America, Australia, and Sweden. In combination with the above values this structure has encouraged greater central authority and facilitated central planning. The élite have, as Berry (1973a) notes, tended to emphasize responsibilities rather than rights in reference to environmental issues. Land for instance has always held a particularly important position in the British value hierarchy, which Clawson and Hall (1973) describe as a sense of 'stewardship of land'. Other values augment this position. Society generally has stressed stability more than progress; conservatism over change; community over mobility; and environmental preservation over consumption. Such values, while different in context and content from those prevailing in Sweden for example (Section 4.2), have produced many of the same outcomes.

The realization of these values in terms of urban development has taken many different forms, only a few of which can be demonstrated here. The important point for deriving any generalizations which are applicable elsewhere is the extent to which underlying attitudes to cities and to urbanization in Britain, set within a historical series of unique circumstances, resulted in the matching of social needs and goals with political priorities for action—which Rodwin (1970) describes as a precondition for effective policy implementation.

### 4.1.2. THE ISSUES: LIMITED SPACE AND THE INDUSTRIAL HERITAGE

Britain was the first of the modern industrial nations and the first massively urban nation (Table 4.1). The age of great cities was recognized in Britain in the early 1800s (Monthly Magazine, 1811; Vaughan, 1843). Consequently it has inherited problems which both ageing and industrialization almost inevitably bring. Most of these problems have been extensively documented in the academic literature and in reports by public commissions and agencies: rapid population growth; out-dated industrial districts; pollution; vast expanses of high-density, squalid housing; health and sanitation problems; and unstable employment and unemployment. The severity of these problems, and their persistence, contributed to a long history of social policy responses beginning in the mid-nineteenth century, responses which were most effective in the areas of housing and urban sanitation. While most of these problems are still present today, our attention here is on statements of post-war issues in a spatial context which underlie recent urban policy responses.

Rapid evolution of planning policies during this post-war period followed from the convergence in time of several mounting pressures. Nationally these problems included the costs of increased congestion and agglomeration around (rather than in) the large conurbations, particularly London and the South-East. The interesting figures in Table 4.1 in contrast reveal a recent decline in the population of the largest conurbations, but as noted in Section II these figures considerably un-

## TABLE 4.1

GROWTH AND DECLINE OF THE MAJOR CONURBATIONS IN ENGLAND AND WALES, 1891–1971

Population (thousands)

|  | 1891 | 1901 | 1911 | 1921 | 1931 | 1951 | 1961 | 1966 | 1971‡ |
|---|---|---|---|---|---|---|---|---|---|
| Six conurbations | **11,670.0** | **13,417.8** | **14,726.9** | **15,315.4** | **16,404.8** | **16,918.4** | **16,901.0** | **16,327.5\*** | **15,928.0\*** |
| Greater London | 5,638.4 | 6,586.3 | 7,255.9 | 7,488.4 | 8,215.7 | 8,348.0 | 8,183.0 | 7,671.2* | 7,379.0* |
| South-East Lancashire | 1,893.6 | 2,116.8 | 2,328.0 | 2,361.2 | 2,426.9 | 2,422.7 | 2,28.0 | 2,404.1 | 2,386.8* |
| West Midlands | 1,268.7 | 1,482.8 | 1,634.5 | 1,773.4 | 1,933.0 | 2,237.1 | 2,347.0 | 2,374.1* | 2,369.2* |
| West Yorkshire | 1,410.1 | 1,523.8 | 1,589.8 | 1,613.5 | 1,655.4 | 1,692.7 | 1,704.0 | 1,708.3 | 1,726.1* |
| Merseyside | 908.3 | 1,030.2 | 1,157.2 | 1,263.3 | 1,346.7 | 1,382.4 | 1,384.0 | 1,337.5 | 1,262.5* |
| Tyneside | 550.9 | 677.9 | 761.5 | 815.6 | 827.1 | 835.5 | 855.0 | 832.3 | 804.4* |

Percentage total population

|  | 1891 | 1901 | 1911 | 1921 | 1931 | 1951 | 1961 | 1966 | 1971‡ |
|---|---|---|---|---|---|---|---|---|---|
| Six conurbations | **40.2** | **43.3** | **40.8** | **40.5** | **41.1** | **38.7** | **36.7** | **34.6\*** | **32.8\*** |
| Greater London | 19.4 | 20.2 | 20.1 | 19.8 | 20.6 | 19.1 | 17.7 | 16.3* | 15.2* |
| South-East Lancashire | 6.5 | 8.5 | 6.5 | 6.2 | 6.1 | 5.5 | 5.3 | 5.1 | 4.9* |
| West Midlands | 4.4 | 4.6 | 4.5 | 4.7 | 4.8 | 5.1 | 5.1 | 5.0* | 4.9* |

West Yorkshire | 4·9 | 4·7 | 4·4 | 4·3 | 4·1 | 3·9 | 3·7 | 3·6 | 3·6*
Merseyside | 3·1 | 3·2 | 3·2 | 3·3 | 3·5 | 3·2 | 3·0 | 2·8 | 2·6*
Tyneside | 1·9 | 2·1 | 2·1 | 2·2 | 2·1 | 1·9 | 1·9 | 1·8 | 1·7*

## Population growth

| | 1891–1901 | 1901–11 | 1911–21 | 1921–31 | 1931–51 | 1951–61 | 1961–6† | 1961–71 |
|---|---|---|---|---|---|---|---|---|
| Six conurbations | **15·0** | **9·8** | **4·0** | **7·1** | **3·1** | **–0·1** | **–3·4*** | **–4·9*** |
| Greater London | 16· | 10·2 | 3·1 | 9·9 | 0·8 | –2·0 | –4·1* | –7·7* |
| South-East Lancashire | 11·8 | 10·0 | 1·4 | 2·8 | –0·1 | 0·2 | –1·0 | –1·7* |
| West Midlands | 16·9 | 10·2 | 8·3 | 9·0 | 7·6 | 4·8 | –0·2* | –0·4* |
| West Yorkshire | 8·1 | 4·3 | 1·5 | 2·6 | 1·1 | 0·6 | 0·3 | 1·3* |
| Merseyside | 13·4 | 12·3 | 9·0 | 6·7 | 1·3 | –0·1 | –3·4 | –8·8* |
| Tyneside | 23·1 | 12·3 | 7·0 | 1·4 | 0·5 | 2·3 | –2·7 | –6·0* |

* Boundary changes (growth figures calculated on adjusted 1961 totals).
† Adjusted for boundary changes.
‡ Preliminary figures.

Source: Hall *et al.*, 1973, Vol. 1, p. 64.

derestimate the population of the daily urban systems in Britain, at least relative to definitions applied in the other three countries under review. Also important were the declining economic base and living environments of the peripheral areas, and the rapid loss of agricultural land through urbanization (Best and Rogers, 1973) in what was argued to be a small country. These issues crystallized during the 1930s, when the conurbations did in fact grow faster than the nation, and most observers expected they would accelerate after the war.[2] At the local and regional levels the critical issues were the physical sprawl of cities into the rural countryside, environmental preservation, and the inherited need for redevelopment and rebuilding of the inner city cores. The cumulative scale of these latter problems was truly massive.

The war, and the widespread damage it brought, provided both the opportunity and the immediate urgency for government action, not only in rebuilding damaged areas but on the broad range of social issues which had their origins in earlier decades. As in other countries, solutions to such issues have been tempered by the need to ensure continued economic growth, in the face of frequent post-war economic and monetary crises, and by the unpredictable pressures of social change, increasing affluence, and technological innovations.

Each of these general issues contains a number of specific problems. One summary, provided by a recent report on national urban settlement strategies released by EFTA (1973), stressed issues of the concentration of the nation's economic and social wealth (notably industrial employment) and power (see Table 3.3) in the large conurbations; the specificity of interregional migration in terms of age, industrial, and occupational structures; and the widening polarization in income distributions within and between the conurbations. Population concentration also has an inverse: the decline of the periphery, which in Britain includes the politically sensitive areas of Scotland, Wales, and Northern Ireland. Not only have these areas and most of northern England suffered from continuous out-migration and depopulation in this century, but they also appear to have borne the brunt of the national costs of transforming a nineteenth-century industrial state into a modern urban economy.

There was sufficient agreement that the issues summarized above

[2] Most readers might not be aware that the decade of the 1930s was, unlike in North America, one of extensive speculative housing construction and widespread suburbanization in Britain, largely, it seems, as a result of low interest rates for available capital in other sectors (see Clawson and Hall, 1973).

represented appropriate priorities to facilitate a government response. The result was an immense range of post-war policies designed to deal with varying spatial expressions of urban problems—particularly at the intra-urban level but also on both regional and national scales. There was also an awareness prior to World War II that the issues were themselves closely interrelated. Urban sprawl and redevelopment of the older city centres could not be divorced from issues of industrial concentration and employment location. However, the policy response was not quite as neatly interrelated. As will be noted in later sections, physical planning at the local municipal level has remained until recently largely independent in both purpose and execution of locational strategies at the national level.

### 4.1.3. THE POLICY RESPONSE: CONTROLS ON LAND AND JOBS

Although the intentional involvement of government in the life of British cities dates back at least to the late nineteenth century, it was none the less half a century overdue. The appalling social problems of urban life in Victorian Britain noted earlier, and the inconsistent public response to changing social conditions, so vividly described by Patrick Geddes (1949 rev. ed.), led to a renewed civic effort at urban and environmental improvement. Most of this effort, as Briggs (1963) demonstrates, came from the local municipal level and depended heavily on aristocratic whim, on private charity, and only when those did not materialize, on local government. Nevertheless, massive improvements in community services, in housing quality and education, as well as in roads and transit (and inevitably monuments), were undertaken as early as the 1830s. Many had become national in scope by the 1880s. One legacy of this history which seems to have persisted to the present is the relatively greater acceptance of local government involvement in regulating urban development than has been the case in North America and Australia.

The period in which the policy perspective expanded from local to regional and subsequently to the national level dates largely from World War II. The specific sequence of events in this evolution is thoroughly summarized elsewhere (Ashworth, 1964; McCrone, 1969; Rodwin, 1970; Cherry, 1972; Cullingworth, 1972, 1973a, b, and c; Hall *et al.*, 1973; Burns, 1973; Clawson and Hall, 1973; Forbes, 1974). Thus this review can be more selective. It will suffice here to note that the first explicit town planning act was passed in 1909. By the 1930s most of urban Britain was covered by local planning legislation and by 1939 urban development in most areas was subject to direct control by planning authorities—with the urging of the central government—controls which in practice were not unlike North American zoning ordinances.

The stage for most of Britain's post-war planning strategies was laid by several key reports published in the early 1940s. One was the report of the Royal Commission on the Distribution of the Industrial Population (the Barlow Report, 1940). Another was the report of the Committee on Compensation and Betterment (the Uthwatt Report), dealing with restrictions on land speculation, published in 1942. A third, published in 1944, was the Greater London Plan prepared by Sir Patrick Abercrombie. A fourth, also released in 1944, was a government white paper on employment policy, industrial location, and problems anticipated in the transition from a war-time to peace-time economy. None of these reports has been surpassed in innovativeness to this day. There were of course many other critical reports, government papers, and public briefs which influenced future planning developments, but these four contain the essence of the current policy debate (Burns, 1973). The watershed decision was the governmental acceptance of the universal recommendation '. . . that national planning is intended to be a reality and a permanent feature of the administration of the internal affairs of the country'.

A variety of regulatory strategies emerged from these studies, although two were prominent: one based on the control of land use and the second emphasizing the location of employment. The objective of the former was to ensure an acceptable and effective use of the land, not simply in the negative sense typical of North American zoning by-laws, but in the much broader context of encouraging rural preservation, recreational amenities, resource conservation, and urban environmental improvements (Clawson and Hall, 1973). Economic efficiency and the maintenance of private property values were of course also important. The primary objective behind the second, the location of jobs, was to achieve a more equitable regional 'balance' in economic growth and thereby in employment opportunities. The land use objective required a firm and explicit system of guiding urban sprawl and reconstruction and a subjugation of private to public interests in the consumption and disposal of land. The employment objective necessitated constraints on the expansion of industry (and later government employment and private offices) in the prosperous regions and incentives to shift new and some existing plants to the depressed peripheral regions. In the following pages we turn to the literature on two areas of national policy, new towns and regional policy, for elaboration.

Before doing so, however, note should be taken of the conditions lying behind these two spatially based planning strategies. There are two fundamental factors here: one is the importance of controls on land. Without that control, as Swedish experience has shown (Section 4.2), regulating urban growth is next to impossible (Blumenfeld, 1974). The other point is equally obvious within the regional policy context: that location incentives must be matched by location controls if a redistribution of economic activity is to be achieved. The early weakness of regional strategy in Britain lay in its emphasis, particularly up until 1964, on manufacturing. This emphasis reflected a limited view of the organization of society generally and specifically of the scale of decentralization needed. It tied policy action to a declining sector of the national economy in terms of total employment and largely to a single level of the income–occupation hierarchy (i.e. technical jobs).

The mechanisms for land-use regulation were established in the Town and Country Planning Act of 1947.[3] This act replaced an interim package of legislation introduced during the war years, which included the creation of a Ministry of Town and Country Planning (now part of the Department of the Environment) from the former Ministry of Works and Planning. The 1947 Act required local planning authorities to produce urban development plans and at the same time gave them control over permissions for land use change. The Act was intended to ensure '. . . the best use of the land . . .' by removing the unlimited right of owners to undertake land conversions and by reducing speculative development values. Through various institutional experiments (such as commissions and boards) and legislative improvements (the Planning Acts of 1968 and 1971 in particular),[4] the new planning system has been

[3] The Town Planning Act of 1947 effectively repealed most of the earlier planning legislation passed between 1909 and the war years. Its many important recommendations included shifting of statutory planning powers from small local government units to the larger County Boroughs and urban districts. The latter together totalled about 90 in number and encompassed most of the nation's urbanized population (see Cullingworth, 1972; Hall *et al.*, 1973).

[4] The Town and Country Planning Act of 1968 (1969 in Scotland) was a legislative landmark in a number of important ways (Cullingworth, 1972). Most relevant here is that the Act stipulated a hierarchy of broad strategies and specific plans which conformed somewhat more closely than the 1947 Act to the spatial organization of urban development. The Act called specifically for two types of plans: (1) structure plans—which were in fact development strategies rather than plans—intended to provide a broad framework for future urban growth in that district or county; and (2) local plans—drawn up by local planning authorities but which would conform in general with the principles of the broader structure plan for that region. The former would have to receive central government approval, the latter in most instances would not. The new system of course has taken some time to institute, limited in particular by the need for local government reform.

## TABLE 4.2

### CONSTRAINTS ON URBAN DEVELOPMENT IN BRITAIN, 1970

| | England and Wales | Scotland (mainland) | Total |
|---|---|---|---|
| | (in thousands of acres) | | |
| Urban Area 1970 | 4,330 | 565 | 4,895 |
| Policy Constraints—Conservation Areas | | | |
| National Parks | 3,366 | 1,530 | 4,896 |
| Forest Parks | 167 | 262 | 429 |
| National Nature Reserves | 77 | 147 | 224 |
| Areas of outstanding natural beauty | 2,746 | | 2,746 |
| Green Belts—Statutory | 1,211 | ⎰ 333 | ⎰ 3,989 |
| —Non-statutory | 2,445 | ⎱ | ⎱ |
| Areas of high landscape value | 5,974 | 5,160 | 11,134 |
| Deduction for overlap with areas listed below | − 583 | n.a. | n.a. |
| Total Conservation Areas | 15,403 | (7,432) | (23,418) |
| Physical Constraints—High Land | | | |
| Land over 800′ a.s.l. not included in above policy constraints category | 1,246 | | |
| Land over 600′ a.s.l. | | 9,840 | |
| Deduction for overlap between policy and physical constraints | | −5,316 | |
| Total Actual and Potential Constraints | 20,979 | 12,521 | 33,500 |
| Total Area | 37,343 | 16,674 | 54,016 |

n.a. = not available.          a.s.l. = above sea level.

Source: Department of the Environment (1971), p. 55. Reproduced by permission of the Controller of H.M.S.O.

relatively successful in achieving this objective, within certain limits. Now a majority of the national land area is under some form of development constraint (Table 4.2 and Figure 4.1).

Abercrombie's Greater London Plan (Abercrombie, 1945) provided frameworks for both the formulation and implemention of urban policies which have in essence persisted to this day (Burns, 1973). He proposed: (1) the physical containment of urban growth and the reduction of densities in the older inner cities; (2) the designation of green

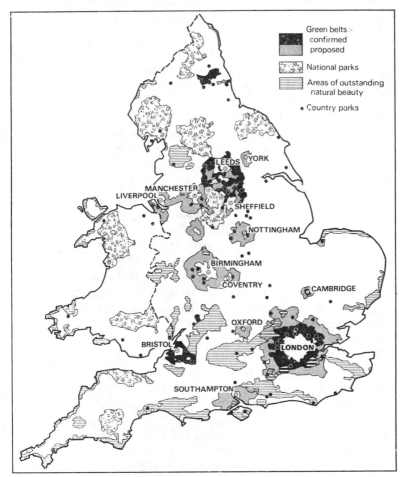

FIG. 4.1. Pattern of Constraints on Urban Development in England and Wales (after *The Economist*, 3 Feb. 1973).

Source: Countryside Commission, Department of the Environment, Ordnance Survey

belts to preserve open space and to facilitate containment; (3) the construction of a ring of new towns (initially eight in number) around London to alleviate urban sprawl and to accommodate populations decentralized from the thinned-out inner city; and (4) strict limits on the location of industries in the London region. All of these were subsequently translated into policy and most have been slowly extended to other areas of the country, although not in the exact form or with the consequences that Abercrombie might have anticipated.

### 4.1.4. NEW TOWNS: GREEN FIELDS AND GROWTH CENTRES

Probably the single achievement of British physical planning receiving the most widespread attention abroad has been the new town programme (Rodwin, 1956 and 1970; Merlin, 1971; Perloff and Sandberg, 1973; Barber, 1973; Berry, 1973a). While the importance of this programme as an urban strategy is often overemphasized, at the expense of the other components of the local planning system discussed above, it is of direct relevance to the theme of this book because new towns represent, or can be interpreted as, an attempt to alter the form of the urban system towards an ideal construct of what that system should look like. The limitation, as will be noted, is that this ideal has been conceived largely at the regional rather than the national level.

The new town concept in Britain has roots going back into the nineteenth century. These roots blur somewhat with the traditional preoccupation with countryside preservation and a 'stewardship of the land' philosophy, embedded in much of English social thought and literature (Cherry, 1972). Nevertheless, the substantive impact of new towns on patterns of urbanization derives almost entirely from late post-war developments. While it is not the intention here to review the historical details of the new town movement or of new town planning *per se*, it is worthwhile to set this movement in the broader context of urban growth and to attempt to evaluate its contribution to national urban strategies in general. This latter task becomes of central importance when one recognizes that the British new town approach has permeated the debate in almost all western countries on the appropriate means of influencing the future spatial structure of urban development.[5]

New towns were in large part a reaction to the congested environment of the nineteenth-century industrial city (Howard, 1898), and then

[5] For instance, see the discussions on new towns in the Australian (Section 5.16) and Canadian (Section 5.27) policy reviews.

the sprawling megalopolis of the twentieth century (Osburn and Whittick, 1969; Schaffer, 1972). The first new towns built, however, were largely private in origin and paternalistic in concept; many in fact were 'enlightened' housing estates constructed for industrial workers. Similar developments also took place in the U.S. (i.e. the Pullman estates near Chicago). Two new towns in Britain, both built at the end of the nineteenth century, are widely known: Port Sunlight near Liverpool developed by the Lever (soap) Corporation and Bournville near Birmingham built by Cadbury.

But the real father of new towns was Ebenezer Howard. His personal efforts to obtain government backing, but in particular the attractiveness of his Utopian philosophy, spawned a generation of planning advocates. His proposal to create a 'social city' in the rural countryside, which in fact consisted not of a single city, but an interrelated set (in fact representing a system in current terminology) of garden cities, directly resulted in the construction of two new towns: Letchworth (1902) and Welwyn Garden City (1920). While neither of these proved immensely successful as commercial ventures at the time (and one later had to be bailed out financially), the planning principles involved persisted. These principles, of orderly urban development on a human scale designed in harmony with the physical environment, have, despite their nineteenth-century rural origin, been maintained almost intact in the new town movement of the 1940s and 1950s and have generally served that movement well.

During the immediate post-war years, new town construction occurred on an impressive scale (Table 4.3). This scale is even more impressive when one considers timing and the difficult circumstances prevailing in the late 1940s. Yet a combination of conditions—on the one hand, severe housing shortages, extensive war-time destruction of urban services, and inner city congestion; and on the other hand, increased centralized public financing deriving from the war effort, political expediency, and widespread public receptiveness to change—facilitated rapid parliamentary approval and construction of the new towns (Figure 4.2).

Formally the movement began with the passing of the New Towns Act in 1946. It was a quick delivery, but not an easy birth. Had it not been for the war, and an unusual degree of consensus as to the desire for firm public action in creating a new and different urban environment, it is doubtful whether the enabling legislation would have been passed. This legislation was in fact only part of a formidably large planning package introduced to deal with economic recovery, reconstruction, and

**TABLE 4.3**

DESIGNATION, POPULATION SIZE, AND OBJECTIVES OF
BRITISH NEW TOWNS

| Name (date of designation) | Population (in thousands) | | Objectives |
| | At Designation | 1972 | Proposed Capacity | |
|---|---|---|---|---|
| Phase One: London | | | | Decentralization/containment |
| 1  Stevenage (1946) | 7 | 72 | 105 | Overspill |
| 2  Crawley (1947) | 9 | 68 | 79 | Overspill |
| 3  Hemel Hempstead (1947) | 21 | 72 | 80 | Overspill |
| 4  Harlow (1947) | 5 | 79 | 90 | Overspill |
| 5  Hatfield (1948) | 9 | 29 | 30 | Overspill |
| 6  Welwyn (1948) | 19 | 41 | 50 | Overspill |
| 7  Basildon (1949) | 25 | 80 | 134 | Overspill |
| 8  Bracknell (1949) | 5 | 38 | 60 | Overspill |
| Subtotal | 98 | 478 | 628 | |
| Phase One: Provinces | | | | Housing/Jobs/Overspill |
| 9  Aycliffe (1947) | 0 | 22 | 45 | Industrial housing |
| 10  East Kilbride (1947) | 2 | 66 | 100 | Overspill——(Glasgow) |
| 11  Peterlee (1948) | 0 | 26 | 30 | Housing improvement |
| 12  Glenrothes (1948) | 1 | 31 | 75 | Industrial housing/growth centre |
| 13  Cwmbran (1949) | 12 | 42 | 55 | Housing improvement |
| 14  Corby (1950) | 16 | 50 | 83 | Industrial housing |
| Subtotal | 31 | 237 | 388 | |

| | | | | Housing/Regional Growth Centres |
|---|---|---|---|---|
| **Phase Two: New Centres** | | | | |
| 15 Cumbernauld (1955) | 3 | 34 | 100 | Overspill—(Glasgow) |
| 16 Skelmersdale (1961) | 10 | 34 | 80 | Overspill—(Liverpool) |
| 17 Livingston (1962) | 2 | 18 | 100 | Overspill/Redistribution |
| 18 Redditch (1964) | 32 | 43 | 90 | Overspill—(Birmingham) |
| 19 Runcorn (1964) | 30 | 44 | 90 | Redevelopment/overspill |
| 20 Washington (1964) | 20 | 32 | 80 | Growth centre |
| 21 Irvine (1966) | 35 | 48 | 120 | Growth centre |
| 22 Newtown, Wales (1967) | 6 | 6 | 13 | Growth centre—Rural migration |
| Subtotal | 138 | 259 | 553 | |
| **Phase Three: New Cities** | | | | Major alternative centres |
| 23 Milton Keynes (1967) | 44 | 47 | 250 | Counter-magnet |
| 24 Peterborough (1967) | 83 | 89 | 187 | Counter-magnet/growth centre |
| 25 Northampton (1968) | 131 | 139 | 260 | Counter-magnet/growth centre |
| 26 Warrington (1968) | 122 | 130 | 202 | Overspill/renewal |
| 27 Telford (1968) | 70 | 82 | 250 | Overspill/renewal |
| 28 Central Lancashire (1970) | 250 | 250 | 500 | Counter-magnet/renewal |
| Subtotal | 700 | 733 | 1,649 | |
| TOTAL | 967 | 1,686 | 3,338 | |

Source: Statistics adapted from *Town and Country Planning*, 40, 1, Jan. 1972: the Department of the Environment; and Barber (1973).

SCOTLAND

Glenrothes

Cumbernauld
Livingston
East Kilbride
Stonehouse

Irvine

Washington
Peterlee
Aycliffe

NORTH

NORTH
WEST
Central
Lancashire
Skelmersdale
Warrington
Runcorn

YORKS-
HUMBER

W.MIDLANDS
Telford

E.MIDLANDS

Corby
Peterborough

EAST ANGLIA

Newtown
Redditch
Northampton

WALES

Milton
Keynes
Welwyn
Hemel
Hempstead
Stevenage
Harlow
Hatfield
Basildon

Cwmbran
Llantrisant

Bracknell

Crawley

SOUTH WEST
SOUTH EAST

FIG. 4.2.  Location and Projected Size of New Towns.

environmental protection, of which the new towns were a secondary and certainly not the most popular element. The legislative support for new towns followed from the urgent problem of housing overspill populations from the war-damaged conurbations.

While the overspill problem was the triggering factor the means of facilitating success was the organization of the new town development corporations and the establishment of enabling machinery for widespread public land acquisition. As these are described fully elsewhere (Thomas, 1969; Town and Country Planning Association, 1972; Schaffer, 1972a; Barber, 1973), a few brief comments will suffice here. It is worth emphasizing that the crucial decisions in the new town legislation were primarily on the management side. The development corporations were set up as semi-autonomous public bodies, entrusted with wide-ranging powers and a direct line of responsibility to the central government. These attributes facilitated rapid development as well as co-ordinated planning. The land acquisition procedures allowed for large-scale land assembly at predevelopment values, thereby keeping costs down, and in the longer term provided the necessary financial independence for the new town corporations.

The objectives of the first phase of new towns was explicitly identified in the responsibilities of the Advisory Committee set up under Lord Reith: 'to consider the general questions of the establishment, development, organization and administration that will arise in the promotion of New Towns in furtherance of a policy of planned decentralization from congested urban areas; and . . . such towns should be established and developed as self-contained and balanced communities for work and living' . . . (Town and Country Planning Association, 1972). With government acceptance of the recommendations of this committee, including those principles embodied in Abercrombie's plan (that is, to house one million people in a system of new towns located 20–50 miles from the centre of London), the movement was launched. Two key phrases in the above quotation are important as guidelines—'planned decentralization' and 'self-contained and balanced' communities. The latter were to be measured by the degree of external commuting and by equality in social–occupational structures. For present purposes, the former, decentralization, is the most relevant objective in terms of national urban strategies.

Thirteen new towns were designated in the first phase (or generation) between 1946 and 1950. In the greater London area these included Stevenage (1946), Hemel Hempstead, Crawley, and Harlow (1947),

Hatfield and Welwyn Garden City (1948), and Basildon and Bracknell (1949). These were paralleled by the designation of others in Scotland—East Kilbride (1947) and Glenrothes (1948); in Northern England—Aycliffe (1947) and Peterlee (1948); in the Midlands—Corby (1950); and in Wales—Cwmbran (1949). All of these shared a number of common attributes—which is not surprising given the speed of designation—such as a predominance of public housing, an emphasis on physical criteria in their design, and modest size (30,000–90,000 population). One additional new town, Cumbernauld, was designated somewhat later (1955) in Scotland.

A substantial break in the new town development took place after 1950. With a change in government, public interests and resources turned to other tasks. It was not until the 1960s that the second series of new towns was designated. Included were overspill towns for those conurbations ignored in the first place, for example: Skelmersdale (1961) for Liverpool; Redditch (1964) for Birmingham; and Warrington (1968) for Manchester. In total, six were designated between 1961 and 1966 and seven between 1967 and 1971. The latter included Milton Keynes (1967), Central Lancashire (1970), and the expanded towns centred on Peterborough (1967) and Northampton (1968).[6]

Most interesting for present purposes is the shift in objectives apparent with each generation of new towns (see Table 4.3 for a summary). The first new towns were primarily, if not exclusively, designed as overspill towns for London's displaced households and for anticipated post-war growth (Thomas, 1969). The Abercrombie plan was explicit in its proposal that these towns were to accommodate the bulk of London's future housing and land needs and that the total population of the urbanized area would remain roughly stable if not actually decline. This strategy, while undermined by the more rapid than anticipated growth in the national population, particularly that in the South-East, was, as Diamond (1972) argues, essentially an intraregional strategy. It was not seen as part of a comprehensive national or interregional strategy for the distribution of population or economic development, nor, it appears, were the planners aware of the full consequences of their decisions in locating the new towns. It is now generally agreed for instance that the location of the first eight new towns in the London region contributed to the relatively rapid growth of population in the South-East and thereby increased existing regional

---

[6] Four new towns (mostly expanded towns) have also been designated in Northern Ireland; Craigavon (1965), Antrim (1966), Ballymena (1967), and Londonderry (1969).

imbalances. It did so in part by providing a more attractive living environment as well as greater possibilities for employment and housing than were generally available in other regions.

Other new towns, designated somewhat later in the first phase, and located in peripheral areas (Scotland, Wales, the North), did of course have other objectives. Some were identified as housing improvement schemes (Peterlee), while others were to provide housing for major industrial projects (Corby). Because most of these were also located in the 'development' areas (see Section 4.15) they did in fact contribute to regional balance, but the effect was indirect and on a rather limited scale.

The second generation of new towns had broader objectives. Although overspill was still a significant factor, there was an explicit attempt to relate their location and design to the objectives of regional policy and urban renewal respectively. The towns were scattered more liberally across the country, somewhat larger in population, and more diversified in their economic base. Three were planned to act as growth centres—Washington, Irvine, and Newtown (Wales), while also serving the overspill function. A further shift in strategy came about in phase three. The towns were considerably larger; in fact most were expansions of existing cities. Milton Keynes has a proposed capacity population of 250,000, and a future-oriented economy based on tertiary and quarternary functions. Others were intended as counter-magnets to the growth of the conurbations themselves (such as Peterborough and Northampton). Still others were virtually redevelopment projects, and one, Central Lancashire new town, was designed to create a new and expanded urban core area, as well as improved social infrastructure, for three almost contiguous problem cities (Preston, Chorley, and Leyland). Their combined present population of about 250,000 is planned to increase to nearly 450,000 by the turn of the century. Parallel proposals, although not specifically using the legislative machinery for new towns, have carried this increase in scale even further. Some plans, such as that outlined for the Reading–Basingstoke area, involve the creation of national growth centres of over 1,000,000 population by encouraging the common development of cities which lie in close proximity and which are, in most instances, economically integrated.

Clearly the emphasis in new town planning objectives has altered over the last decade. Increasingly the new town legislative and administrative machinery (now under the New Town Directorate in the Department of the Environment) has been employed to achieve a variety of planning objectives. Since 1963 at least, these have included the goal of achieving regional balance, particularly evident in the designation of most new towns as growth centres, but a view also reflected in the locations selected for these towns. They have as well, for better and worse, witnessed an increase in the scale of development and in the range of activities, households, and interests accommodated. There is considerable disquiet at both of these trends. Nevertheless, the new towns strategy still reflects a central interest in housing supply (Barber, 1973) and urban land use containment, and they are seldom seen as new nodes operating within a national system of cities.

Future plans are uncertain.[7] It is likely, however, that no major new cities beyond those already designated will be built—because they are not needed in absolute terms given falling rates of population increase, and because of the increasingly competitive demands made on public resources for improving employment opportunities and environmental quality in existing cities. Even so, the new town machinery may have, with this shift in policy, an important 'in-town' application in the design and implementation of major redevelopment schemes, such as in that of the dockland area of London. While there are difficult political problems in such inner-city areas, the administrative lessons of the new town programme should be immensely valuable.

4.1.5. REGIONAL POLICY

The other strong arm regulating the spatial structure of economic (and urban) development in Britain has been regional policy. In a recent review, prepared by the conservative Institute of Economic Affairs (1973), the basic rationale of regional policy was summarized in the following terms: 'Regional problems ... are the symptoms of inadequate adjustment to changes in the *spatial economy*. Thus the underlying aim of regional policy should be to ease the transition to a new equilibrium.' The elements to be balanced in achieving this equilibrium are rates of unemployment and migration between regions. Since direct stimulation of the latter as a solution to the former has not been politically popular in Britain (nor in most countries), and given that the direction of most regional emigration is toward the South-East and the Midlands, both already thought to be seriously congested, policy has traditionally emphasized differences in unemployment and the relocation of basic industry to areas of high unemployment.

[7] These additional new towns have been proposed: Stonehouse near Glasgow, essentially an overspill town; Llantrisant, which would act as a new growth pole in the South Wales industrial area; and a new town to serve the now defunct third London airport and port complex near Maplin.

The national objective of 'regional balance' is not recent. By the 1930s a continuation of the disturbing trends in the distribution of economic development noted above, trends which followed from and augmented the transition to a new organizational and industrial structure, generated a concern for achieving '. . . the proper distribution of industry . . .' in the national interest (Burns, 1973). The two consequences of these trends most widely recognized were the 'drift' to the south (congestion) and the decline of industrial employment on the periphery (stagnation). The solution proposed was twofold: to limit industrial expansion in the congested areas (the stick), and to promote the location of industries in depressed regions through direct incentives (the carrot). In 1934 the first problem areas were designated in a Special Areas Act and subsidies for industries moving to these areas and for rehabilitation of existing industries were initiated.

Since the war, and release of the Barlow Report, a long and complex series of legislative measures have been used to encourage regional balance and to reduce high levels of unemployment in the depressed regions. Formal controls on industrial location were introduced in the Distribution of Industry Act of 1945 and have been refined and redefined continuously since that time. An extensive literature documents this history (McCrone, 1969; Holmans, 1964; Needleman and Scott, 1964; Department of Economic Affairs, 1967; EFTA, 1968 and 1973; Chisholm and Manners, 1971; Brown, 1972; and Cullingworth, 1973a). The specific policy instruments used, briefly summarized in Table 4.4, are far too numerous to comment on here. They have included an array of measures: industrial development certificates (IDCs) through which the government can influence industrial location decisions; regional employment premiums (REPs) which are subsidies paid to private firms located in the depressed regions, based on the number of employees involved (now about $3·45 per employee per week); and capital subsidies and tax allowances to reduce new construction costs as an incentive for plant relocation. These measures have been modified frequently over the years, as have the geographic areas designated for incentives[8] (see Figure 4.3), usually following a change in government or economic priorities. In spite of numerous legislative

[8] Three types of area designations have been used to determine the level of subsidy provided: development areas (DAs), the clear problem areas; intermediate areas (IDAs); and special development areas (SAs) suffering from unusual economic and social problems. New investments in the DAs receive an average of 18 per cent government subsidy on capital costs, the IDAs 4 per cent, and the special areas 20 per cent.

**TABLE 4.4**

**EVOLUTION OF MAJOR REGIONAL POLICY MEASURES IN BRITAIN, 1934–72**

| Legislation | Areas designated | Financial incentives | Development controls | Other features |
|---|---|---|---|---|
| Special Areas Acts, 1934, 36, 37. | North-east England, west Cumberland, South Wales, Clydeside | Loans to firms moving to SAs. Contributions to rent, rates, and tax. Exemption from national defence contributions. | None | Policy run by two commissioners. Trading estates formed to provide industrial sites and premises. Funds for physical rehabilitation. |
| Distribution of Industry Act, 1945. | South Lancashire (1946), Merseyside (1948), part of Scottish highlands (1949), and north-east Lancashire (1950) were added to the SAs. | Loans for sites, buildings. Treasury loans and grants on 'lender of last resort' basis for approved projects. | None (though building licences favoured DAs). | Board of Trade (now DTI) takes over supervision. Industrial estates. Advanced factories until 1948. |
| Town and Country Planning Act, 1947. | | | IDCs needed for over 5,000 sq. ft. and favoured DAs. | Stick to complement the carrot of the 1945 Act. |
| Distribution of Industry Act, 1958. | Concentrated on areas, in or out of DAs where unemployment more than 4¼. | Extended Treasury loans and grants. | None. | With low unemployment in most of the DAs, 1945 Act powers allowed to lapse. |
| Local Employment Act, 1960. | Replaced DAs with Development Districts—areas with over 4½% unemployment. | Loans and grants without 'lender of last resort' restrictions. Building grants. | IDCs to favour DDs. | Industrial estates reorganized. |
| Local Employment and Finance Acts, 1963. | As 1960 Act. | 25% building grant, 10% plant and machinery grant. Accelerated depreciation. | None. | Advanced factories programme stepped up. |

| | | | |
|---|---|---|---|
| Industrial Development Act, 1966. | Back to DAs: most of Scotland and Wales, Merseyside, Cornwall, north Devon, and north of England. | 40% investment grants replace all investment tax allowances. | IDC limit lowered and ODP started. |
| Further Labour action, 1967. | Special DAs added: Northumberland, Durham, Cumberland, and Scottish and Welsh coalfields. | REP introduced for DAs and SDAs. 35% building grants in SDAs. Investment grants raised to 45%, 1967–8 only. | Extra help for hard-hit areas in SDAs, e.g. collieries. |
| Local Employment Act, 1970. | Creation of intermediate areas: Leith, north-east Lancashire, Yorkshire coalfield, north Humberside, Notts/Derby coalfield, south-east Wales, and Plymouth. | 25% building grant: training grants. | Advanced factories. |
| Conservative action, 1970–1. | SDAs extended to include: Clydeside, Tyneside, north-west England, and South Wales. | Investment grants replaced by 'free depreciation'. Larger building grants. 30% operational grants in SDAs. | £160m. allocated to 'public works' in DAs and SDAs. |
| The Industry Act, 1972. | DAs and SDAs remain the same. | Back to investment grants: 20% in DAs, 22% in SDAs; free depreciation to remain. | Regional executive created with power to give additional grants and loans; budget of £250m. |

Notes:  SA = special areas.
DA = development areas.
DD = development districts.
IDC = industrial development certificates.
ODP = office development permits.
REP = regional employment premiums.
SDA =special development areas.

Source: *The Economist*, 'A Bit Here, A Bit There', 21 April, 1973, p. 60.

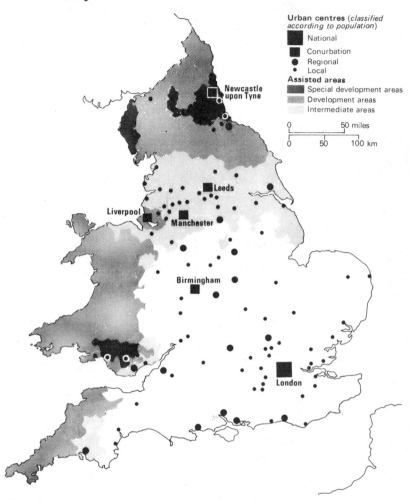

FIG. 4.3. Urban Centres and Assisted Areas in England and Wales, 1972. Reproduced by permission of the Controller of H.M.S.O.

changes, a consistent evolution in regional policy is apparent—that is, towards a more comprehensive view of the nation's space economy, and an awareness of its domination by large cities, and the use of a broader range of location controls and incentives than in the past.

One example of the former perspective in regional policy is the recognition of the growing role, as a source of employment and of multiplier effects, of the tertiary sector of the economy. Recently attention has focused on offices and specifically on reducing the consequences of their increasing concentration in central London (Table 3.3). In 1963 the Location of Offices Bureau (LOB) was established (located in Central London of course, not in the development regions), and in 1965 new office construction over a minimum threshold size was limited in selected regions through development permits (ODPs) similar in form to the IDCs.[9] The results have been followed with considerable interest (LOB, 1969 and 1972; Cowan, 1969; Rhodes and Kan, 1972; Goddard, 1973; Yannopoulos, 1973; Donnison and Eversley, 1973).

In concert with these controls the government undertook, as in Sweden, to decentralize its own office employment from London and the South-East, much of it allocated to the development areas. By 1973 over 22,500 jobs had been dispersed and another 8,000 awaited dispersal. Adding to these nearly 9,500 jobs set up outside London in newly created positions brings the total decentralized employment to 32,000, and with a further 10,200 possible relocations in proposed positions, the total surpasses 50,000 (Table 4.5). A recent government report (Hardman, 1973) recommend that a further 30,000 jobs *could* be dispersed over a period of years without a significant loss in efficiency of communication. Rhodes and Kan (1972) concluded their review of regional policy by suggesting that on 'the question of office dispersal, and particularly with respect to long-distance decentralization, the government has set a good example'. Among the decentralized jobs most have gone north—to Scotland (20·2 per cent), the North-West (18·7 per cent), and the North (10·5 per cent), with only 28·3 per cent relocating within the South-East. In contrast, within the private sector, most decentralized offices have remained close to London; few seem to have found movement to a development area either necessary or worthwhile.[10]

The problem with such controls in the private sector, as the recent Layfield report documented, is that the government has no widely accepted criteria for deciding which offices should or should not be allowed to be located in London, or anywhere else for that matter. While recent research on the spatial contact patterns and communication needs of different office functions (Hardman, 1973; Goddard, 1973) has provided some of the information necessary for establishing such criteria, the relative merits of the ODPs are still unresolved.

[9] Under revisions introduced in 1971, ODPs were only necessary in the South-East and for office buildings of over 10,000 square feet in area.

[10] For example, of private-sector office clients using the Location of Offices Bureau up to 1972, over 45 per cent moved within the Greater London area and 80 per cent moved less than 40 miles from the city centre (LOB Annual Report, 1971–2).

TABLE 4.5

GOVERNMENT OFFICE EMPLOYMENT POSITIONS
RELOCATED, OR SCHEDULED FOR RELOCATION
FROM LONDON, 1972

| Region in which Cities Receiving Office Jobs are Located | Jobs Relocated May 1963–Oct. 1972 | | Jobs Scheduled for Relocation at Oct. 1972 | |
|---|---|---|---|---|
| | No. of Positions Relocation or Established outside London | % of Total | No. of Positions to be Relocated from London | % of Total |
| Scotland | 6,481 | 20·2 | 4,476 | 24·6 |
| Northern | 3,377 | 10·5 | 790 | 4·3 |
| North-West | 5,997 | 18·7 | 1,918 | 10·5 |
| Yorkshire and and Humberside | 783 | 2·4 | 55 | 0·3 |
| Wales | 2,826 | 8·8 | 7,784 | 42·7 |
| East Midlands | 746 | 2·3 | 140 | 0·8 |
| West Midlands | 279 | 0·9 | 0 | — |
| East Anglia | 1,192 | 3·7 | 0 | — |
| South-West | 1,332 | 4·2 | 1,185 | 6·5 |
| South-East | 9,004 | 28·1 | 1,861 | 10·2 |
| TOTAL | 32,017 | 100·0 | 18,209 | 100·0 |

Source: Hardman (1973).

The operational unit of spatial planning at the macro-level in Britain is the region. Ten economic regions were set up for planning purposes in 1965; eight in England, and one each for Scotland and Wales. Each was to have an Economic Planning Board and a Regional Economic Planning Council; the former was to act to co-ordinate activities of various regional offices of the central government, while the latter was to serve as the link in a tripartite arrangement between local government statutory planning bodies and similar functioning bodies at the national level. A broad 'strategy' plan was to be prepared for each region as a guide-line for the detailed plans of local authorities. This complex process is now well documented.[11] The first such plan, for the South-

[11] Excellent reviews of this process are provided in McCrone (1969), OECD (1970), Cullingworth (1973b), McLoughlin and Thorney (1972 and 1973), and Hall *et al.* (1973).

East region (population 17·4 millions), has attracted wide attention (South East Joint Planning Team, 1970). In its design, recommendations, and success it seems to emulate the famous Abercrombie plan for London. The South-East region by its size and complexity is roughly equated by some officials to the scale of national problems in regional planning faced by smaller European countries. This is a debatable point, but it is revealing of a certain perspective. Most other regions in Britain have yet to produce strategy plans, and the Department of the Environment's attempt to co-ordinate the regional actions of government departments, notably in housing, transport, and industrial location, has been only marginally successful. To what extent interregional co-ordination will take place through, or in spite of, this regional planning framework is as yet difficult to estimate.

### 4.1.6. LOCATIONAL STRATEGIES AND THE EEC

Britain's planning strategies, both urban and regional, became rather more complicated upon her entry into the European Economic Community (EEC). One secondary condition of membership of the Community as laid down by the treaty of Rome was the internal standardization of regional and industrial location policies. This meant that regional incentives and subsidies given by member countries were not to conflict with the emerging (but as yet undefined) regional strategy of the EEC nor extend unfair advantage through subsidies or indirect means to any one sector or area. Britain, with the longest and most firmly established regional programme, and the highest level of expenditures (in Europe) on regional subsidies, almost certainly has the greatest adjustment to make of any of the new members. Some of the necessary adjustments were anticipated (McCrone, 1969), others were not (Burns, 1973). The debate is still going on.

The financial implications of Community membership in the area of regional policy are probably less severe than the administrative. Britain, by most international yardsticks (current income), now ranks below nearly all its Western European partners. While this ranking is misleading, in part because it ignores other forms of national wealth, none the less it has been and is likely to continue to be an important decision-making criterion on EEC policy. Relatively high rates of unemployment and emigration and low per capita incomes in all areas but the South-East and the West Midlands place Britain on about the same absolute scale as Italy. More specifically, peripheral areas such as the North, Scotland, Wales and Northern Ireland qualify in terms of degree of

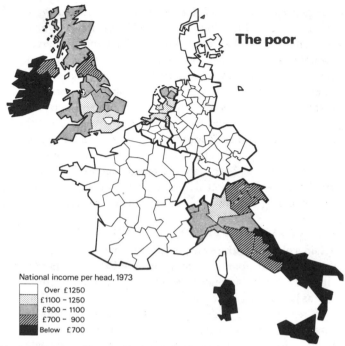

The poor

National income per head, 1973

Over £1250
£1100 – 1250
£900 – 1100
£700 – 900
Below £700

FIG. 4.4. Patterns of Income Variation within Britain and the Expanded EEC.

Source: *The Economist*, 21 April 1973. Adapted from EEC data and updated.

economic retardation with areas in southern Europe (*The Economist*, 1973; see Figure 4.4). Consequently, Britain can expect a greater share of expenditures over the long run from the Community's as yet unspecified regional fund than it puts in.[12] The areas qualifying for assistance, however, may be less extensive under EEC rules than under present British rules.[13] First, the former rules are more restrictive spatially, and second, the degree of regional imbalance in income within Britain is considerably less than on the Continent (Figure 4.5). In any

[12] Some observers have argued that Britain's role in the EEC regional policy debate has been more a device for repatriating her initial financial payments on membership than a means of identifying a common policy approach.

[13] A specific problem centres around the designation of areas eligible for Community support from the EEC regional fund and the limits on the degree of assistance for industrial location within these areas. EEC policy at present recognizes only two types of areas, central and peripheral, with only the latter qualifying for support and that limited to a maximum of 20 per cent on net capital investment. Consequently, Britain may lose the authority to subsidize investment in those areas designated as intermediate development areas.

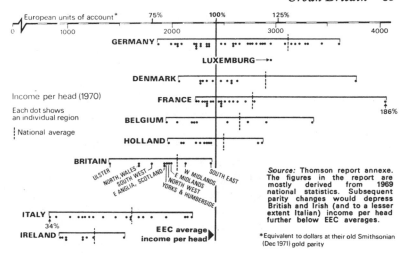

FIG. 4.5. Relative Inequalities: Britain and the EEC Countries.

Source: *The Economist*, 14 April 1973.

event, Britain is likely to benefit on average, but improved co-ordination of incentive programmes and a considerable rethinking of regional strategies will be necessary over the next decade. By that time North Sea oil and gas revenues may eradicate many of the differentials between the North and West, particularly between Scotland and Wales and the rest of Europe, thereby changing the criteria for regional assistance again.

Other conditions of EEC membership will also have important long-term locational consequences. Among these conditions are legislation facilitating labour mobility among member countries, greater export competition and its effects on the type of economic growth, as well as wider options for investors in industrial location and for governments in setting subsidies for sectors such as transport. Some of the consequences, including closer integration with the rapidly growing Rotterdam–Ruhr–Paris industrial triangle, may run directly against the stated objectives of regional balance and urban containment by encouraging further drifts of industry and population to the South-East. The now defunct Channel Tunnel and third London airport would most certainly have added to these pressures.

4.1.7. SOME SPATIAL CONSEQUENCES OF PLANNING:
AN EVALUATION

The impact of planning—regional and town planning—on the processes and patterns of urban development has seldom been explicitly documented in any country. It is clear, however, that urban planning in Britain has had little over-all effect on the national (interregional) distribution of population or employment. Regional planning, on the other hand, notably the industrial and office development controls and related relocation incentives have had a significant redistributive effect. Urban land use, new town, and related legislation, in the opinion of the PEP study group (Hall *et al.*, 1973), has had three major impacts: (1) the *containment* of the English megalopolis—that is, minimizing both the aggregate amount of land consumed by urbanization and the local shadow effect of urban expansion on adjacent urban areas; (2) *suburbanization*—accelerating the outward movement of population and employment from the metropolitan cores to outlying urban centres, housing estates, and new towns; and (3) *inflation*—adding to the rapid increase in land prices and thus to the costs of housing and urban development.

Of the three effects only the first, containment, might be considered a direct and anticipated consequence of planning objectives. In fact urban containment is to most observers the crowning achievement of British urban planning. The new towns are part of this achievement, but only part. Green belt legislation, environmental and recreational conservation areas, historical and agricultural preservation laws are some of the other parts. These, combined with a rigorous public sector control over the release of rural land for urban use, have created a more orderly, but probably somewhat higher-cost and higher-density, accommodation of post-war population growth than that achieved in the 1930s. Consequently, the impact of urban growth, in terms of rural land conversion and environmental destruction, has likely been less severe than would have been the result of any other urban form which might have arisen through different planning priorities or through *laissez-faire* practices.

The other two consequences are in part outcomes of the success of urban containment policies. Suburbanization is the most difficult to explain, but in Clawson and Hall's (1973) review it includes two results. On the one hand, containment policies have succeeded because they conformed to the so-called natural forces of intraregional population decentralization. These policies have in fact extended the effects of those forces further and further outward (i.e. extending daily urban fields) from the central cores of most English cities. Initially at least they lengthened the journeys to work, to friends, and to services faced by most suburban residents. On the other hand, restrictions on the provisions of services to new suburban zones attached to the existing built-up areas have increased many of the disadvantages and costs of living in these areas relative to exurban locations. Inflation in land prices meanwhile is a universal phenomenon and therefore is less directly attributable to the existence or success of any set of national policies. Rather, land inflation is more closely related to the number of links and time involved in the planning process, and of course to the level of demand for urban space. Many other countries, Canada and Australia for example, have similar degrees of land inflation, but without most of the benefits deriving from containment as a trade-off against higher costs.

Obviously there are other consequences of containment specifically, and of British urban planning practice in general, which are interrelated with the above. The interested student of planning would be wise to explore some of these thoroughly to decide whether they represent severe trade-off decisions or not. One such problem is the possible effect of reducing household mobility and housing choice among that sector of the population which is subject to containment. Those who can afford the price of a rural town or country house, and can bear the costs of commuting, are not directly affected by containment. They would probably not be interested in alternative residential locations on the built-up urban fringe in any case. Another possible consequence is to inflate demand schedules for land in areas available for development, thereby creating monopoly profits for a selective proportion of the population—again primarily directed to those who already own land and those not subject to containment. There are clearly redistributive mechanisms within the planning process operating in different if not opposite directions to those advocated or anticipated by most planners.

Among the other possible consequences of planning which the PEP group considered in its report are the negative effects of urban growth containment practices, in combination with regional policy, on the rate of national economic growth. Most readers are aware of the existence of such relationships and the strong possibility that tight planning controls have reduced locational efficiency and thereby lowered the rate of overall expansion in the economy. While this issue was not made explicit in the planning literature at the outset (if anything, the reverse position was taken), it has since become an important point for debate. No doubt the British public would have accepted lower economic growth if given the choice. But how much lower, and at what cost to whom? And there are few in other countries who would not now accept some reduction in growth rates as a necessary cost to achieve the benefits of containment and stricter environmental controls. But are they necessarily trade-offs? Or is it that government bureaucracy together with ill-conceived plans and rigid planning mechanisms have a cost in terms of economic growth which planning *per se* need not have? These are of course complex questions, which cannot be answered here, but they must at least be openly assessed in developing a national strategy for regulating urban growth.

What of the success of British new towns? There seems to be little doubt that they have been, despite some teething problems, a resounding success in terms of their initial objectives.[14] Besides breaking even financially, have they provided an alternative to contained growth of megalopolis? Have they improved the distribution and efficiency of public services for new urban growth? Have they achieved self-containment and socially balanced communities? To each the obvious answer is yes—but to a limited extent. They have provided one alternative to the conurbations and to suburban sprawl.[15] While they have taken less than 10 per cent of post-war population growth and currently receive about 3 per cent of the nation's housing construction, the benefits nevertheless have gone in large part to a particularly important group—lower-working-class residents of the congested inner cities. While housing for this group could clearly have been provided by extending existing built-up urban areas, the resulting public economies would almost certainly not have been as great or as widely distributed through the social order.[16]

[14] The impressive scale of new town development is evident in the following statistics: a population of 1·7 million resided in 28 new and expanded towns at the beginning of 1973, nearly 800,000 having been added since their designation; over 200,000 dwellings have been constructed in these towns, representing 10 per cent of the nation's (rented) housing programme (but only 1 per cent of private housing); and over 160,000 jobs in industry have been provided. Total government investment in the new towns is estimated at over £1,000 million.

[15] It should also be stressed that the new town programme forms only part of an over-all decentralization strategy. Considerable numbers of overspill population have been added as increments to established towns at varying distances from the conurbations. Usually an arrangement is made directly between the conurbation and the receiving town (or city), and generally the population movement involved is not as great as that in new or expanded town developments. Examples include Basingstoke and Swindon, both receiving relocated population from London.

[16] In terms of the distribution of social benefits in planning one must also take into consideration the acquisition of development values on land in the new towns by the communities themselves through the practice of public landownership. As this land was generally purchased or expropriated at predevelopment values there is little evidence of extensive speculative profits being made in the private sector.

Otherwise the main effect of the new towns has been to encourage intraregional decentralization—at first on a local scale but later over much greater distances—while at the same time improving the neatness of the urban fringe. Both of these effects have been extremely important. In a few cases the new towns have served to stimulate economic development in selected regions, foremost in the South-East, but also in some of the designated development areas. As for stimulating a reordering of urban development and population distribution at the national level, their effect as yet has been minimal. If anything, they have had the reverse effect to that anticipated. Their success at the regional level, as previously noted, comes largely from the fact that the policy was in direct accord with established spatial trends toward decentralization—trends which accelerated in the post-war years. Their failure at the national level is due in part to the apparent conflict between maintaining acceptable rates of economic growth over-all while arresting the continued 'drift to the south'; and in part to the fact that population growth and the pace of social and technological change were substantially greater than predicted in the early post-war years. Consequently the new towns were insufficient in both number and size to accommodate a significant proportion of the nation's new population and to redistribute industrial growth. None the less, they did set a precedent which has been followed in local decentralization strategies in many other countries.

Evaluating regional policy is somewhat easier, although many of the same reservations apply. Britain's investment in the two arms of regional policy—industrial location controls and incentives and the decentralization of office employment—has been relatively large and the results impressive, particularly given the slow growth in the economy over-all. To some observers, however, Britain may have done better at telling activities where they may not be located than where they may. While no one would expect the problems of regional imbalance to be solved in three or four decades, there is conflicting evidence as to whether the incentives have been properly designed and worthy of the expense (Chisholm, 1970; Brown, 1972; Manners, 1972). The development areas still lag behind the national average in new jobs created, personal income, and service growth, and remain above the national average in unemployment rates, substandard housing, derelict industrial structures, as well as in rates of out-migration to other regions and emigration abroad. At a minimum such policies may have prevented a serious situation from becoming worse (Kan and Rhodes,

1972). From the scattered figures that are available (Table 4.6), it appears that the development areas have secured more than their share since 1965 of a rapidly declining national employment base in the manufacturing sector, and are only now beginning to receive significant allocations of national growth in the office and management sector.

How much worse (or better) off these areas would be without such

**TABLE 4.6**

IMPACT OF REGIONAL POLICY: EMPLOYMENT CHANGES
IN MANUFACTURING IN THE DEVELOPMENT AREAS

|  | Development Areas | Non-Development Areas | Britain |
|---|---|---|---|
| Manufacturing employment (in thousands) | | | |
| 1952 | 3,019·6 | 5,576·4 | 8,596·0 |
| Annual change in employees (in thousands) | | | |
| 1952–8 | +14·7 | +77·6 | +92·3 |
| 1959–64 | +4·3 | +73·2 | +77·5 |
| 1965–7 | +0·7 | −14·9 | −14·2 |
| 1968–70 | +32·4 | +32·9 | +65·3 |
| Average percentage change | | | |
| 1952–8 | +2·9 | +8·3 | +6·2 |
| 1959–64 | +0·7 | +6·6 | +4·6 |
| 1965–7 | +0·1 | −1·0 | −0·7 |
| 1968–70 | +1·0 | +0·5 | +0·7 |

Source: Kan and Rhodes (1972), 171.

policies is impossible to estimate. On the negative side, it may be that such policies have perpetuated a dominance of declining industries and low-paying jobs in the development areas (as in Table 4.6). They may also have reduced the potential improvement in living standards for those who in the absence of such policies would have migrated to more prosperous areas such as in the Midlands and the South-East. By placing restrictions on the location of new industries in these areas the level of national economic efficiency and, as noted, the rate of national income growth, may have been seriously dampened (Burns, 1973; Hardman, 1973). While these arguments are the same in any country, their relative importance is greater in Britain. Even so, a severe shortage (perceived rather than real) of land and a long-standing policy objective in Britain of maintaining and improving existing communities and rural areas have tipped the scales in favour of both urban containment and the interregional redistribution of employment as planning objectives rather than the achievement of greater economic efficiency and maximum social choice. Nevertheless, one of the best regional policy measures, in the limited terms in which it is normally set, is still considered to be more economic growth.

### 4.1.8. CENTRALITY IN BRITISH PLANNING

One final point in review is to note the apparent centrality of planning innovation in Britain. Many of the concepts and legislation in urban and regional planning policy, as in other European countries, were developed to deal with the national capital, London, and its unique and widely publicized problems (Foley, 1963 and 1972; Hall, 1969; Hall *et al.*, 1973; Donnison and Eversley, 1973). Some were developed for London and then subsequently were applied elsewhere, others were designed for London alone. There was for instance little interest in a deliberate policy of urban containment outside of the London region during the intensive planning debate of the early 1940s (Barlow Report, 1940). The new town scheme was initially a London overspill policy; the green belt concept and the underlying principles of the Abercrombie plan were not quickly replicated elsewhere; industrial development and office location restrictions applied specifically to London, as did other policies relating to housing construction and transport. The Strategy Plan for the South-East region has become a model for regional planning throughout the country. This emphasis is certainly reasonable given London's size, importance, and unique position in the national social order. The failing if any of this emphasis was that London was not viewed as a member of a functioning urban system (or systems) and of an integrated national space economy in which actions taken in one area or sector would have many and varied side-effects in other areas and sectors.[17]

[17] The same principle holds true in other sectors, witness the planning for the third London airport at Maplin. There is now a growing feeling that had the Maplin decision been set explicitly within the framework of a national system of airports (and therefore the urban system), it might not have been proposed in the first place, at least in its present form. Current proposals now centre on a strengthening of the regional airport system, which also has numerous positive advantages for improving regional balance (*Sunday Times*, London, 24 March 1974).

4.1.9. COMMENTARY

Britain has developed a relatively complex set of strategies and policies for regulating urban development and its social and spatial consequences. These may be summarized as: (1) limiting the geographic spread of cities through land-use controls—planning permissions, green belt, and conservation policies—and the relocation of some of this growth into new and expanded towns; (2) limiting the location of new jobs—industrial and office—in already congested areas and their redirection to depressed areas through capital and employment incentives and government decentralization; and (3) on the local level, limiting private redevelopment of the existing urban landscape in combination with massive incentives for public slum clearance and environmental improvement.

These achievements reflect a number of background conditions: a sufficiently broad consensus on the problems and benefits of urbanization (notably on problems), and on the goals of the planning process itself; and a prevailing and persuasive image of what the ideal urban form should be. This image, deriving largely from rural preservation and garden city concepts, guided the translation of goals into planning practices. Neither a similar consensus nor an acceptable ideal form for cities has existed or is likely to exist in North America. The regulation of urban development has also been facilitated in Britain by a highly centralized political system and by a rather elitist social structure.[18] Clearly, Britain has at least partially satisfied Rodwin's (1970) preconditions for effective urban policy implementation noted in the introduction to this volume: that problems must be recognized as problems and they must appear capable of solution by political means. To these must be added the prerequisites which Berry (1973a) describes as the will to plan and the means to plan. World War II may have been the specific stimulus bringing together many of the issues which demanded policy action and encouraged a political and social desire for directing change, but this stimulus simply captured trends already present in the social climate of the 1930s.

Despite the enormous array of planning guide-lines, and partly in response to it, evaluations and criticisms of British planning have been

---

[18] Proposals for some decentralization of central government powers may significantly alter this factor. The report of the special commission on local government, the Kilbrandon Report, recommended considerable decentralization of policy-making responsibility, and government reorganization. Seven regional assemblies were advocated, five for England, and one each for Scotland and Wales. The realization of these recommendations was not viewed with much support, at least until the February 1974 election (*The Economist*, 16 March 1974, p. 26).

frequent (i.e. Cowan *et al.*, 1973; Clawson and Hall, 1973; Hall *et al.*, 1973). These criticisms have identified the originating principles, the underlying ideal urban constructs, and the means of implementing planning policies as well as the general failure to evaluate the true distribution of social costs in regulating urban growth and to reassess planning philosophies. Senior (1973, p. 125), for example, has commented on an increasing trend toward 'professional elitism and impending omnicompetence' in planning. While this is certainly not a recent development, its increase in recent years may fly in the face of current directions of social change. Donnison (1973, p. 98) has gone further in forecasting 'a new climate of opinion in which planners will have to cope with a public that is better informed, more demanding and more aggressively organized'. An elitist planning movement, largely guided by professional rather than public values and preferences, has served the nation well under early post-war pressures, but is less likely to do so in the future.

The results of this legislation have been most apparent at the local level. While beyond the scope of this essay the possible conflict of local v. national objectives should be raised. British planning has been successful in regulating the internal structure, and particularly the rural margins, of the conurbations, and in reducing the negative impact of economic and technological change in specific peripheral locations. But at the more aggregate level the urban regulation and redistributive results have been considerably less significant (except in housing), and in some instances the successes of local planning have been at the expense of stated national objectives. The ideal urban form which has underlain the containment of urban sprawl has not been followed by a similar concept of the organization of the nation's urban system.

This raises the interesting question of whether the current set of policies adds up to a national development strategy. It can be argued that Britain has an emerging national regional policy and a regional urban policy, but no national urban policy. Nor does it appear that the national urban system approach has much political sympathy given the complexity of regional economies and the strength of regional over urban interests and politics. This leads to an intriguing point for speculation concerning the degree to which the established and well-tested policies of regional planning and industrial location on the one hand, and the land use and new town components or urban planning policies on the other hand, are converging on a focus which is both urban and national. That is, a focus explicitly based on the interdependences of location decisions between cities and regions.

This section has outlined the evolution of the new town movement and regional policy and suggested that their emphasis has in fact shifted towards a growth redistribution policy which is national as well as regional. Historically, regional policy has held a discrete and rather polarized view of the regional make-up of the country's economic structure. Location incentives have been largely of the blanket type—that is, available throughout broad development areas. Most recently pressures have been exerted to concentrate incentives on viable growth centres within the development areas, although political resistance to this concentration remains strong. The growth centre concept has also emerged in the discussion of new towns, providing one possible link toward a national urban and regional development strategy. Another possible link is the closer integration at the national level of regional strategy and structure plans. How and when this integration might be achieved remains to be answered.

## 4.2. URBAN SWEDEN

Most readers will agree that Sweden is one of the world's most advanced countries, both technologically and in terms of social policy. A recent report on the state of the Swedish economy, by the Organization for Economic Co-operation and Development (OECD, 1972), concluded that: 'Sweden is probably one of the first countries to enter the new era of post-industrial society, increasingly devoting its pilot forces to problems of environment, systems management, research and social developments' (p. 22). This statement acts as a barometer on social evolution and is an important component in understanding recent developments in Swedish urban policy. Sweden's long and relatively successful endeavours in the fields of urban planning, and in regulating economic development, form part of a much broader approach to social development. This approach serves as a useful introduction to Sweden's recent urban policy experience.

While a great deal has been written about Swedish planning in the English-language literature, and need not be duplicated here, much remains hidden behind the language screen. The most recent and often the most valuable policy literature is generally not available in English. Nevertheless, sufficient material is published to provide the novice with ample, if not somewhat biased, insights. Among the excellent summaries available in English of Swedish planning practices are those by Astrom (1967), Strong (1971), Berry (1973a), and the Ministry of

Labour and Housing (1973). Reviews of recent research on housing and environmental planning (Swedish Council on Building Research, 1972; Plan, 1972; Ödmann, 1973), on urbanization trends (Hägerstrand, 1970), and on regional development (ERU, 1970; EFTA, 1973; Andersson, 1973) are numerous and substantial. Particularly appropriate in timing and content, given the emphasis here on the spatial aspects of urbanization, is Pred's (1973c) summary of the Swedish-language literature on geographical research, urbanization, and planning.

This literature review is important here. Throughout this section it is argued that social science research has had a very profound influence on policy development in Sweden. While this success has been facilitated by the relatively small size of the Swedish professional research community, it also identifies another important factor in explaining past successes in anticipating and planning for new directions of social change and policy needs.[1]

## 4.2.1. BACKGROUND: THE SOCIAL WELFARE ENVIRONMENT

The evolution of Swedish national planning suggests an unusual degree of consensus on the importance of planning *per se* and on the identification of social goals. One frequently stated national priority is that improvement in social welfare must be equal in weight to, and in many instances supersede, that of material growth. Recently the prevailing social philosophy has shifted from a focus on welfare to one of 'social renewal'. Although this terminology is partly a political gimmick, there is a clear sense that Swedish society, despite the continued dominance of economic goals, is closer to accepting social criteria for national and regional development planning than are most other Western European countries.

Similar social principles have underscored the growing interest in regulating urbanization. During the post-war years, if not before, a significant portion of the attention span of politicians has been given over to problems of reducing social, sectoral, and spatial imbalances, and of environmental protection. This attention has produced many forms of policy response, including the transfer of resources to the socially disadvantaged, more egalitarian income distributions, selective improvements in physical and cultural infrastructure, and pollution

[1] Devising appropriate public policies is heavily conditioned by the amount and quality of data available on the growth processes involved. Swedish efficiency in information collection, storage, and processing has also contributed substantially to interregional research and policy analysis.

control. Most recently, explicit spatial and urban systems components have been added to this philosophy.

All of these measures must be set in their relevant time frame. Swedish policy and research, in many sectors of national development, have been accompanied by an unusual political emphasis on planning for long-term outcomes. In part this emphasis represents a social perspective, and in part it mirrors the continuity and stability of government. Whatever the reason, this perspective provides a degree of freedom in the area of policy formulation which few other nations have had or seem willing to accept. Granted Sweden's urban problems are by international comparison minor in scale, severity, and urgency, and there may be other problems of at least equal importance which are not debated and which escape the usual criteria (Hancock, 1972; *The Economist*, 1974), yet this social policy position is one that will no doubt bear significant benefits in the long run, particularly in such specific policy areas as environmental protection and health care delivery. This same perspective is evident in the Swedish approach to issues of urban system regulation; issues which by their very nature are susceptible largely to long-term actions.[2]

In each of these cases, planning in general and the regulation of urban growth in particular are made more palatable by relative prosperity. Continued high rates of economic growth and job formation, relatively low unemployment rates, and modest over-all population growth are obvious advantages in policy-making. These conditions have facilitated efforts at resource management and provided scope for industrial relocation and the reallocation of government services which many countries have not had. Even so, such policies have been tempered by the need for Sweden to remain competitive in Europe which some argue includes permitting Stockholm to continue to grow.

### 4.2.2. THE ISSUES: THE NORTH AND STOCKHOLM

The factors leading to a greater awareness of locational and urban problems in Sweden are much the same as elsewhere although their exact expressions differ. The transformation of Swedish society from a depressed rural state in the nineteenth century to a modern industrial state was one of the most recent, rapid, and complete in Europe.

[2] As in other developed countries, the Swedish urban system is characterized by remarkable historical stability in terms of city-size distributions (Byland, 1972). No major changes in ranking have occurred for several decades. The only change expected by the year 2000 is that Malmö may pass Göteborg to become Sweden's second largest centre, reflecting the increasing economic pull of accessibility to Continental European markets.

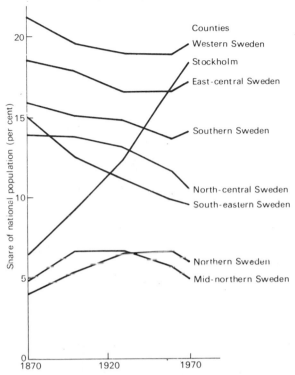

FIG. 4.6. Relative Growth of Regional Population in Sweden, 1870–1970 (after Ministry of Labour and Housing, 1973).

Stockholm grew rapidly, at the expense of most other regions (Figure 4.6). Consequently political attention focused initially on the depopulation of the rural countryside, and the resulting problems of social and economic deprivation which frequently accompany heavy net emigration (Table 4.7). The dominance of the rural political voice in national government saw to this interest. At this early stage in the country's urban history there was no need to cope with problems at the other end of the geographic scale—the overgrown metropolis—because it was argued that such a city did not exist (Holm, 1957). However, war-time conditions applied pressure for increased government intervention in the pattern of economic growth. Military considerations encouraged arguments for decentralization particularly of heavy manufacturing industries and utilities. Although these are no longer very significant they

## TABLE 4.7

REGIONAL DIFFERENTIALS IN SWEDEN, BY LEVEL IN THE
URBAN SYSTEM HIERARCHY

| Urban Level* (by population size in thousands) | Average rate of net migration | Average Income/Employee (in thousands Skr) | No. of job vacancies/no. of unemployed | Participation Rate: No. employed/100 population |
|---|---|---|---|---|
| 29– 59 | –7.0 | 19.3 | 1.04 | 41.4 |
| 60– 95 | –4.0 | 19.4 | 1.15 | 41.4 |
| 96–132 | –1.4 | 19.7 | 2.04 | 42.6 |
| 133–184 | +0.4 | 20.6 | 1.92 | 43.8 |
| Small metropolitan centres** | +6.8 | 23.8 | 4.55 | 45.9 |
| Stockholm/Södertälje | +6.9 | 26.7 | 6.67 | 47.6 |

* These levels are modifications of the definition of "municipal building blocks". These municipal blocks (regions), of which there are 300 in Sweden, embrace the entire population and populated area of the country and do away with what Swedish authorities believe to be an artificial distinction between urban and rural. For details of the definition see note 13.

** Göteborg/Malmö/Lund/Helsingborg/Landskrona.

Source: Royal Ministry for Foreign Affairs (1972b).

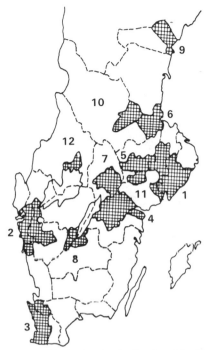

FIG. 4.7. Spatial Structure of Urbanization in Sweden: The Twelve Largest Urban Regions (numbers refer to Table 4.8).

did set the stage for more direct public involvement in national development.

Rapid economic growth and technological change in the post-war years brought a further reordering of Swedish society and a restructuring of the spatial economy. As background, Figure 4.7 and Table 4.8 identify the twelve largest urban regions in Sweden. This reordering accelerated the depopulation of northern and rural Sweden and the growth of the metropolitan centres (Andersson and Jungen, 1968). Income differentials, environmental problems, and social service costs increased accordingly, and peripheral areas suffered from deteriorating municipal services and diminishing employment opportunities (Royal Ministry of Foreign Affairs, 1972b).

Although statistics on the regional problem are notoriously difficult to obtain, and are even more difficult to interpret, several crude indices are available for Sweden (Table 4.7 and Table 3.2). These indices show

**TABLE 4.8**

POPULATION GROWTH AND URBAN CONCENTRATION IN THE LARGEST URBAN REGIONS IN SWEDEN, 1930–65

| | Population (thousands) | | | | Percentage increase per annum (cumulative) | | | | | Population 1930–65 | |
|---|---|---|---|---|---|---|---|---|---|---|---|
| | 1930 | 1950 | 1960 | 1965 | 30–50 | 50–60 | 60–65 | 50–65 | 30–65 | Index | Increase (thousands) |
| 1 Stockholm | 819 | 1182 | 1365 | 1484 | 1·85 | 1·45 | 1·75 | 1·55 | 1·70 | 182 | 665 |
| 2 Göteborg | 542 | 709 | 807 | 873 | 1·35 | 1·30 | 1·55 | 1·40 | 1·35 | 161 | 331 |
| 3 Malmö (West Skåne) | 476 | 560 | 612 | 661 | 0·85 | 0·90 | 1·55 | 1·10 | 0·95 | 139 | 185 |
| 4 Norrköping | 237 | 284 | 299 | 309 | 0·90 | 0·55 | 0·70 | 0·60 | 0·75 | 131 | 72 |
| 5 Västerås | 79 | 118 | 143 | 161 | 2·00 | 2·00 | 2·40 | 2·15 | 2·05 | 204 | 82 |
| 6 Gävle | 114 | 130 | 143 | 150 | 0·65 | 0·95 | 0·90 | 0·95 | 0·80 | 132 | 36 |
| 7 Örebro | 112 | 127 | 138 | 143 | 0·65 | 0·85 | 0·75 | 0·80 | 0·70 | 128 | 31 |
| 8 Jönköping | 74 | 96 | 105 | 111 | 1·30 | 0·90 | 1·10 | 0·95 | 1·15 | 150 | 37 |
| 9 Sundsvall | 80 | 80 | 89 | 93 | 0·05 | 1·05 | 0·85 | 1·00 | 0·40 | 116 | 13 |
| 10 Falun | 64 | 74 | 84 | 87 | 0·70 | 1·25 | 0·70 | 1·10 | 0·85 | 136 | 23 |
| 11 Eskilstuna | 56 | 76 | 81 | 87 | 1·55 | 0·65 | 1·45 | 0·90 | 1·25 | 155 | 31 |
| 12 Karlstad | 50 | 63 | 73 | 78 | 1·15 | 1·45 | 1·40 | 1·45 | 1·25 | 156 | 28 |
| Regions 1– 3 | 1838 | 2451 | 2784 | 3018 | 1·45 | 1·30 | 1·65 | 1·40 | 1·40 | 164 | 1180 |
| 4– 7 | 542 | 658 | 723 | 764 | 0·95 | 0·95 | 1·10 | 1·00 | 1·00 | 141 | 222 |
| 8–12 | 323 | 389 | 432 | 455 | 0·95 | 1·05 | 1·05 | 1·05 | 1·00 | 141 | 132 |
| 1–12 | 2703 | 3498 | 3938 | 4237 | 1·30 | 1·20 | 1·45 | 1·30 | 1·30 | 157 | 1528 |
| Whole country | 6142 | 7044 | 7495 | 7773 | 0·70 | 0·65 | 0·75 | 0·65 | 0·75 | 127 | 1631 |

what is in most instances common knowledge, that income increases with city size, and that both income and size are positively related to net migration rates, the local employment mixture, and labour force participation rates. Each reinforces the other in the cumulative self-fulfilling fashion which Pred (1973c) has identified. The impact of urbanization in this context of regional imbalances is extensively documented by Ödmann and Dahlberg (1970) and by Hägerstrand (1970). In Sweden, at least, the traditional public response at both national and regional levels to these differentials (they may or may not be social inequalities) has been primarily in terms of labour market and mobility policies.

Spatially, the issues have crystallized around the two obvious extremes—the North (Norrland) and Stockholm. The Norrland question will be taken up later; of more immediate interest is that of metropolitan growth. The political and academic fascination with the 'big city' problem has pervaded recent planning strategy in Sweden as it has elsewhere, despite frequent assertions to the contrary (Holm, 1957). It is now stated government policy to limit the growth of the larger metropolitan centres, i.e. Stockholm, Göteborg, and Malmö. The issue it seems is not so much the size of the urban agglomeration, but one of distributing limited urban resources more evenly across the country.

In a small country, it is argued by Swedish authorities, employment and consumer opportunities are limited in number. It is considered unacceptable to allow a continued concentration of these finite opportunities in the capital city, or in a small number of urban centres. The decision to limit the growth of Stockholm specifically was based on these grounds, but with little or no debate on the secondary issues involved. Nevertheless, the principle does hold important implications for the theme of this volume. A decision to limit Stockholm's growth, or that of other single metropolitan areas, essentially focuses on local action. However, a decision to redistribute national resources resulting from limits to growth applied at selective locations implies the existence of some model of the urban system and how it operates in both spatial and hierarchical terms.

### 4.2.3. THE POLICY RESPONSE: URBAN AND REGIONAL POLICY

Urban planning at the local level in Sweden is at least three centuries old. Current national planning practice, however, as in most of Europe, effectively began with public debates during the 1940s and in Sweden

specifically with the Building Act of 1947 (Jungen and Lönnroth, 1972).
A chain of legislative actions followed in the immediate post-war years,
induced by rapid economic growth and social change and in many cases
extending public control over activities in the private sector.[3] At least
two principal thrusts were evident in this historical progression, one in
housing and the other in regional economic policy (Ödmann and
Dahlberg, 1970). Housing in Sweden as in other European countries has
been the cornerstone of central government economic policy (Holm,
1957), largely because such governments control the financial strings for
that particular sector (Strong, 1971). But in Sweden housing has also
been used as a direct urban policy instrument.

It is in terms of regional policy that the Swedish experience is most
closely related to national urban strategies. During the post-war years,
particularly in the 1960s, an active location policy emerged in concert
with long-term economic planning in other sectors. The first national
economic review was produced in 1948, but it was not until 1964 that
the Swedish Parliament (the Riksdag) adopted an explicit programme
for regional development. It was apparent to the supporters of this
programme that to design a regional settlement pattern for work and
living, which matched the social objectives noted above, defined the
need '... to plan the geographical distribution of manpower and social
capital investment' (Royal Ministry for Foreign Affairs, Royal Ministry
of Agriculture, 1972, 44), and '... to co-ordinate sectoral planning with
the objectives laid down by regional policy' (Ministry of Labour and
Housing, 1973, 30). The spatial structure and evolution of economic
development were, therefore, an integral part of national planning.
Although the 1964 policy statement was not primarily urban in focus, it
did imply '... identifying those localities and municipalities where the
efforts of regional policy shall be primarily concentrated' (Guteland,
1972, 7). The criteria on which these municipalities were to be subsequently identified have only recently been clarified.

The main instruments on which Swedish government agencies rely in
activating regional policy are, with a few important exceptions, similar
to those employed elsewhere (EFTA, 1973). The emphasis has been
largely on subsidies for labour market diversification and industrial

---

[3] These changes have been accompanied by major revisions in the map of local government in
Sweden. The number of local municipalities has been reduced from over 3,000 in 1952 to 1,000 in
1964 until, on 1 January 1974, only 275 remained. Most of these units include a small town or city
with the adjacent tributary or commuting area, with a minimum population of about 6,000 (see
note 13).

relocation assistance, applied most generously in Norrland. The incentives are of two basic types:

(1) *location aid:* contributions for the establishment or expansion of industry in designated urban centres, including loans, outright grants, guarantees, and refunds for removal costs.

(2) *employment aid:* including various forms of training grants, employment premiums, removal grants, and transport costs, applied primarily to industrial employment in the development areas.

In addition there are other policy mechanisms available:

(3) informal controls on the siting and expansion of specific types of enterprises in the three largest metropolises, relying primarily on persuasion.

(4) information and advice to enterprises on alternative locations, provided through the National Labour Market Board.

(5) strengthening of community planning controls at the county level.

As in most countries these incentives are applied differentially within a hierarchy of development regions: (1) inner aid area (interior Norrland); (2) general aid area (southern and coastal Norrland); and (3) special areas outside of (1) and (2) in central Sweden where consideration is given for assistance (Figure 4.8). None of these incentives is particularly novel; nor in their influence on the location of industrial activity and unemployment have they been all that successful.[4]

The form and design of the policy incentives used of course reflects the location of decision-making power in Swedish government.[5] The location of power in turn reflects the government's unusual ministerial structure and its long planning inheritance. More will be said on this factor later in the section. At this point it is sufficient in evaluating policies to state that they have tended to be spatially and sectorally discontinuous, and to concentrate on problems of extreme locations (Norrland) or on specific economic sectors (manufacturing industry).

Subsequent policy evolution has demonstrated an increasing urban

[4] The impact of the capital investment subsidies in the regional programme has been limited. For example, regional variations in unemployment declined during the 1950–65 period, but increased in the 1965–70 period. In 1971 unemployment rates varied from 2·7 per cent in Stockholm to 11·2 per cent in northern peripheral areas (OECD, 1973c).

[5] At the time of writing, Sweden was faced with an uncertain general election outcome. However, even if the long-running Social Democratic coalition is unseated, it is unlikely that major changes in the direction of national planning will take place. The extensive legislative machinery set in motion over several decades will ensure that revisions to locational policy are small (Personal communication, Sture Öberg, ERU Stockholm, 27 March 1973).

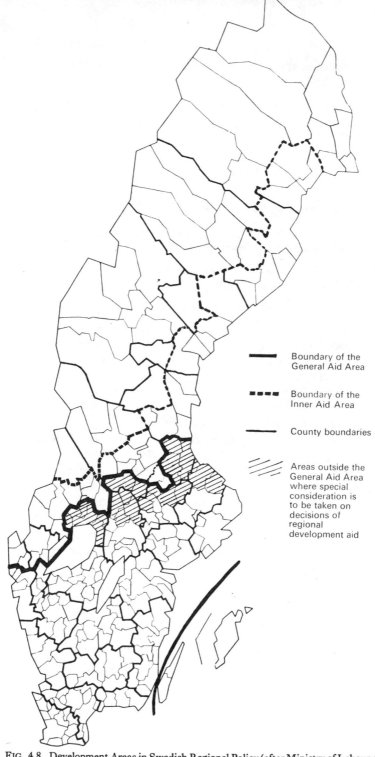

Boundary of the
General Aid Area

Boundary of the
Inner Aid Area

County boundaries

Areas outside the
General Aid Area
where special
consideration is
to be taken on
decisions of
regional
development aid

FIG. 4.8. Development Areas in Swedish Regional Policy (after Ministry of Labour and Housing, 1973).

focus to national development planning and a refinement of the decision criteria for regional investment allocation (*Plan*, 1972).[6] In February 1967 the government issued instructions to the local planning authorities, that is the County Administrative Boards, outlining a broad programme for continuous and long-range development planning (*Plan*, 1968). This strategy, introduced under the title of the County Programme in 1970, sought to establish priorities among municipalities with respect to their needs for growth-promoting measures, for social subsidies to ensure acceptable levels of living conditions, and for means of co-ordinating public sector investments.[7] These principles were accepted by the Riksdag in 1970.

The actual legislative programme based on this strategy was formally introduced in the autumn of 1972 (Thufvesson, 1973). In both concept and practice this programme is the most comprehensive and the most explicitly urban in emphasis among those introduced in the four countries under study. The programme consisted of three parts: (1) forecasts of population levels for counties up to 1980; (2) a 'regional structure plan', including a normative description of the functions municipalities of different sizes and locations should have at future points in time; and (3) an enumeration of what are referred to as guide-lines for the implementation of specific regional policy measures. In many instances data and ideas for the programme came from the local and county levels to the central government where they were collated, assessed, and then recycled to the counties for comment.

### 4.2.4. RECENT POLICY EXTENSIONS

Other regional policy measures have been introduced in more recent legislative actions (Thufvesson, 1973). Among these are several which demonstrate the enormous importance attached to locational considerations in Swedish planning and the expanding scale and diversity of government measures to achieve regional balance. These measures

[6] One additional technique used to influence the nature and location of industrial investment decisions is an Investment Fund. The Fund was established in 1938 initially to assist in regulating national economic cycles, but has been employed since 1963 as a component of the government's locational policies. Corporations have the right to make tax-free depositions of up to 40 per cent of before-tax profit into a fund with the National Bank of Sweden. This fund may then be drawn upon, subject to certain conditions. If the use of the money conforms with government priorities in specific sectors or locations, a further tax-free allowance is made.

[7] In 1971 the Riksdag agreed to proposals to relocate 30 government administrative offices from Stockholm to selected primary centres, mostly in northern and central Sweden, involving over 6,100 employees. Needless to say, there has been considerable resistance among many existing employees to the relocations.

include: (1) expanded tax equalization grants to local municipalities, emphasizing those located in northern Sweden; (2) direct government support in establishing industrial complexes in the inner aid (maximum development subsidy) areas; and (3) the geographic smoothing of telephone charges across the country, including reductions in charges of up to 50 per cent for northern regions. All three of these examples deal essentially with the quality of local infrastructure and its role in economic growth, while the third explicitly recognizes the obvious but seldom-acted-upon importance of communication costs in shaping patterns of urban and regional development (Hägerstrand, 1965; Törngvist, 1970; Thorngren, 1970).

From July 1973 three further extensions to regional policy have taken effect. One formally extended locational assistance to include other types of employment-generating activities, such as wholesaling, business services, and consultants, although these were still designed largely as support for the manufacturing sector. In addition, there were improvements in locational consultative services available to those industries considering expansion within or relocation to the major metropolitan areas, as well as increases in the size and proportion of direct capital subsidies to firms settling in the inner aid areas.[8] Further measures included an increase in the grant for each new employee added in the inner area, and increases in transport subsidies for the long-distance movement of goods by rail and road from these same areas to southern Sweden. In each case recommendations have been made recently for even wider measures to reduce the differentials in transport and interaction costs at varying locations within the national urban-economic system.

Before elaborating further on the regional programme, and in particular on the structure plan, brief mention should be made of one other recent component of Swedish locational policy—national physical planning. A new Ministry of Physical Planning has been set up to monitor management of the country's natural resources of land and water (Royal Ministry for Physical Planning and Local Government, 1972). The Ministry's objective, which is part of a broader but as yet undefined environmental policy (Emmelin, 1973), is to prepare a national plan for resource utilization and conservation which minimizes conflicts over scarce natural resources. As such it draws much of its stimulus from the increasing demands generated by the growth of the urban system for

---

[8] The increase in the proportion of the subsidy was from 50 to 65 per cent of building investment costs.

recreational space, energy, industrial concentration, and social services. In early 1973 the Riksdag accepted the general plan in principle, providing local authorities with considerable regulatory powers in land-use development and environmental planning.

Obviously, close integration and co-ordination between regional location policy and the national physical planning for land usage and conservation will be essential for either programme to work effectively. Each is a prerequisite of the other. While the separation of these policies follows from the structure of ministerial responsibilities, notably the immense importance of the Department of Labour and Housing, which held responsibility for housing and labour markets as well as regional policy, it is in theory no better or no worse than another separation of an environmental whole. How much importance can be read into this institutional structure in terms of the success of Swedish regional policy is debatable, but it certainly has been a contributing factor.

### 4.2.5. POLICY OBJECTIVES IN A SPATIAL CONTEXT

At this point we step back to review the specific objectives underlying Sweden's various 'locational' strategies. The objectives are essentially twofold. One is directed at the creation of labour market areas which meet certain minimum social criteria, primarily of size, diversity, and stability. The intention is to ensure that as large a proportion as possible of the Swedish population is resident within labour markets which offer employment sufficient in both number and range to render household migration unnecessary on an interregional scale, except by choice. Related to this objective is the desire to minimize the regional effects of cyclical swings in the national (or international) economy such that the impact of these swings on households should not depend heavily on where that household lives. In addition to labour market stability this objective calls for specific measures to decrease locational specialization in those employment sectors most sensitive to external (international) market behaviour.

The second objective, which is increasingly central to the evolving strategy for urban development, seeks to reduce differentials in the access which individuals and households have to public services. Again it is argued that the available range and quality of public services, social 'opportunities' in general, should not be unduly affected by where one lives. It is recognized that certain specialized services, including institutions of higher learning, advanced medical research facilities, and those which are intensely technologically based, such as in the fields of information and management systems, are by definition limited in number and, to some extent, cannot be subdivided by region. And it is recognized that some concentration is necessary in the major urban centres if further agglomeration economies are to be achieved in those sectors which are in direct competition with Continental cities. But it is also felt that recent trends towards an increasing locational concentration of such services are greater than necessary or socially desirable.

**TABLE 4.9**

CONCENTRATION OF CENTRAL GOVERNMENT
EMPLOYEES IN MAJOR URBAN AREAS IN SWEDEN,
1966 AND 1970

| Urban Area* | Number of Government Employees | | Percentage Growth |
|---|---|---|---|
| | 1966 | 1970 | 1966–70 |
| Stockholm | 93,000 | 107,000 | +15·6 |
| Göteborg and Malmö | 44,000 | 51,000 | +17·8 |
| Other major towns | 93,000 | 106,000 | +13·4 |
| South-central Sweden | 50,000 | 55,000 | +11·5 |
| Northern densely populated areas | 31,000 | 34,000 | +9·9 |
| Northern sparsely populated areas | 15,000 | 16,000 | +6·3 |
| Sweden: total | 326,000 | 369,000 | +12·7 |

* Defined as municipal blocks (see note 13).

Source: Royal Ministry of Labour and Housing (1973).

Government employment growth has in fact in the past contributed to this concentration (Table 4.9).

Two solutions to this distributional problem are thought possible: (1) the redistributing of existing public services and, wherever possible, to encourage new and expanded facilities to settle in disadvantaged regions through decentralization and increased subsidies; and (2) an increase in the direct accessibility of households to services through improved transport systems and by co-ordinating transport policy with regional policy. Both approaches are advocated in the new regional programme, although the latter options are as yet only weakly defined.

Similar objectives, with different labels, are basic to the locational policies of any country which has such policies. Yet in Sweden the emphasis on social criteria appears to be greater, and the arguments in support of these objectives are frequently couched in a broader context. Society is viewed as consisting of a set of organizations—spatial and hierarchical—whose various linkages and redistributive mechanisms determine the extent and quality of economic growth and social opportunities. This interpretation, while also appreciated elsewhere, is probably nowhere more clearly voiced.[9] This emphasis reflects the Swedish national preoccupation with organizations, but it also mirrors the interest in organization systems in Swedish urban research noted above, and which Pred (1973c) has recently summarized in detail.[10]

This long-standing focus on both labour markets and service accessibility necessitated that a convergence of policy interest on the question of regulating urban growth at the national level take place. The guiding concept in this convergence has been that of improving the welfare structure of the urban system (Figure 4.9a and b). One specific proposal to achieve this goal is to encourage what Hägerstrand (1972) has called an 'equitable urban structure'. While this structure could take many forms, the extreme alternative is one which attempts to equalize city sizes throughout the urban system. The system then becomes non-hierarchical, and social choice is presumably equal throughout. Whatever the form, an equitable structure implies at a minimum limits on the growth of the major metropolitan centres. These centres are said to be considerably 'overpopulated' in terms of the quality and quantity of services they offer relative to the rest of the nation, and a choice in employment which is larger than that desired or necessary for most households. The numerous arguments in support of such limits, while not necessarily favouring a non-hierarchical urban system as Hägerstrand suggests, do support recent initiatives for the more active encouragement of growth in selected centres outside the metropolitan areas.

### 4.2.6. THE PLANNING PROCESS

These objectives should be interpreted within the historical structure of government and of planning systems in Sweden. Both are sufficiently

[9] It should also be emphasized that in Sweden social as well as spatial objectives have been historically associated with physical, sectoral, and intersectoral planning to an extent unusual in western economies.

[10] Also see Wärneryd (1968 and 1971), Godlund and Wärneryd (1968), Thorngren (1970), Törnqvist (1970), Törnqvist *et al.* (1971), Hägerstrand and Kuklinski (1971), and Carlestam and Lundahl (1972).

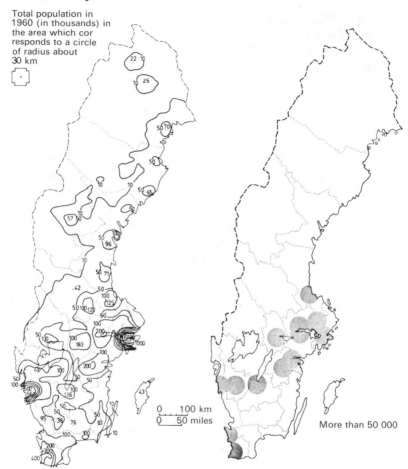

FIG. 4.9. Welfare Structure of the Swedish Urban System: Population Distribution and Accessibility to Urban Concentrations.

(a) Isarithmic map of
     population distribution

(b) Approximate geographic areas of 30 km
     radius around urban centres of 50,000
     or more population

Source: Hägerstrand (1970).

different from those of the other three countries under review to warrant a brief elaboration here. The planning systems are hierarchical in spatial as well as in sectoral terms. Urban planning *per se* is almost the monopoly of local government—principally the communes—although the central government has considerable regulatory powers through the counties. The communes are in many instances directly responsible to the county, and it is with these county administrations that the central government is most involved in terms of locational policies. Of course

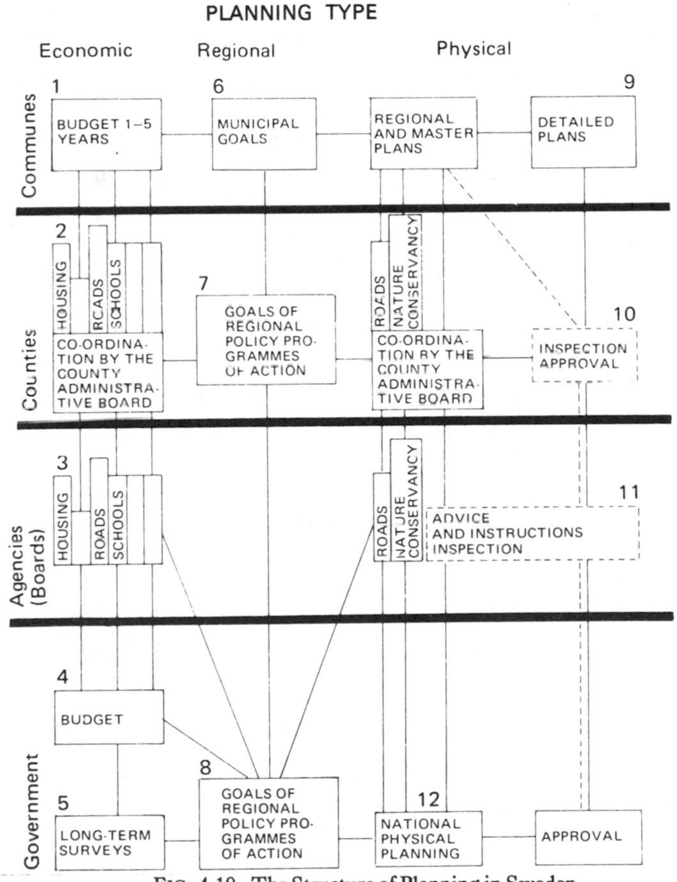

FIG. 4.10. The Structure of Planning in Sweden.

Source: adapted from Royal Ministry of Labour and Housing (1973).

the objectives, the criteria, and the instruments of such policies vary with the different levels of government.

The organization of planning in Sweden is dependent on this political structure. Planning is of three general types: physical, economic, and regional. In most instances the planning process is conducted by each of three levels of government (communes, counties, and national government ministries and boards), for individual sectors of society, between sectors, and for differing geographic areas. Figure 4.10, adapted from a recent report of the (Royal) Ministry of Labour and Housing (1973), attempts to summarize the planning functions of and linkages between these levels and sectors.

Each level of government is responsible for different but overlapping components of the planning process: physical planning, as noted earlier, is primarily a municipal responsibility; economic planning is vested in the counties, under central government budget constraints; and regional planning policy originates with the central government. In the latter, agencies (and boards) are responsible for sectoral planning and ministries for intersectoral planning. The counties, particularly the County Administrative Boards, hold a pivotal role in co-ordinating municipal plans for physical development and investment, and in translating national policy goals into effective intersectoral planning at the local level.

Three points in the structure are critical in understanding how the planning process works. One is that each level has some decision criteria in common (including, recently, locational criteria) by which to evaluate proposals. A second aspect is the extent to which central government functions have been decentralized to regional offices (see Vinde, 1971). Third, at the central government level there is a clear separation of responsibilities for policy-making, held by ministers, from the implementation of those policies, which is vested in central agencies and boards.[11] While cumbersome, the system seems to work relatively smoothly.

### 4.2.7. REGIONAL STRUCTURE PLAN 1973

With the preceding objectives as background, Swedish researchers within the Ministry of Labour and Housing, the Expert Group for Regional Studies (ERU),[12] provided the government with a generalized framework for location decisions set in the context of the national urban system. This framework contained a classification of urban centres based on the present and potential labour market and service characteristics of those centres. This classification served as the backbone of the Regional Structure Plan approved in 1972. The criteria

---

[11] Prior to the last election there were 12 ministries and 70 national administrative boards. The relatively small number of ministries, and the absence of programme implementation responsibilities from these ministries, greatly facilitate intersectoral policy co-ordination at the national level in Sweden.

[12] Expertgruppen för regional utredningsverksamhet.

employed in classifying centres were both functional and political, that is, both descriptive and perscriptive. In the final version (Emmelin, 1973) four types of centres were identified, although in earlier versions there were five (Royal Ministry for Foreign Affairs, 1972) or as many as seven types (Ödmann and Dahlberg, 1970).

The four types of centres, allowing for rough translation of titles, are:

(1) the three major metropolitan centres (Stockholm, Göteborg and Malmö);

(2) primary centres (22 named, one added later by Parliament);

(3) regional centres (70 proposed);

(4) municipal centres or communes (150 proposed).

The distribution of these centres is given in Figure 4.11. Although the term hierarchy is not used as a means of describing the scheme, it is in fact a strict hierarchical one, a condition which may produce problems in the future by building in rigidity in the planning process.

The method of grouping the three dominant metropolitan areas needs little elaboration (EFTA, 1973). In size alone they vastly exceed cities in the second tier. The planning priority in all three areas will be to slow growth and thereby to reduce their '. . . drain on the rest of the country' (Emmelin, 1973), and to encourage the relocation of development elsewhere. Their rapid growth in recent decades has generated sufficiently numerous social and environmental problems (Andersson and Jungen, 1968; Stockholm, 1972) to warrant national concern. In Stockholm, in particular, a reduction in growth rate, if not in absolute population, is to be achieved in part by the relocation of government agencies and employment. The first round of this policy is now in operation (Department of the Interior, 1970), and the second round won Parliament's approval in March 1973.

Below the metropolitan areas, the plan in Figure 4.11 identifies 23 primary centres.[13] These represent urban-centred regions with populations of 90,000 or more residing in a labour market area extending

[13] Municipal building blocks in Sweden are defined as small nodal regions with populations of more than 6,000. They are classified into six groups on the basis of: (1) the size of the local population within a radius of 30 km of an urban centre, and (2) the size of the regional population within a radius of 100 km. The former is based on the concept of *local potential* labour market, that is within the range of daily commuting. The latter is based on the notion of *regional potential* hinterlands which allows for weekly access to functions and services. An individual urban area may be part of the potential market for more than one larger urban area. The essence of the classification is the difference in population density within labour market and service areas. (For further elaboration see Department of the Interior, 1970 and 1973; EFTA, 1973, as well as Hägerstrand, 1970, and Ödmann and Dahlberg, 1970.)

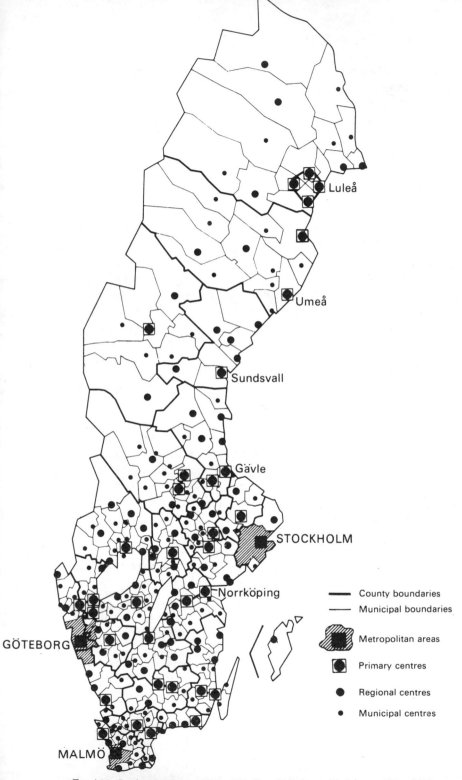

Luleå

Umeå

Sundsvall

Gävle

STOCKHOLM

Norrköping

GÖTEBORG

MALMÖ

| | County boundaries |
| | Municipal boundaries |
| | Metropolitan areas |
| | Primary centres |
| | Regional centres |
| | Municipal centres |

Fig. 4.11. Regional Structure Plan 1973. (Royal Ministry of Labour and Housing.)

out 30 kilometres from the centre. The 30 kilometre figure is defined as the average commuting distance at the margin of the 'daily urban system', but is extended somewhat in less densely populated northern regions. In those instances where several urban centres are located in close proximity they have been joined to reach (or come close to) the 90,000 population threshold for inclusion as a primary centre (although centres in the north again may have lower populations). This population figure is considered to be an approximate minimum for adequate labour market diversification and to achieve scale economies in the provision of public services. Interestingly, there is at least one primary centre designated in all but one (Stockholm) of Sweden's historic 24 countries. This is generally acknowledged to be far too many for an effective strategy of locational consolidation, but was politically unavoidable. No doubt strong regional politics will influence the form of urban policies in other ways; and in fact may seriously hinder those formal redistributive practices at the national level which explicitly require a differentiation between urban places.

In each county there is also at least one 'regional' centre. These centres, the third step in the hierarchy, are intended to operate as small growth centres within local labour markets containing a nucleus population of at least 30,000. They will receive the bulk of government investment in their respective tributary regions, and may therefore act to intercept migrants who would otherwise go to larger cities outside that region. The plan is to accommodate a range of intermediate and lower-level public services in these centres and to ensure a degree of labour market stability and diversification sufficient for most household choices and needs.

The regional centres in turn then act as foci for a surrounding tributary region consisting of many smaller municipal centres or communes. Among these communes the plan selects those which offer some prospects of greater stability in local employment and services in the future. Here the selection problem becomes even more difficult politically, which may account for the large number chosen. It is understood that local county administrative councils will play a prominent role in the execution of the strategy. The government's acceptance of the classification means that it is willing to underwrite the construction and maintenance of public services in some communes but not in others. The intended result is one of urban concentration, but concentration within a spatial framework which reaches most of the population through commuting to work, daily access to services, or, only if necessary, through relatively short-term migration and household relocation over short distances.

How will this strategy actually work? In part the procedure will be a matter of defining social priorities, some of which may be clarified in forthcoming reports on urban systems research deriving from ERU and the Ministry of Labour under the theme 'cities in co-operation'. The political connotation of the title, optimistic as it is, suggests the mechanism. The plan and its appended documents are intended to serve as a means of formally and informally 'co-ordinating' locational decisions within and between public and private sectors. All major investment decisions may be screened to encourage their compliance with government regional policy objectives. That is, the legislation should provide more direct control over specific sectoral investment allocations—such as in roads, airports, ports, etc.—and encourage closer integration of major government programmes—in the location of new universities and the spatial reorganization of the medical system, for instance.

The emphasis on co-ordination is critical. While this has always been an explanation for Sweden's relative success in social planning, it is evident that the immediate benefit of the urban system scheme will be the opportunity for greater co-operation among central government offices and between different levels of government. It is largely indirect co-ordination obviously, but this approach is a recognition of the political realities and the difficulties of selecting other routes for implementing an urban system strategy.[14]

### 4.2.8. NORRLAND

As the historically dominant focus of Swedish regional—and thus locational—policy, it is impossible to avoid commenting on the role of the 'Northern' problem in the evolution of such policy. Traditionally, regional policy in Norrland has been directed at expanding an employment base weakened by extensive mechanization in the mining and forest industries, while also improving the quality of local community and social services (Royal Ministry for Foreign Affairs and Agriculture, 1971; Bylund, 1969 and 1972). From this base, the concepts have slowly

[14] Admittedly, the classification is extremely simple and it can be criticized as being both static and inflexible. While these problems could seriously affect its success, to criticize on these grounds and probe no further would be to miss the important philosophy underlying the proposal. This philosophy is one of defining a spatially based decision framework which will stimulate discussion on an ideal form for the national urban system. The fact that it is simple provides the flexibility needed for political acceptance in the present.

(but only recently) been expanded to cover the regional problems of the whole country.

The success (or lack thereof) in regional policy in the north has been the subject of considerable debate (Royal Ministry of Labour and Housing, 1973). As noted earlier the focus of policy incentives in the past has been on capital investment and employment growth resulting from industrial expansion and relocation. From what scattered evidence there is available it is acknowledged that industrial firms receiving assistance in the general aid area in the southern and coastal portions of

**TABLE 4.10**

REGIONAL POLICY IN SWEDEN'S NORTH:
CHANGES IN EMPLOYMENT OF INDUSTRIAL FIRMS
RECEIVING GOVERNMENT SUPPORT, 1963–70

Index: 1963 = 100

|  | 1963 | 1964 | 1965 | 1966 | 1967 | 1968 | 1969 | 1970 |
|---|---|---|---|---|---|---|---|---|
| All firms receiving support 1965–70 | 100 | 109 | 117 | 125 | 124 | 127 | 137 | 147 |
| All industrial firms in forest counties[a] | 100 | 107 | 109 | 109 | 106 | 100 | — | — |
| Total industry | 100 | 104 | 105 | 104 | 99 | 98 | — | — |

[a] Roughly equivalent to the General Aid Area.

Source: Ministry of Labour and Housing, 'Report on Regional Policy in Sweden', 3 March, 1973.

Norrland have shown higher rates of employment growth than all industry in Sweden (where the numbers have actually declined since the mid-1960s), but much lower rates than firms receiving support in other areas of the country (Table 4.10). The total number of jobs created in the general aid area is, however, only around 20,000, and when employment losses are subtracted the net balance is just 13,000. Compared to northern areas in Canada and Australia, on the other hand, this achievement is still considerable.

The current northern development strategy, one that has implications for both Australia and Canada, is that of concentration and consolidation. There is an implicit and largely unstated political assumption of gradual depopulation. The strategy is to a considerable degree an urban one. It is intended to slow the rate of depopulation and at the same time to direct emigration, when it must occur, from the interior to growing coastal centres on the Baltic such as Luleå, Umeå, Ornsköldsvik, and Sundsvall, rather than to the south. New and expanded social services in Norrland, an area north of a line from Strömstad near the Norwegian border to Gävle on the Baltic, are to be concentrated in those primary centres identified in the regional structure plan. Other smaller centres will not be assigned new investments for services, but the populations involved will not be overlooked. Most areas, though improved transport facilities and subsidies, will have greater access to the expanded primary centres than they do at present. Thus, the extreme environmental conditions in Norrland, vast distances, low population densities, and relatively poor services, may help explain why the specific concern for minimum thresholds of accessibility to services and urban labour market diversification currently dominate Swedish national locational strategies.

### 4.2.9. COMMENTARY

Clearly Swedish regional and location policy has evolved rapidly in the post-war years. This evolution has also seen a convergence between two separate streams of planning which impinge on urbanization: (1) national economic and sectoral planning; and (2) local physical planning for individual urban areas. The latter, although in detail beyond the scope of this review, is probably the best known outside of Sweden (Adams, 1973). The former has in the past tended to be piecemeal and largely uncoordinated, but this has slowly given way to a more integrated and comprehensive practice of multi-sectoral (and spatial) planning involving three levels of government. Regional policy, as one bridge between the above two, has also matured from an emphasis on extreme problem cases—the north and the capital city—to an approach that looks at regional systems in their entirety.

If a formal association between sectoral and locational planning does come about, it will probably follow from the concepts contained in the urban system structure plan. This plan provides guide-lines for decision-making which are simple and sufficiently flexible. The planning programme that is developing around the plan, attempting to encompass the entire urban hierarchy in a regional context, is designed to direct that hierarchy towards a specified equitable structure. While the approach can be criticized at present as an exercise in comparative statics, it also appears to be moving in the direction of an integrated and dynamic strategy for regulating urban growth. Even so, it may remain regional in name at least as the municipalities remain largely a responsibility of the counties, and because the current wide-ranging definitions of labour market areas encompass all of the national territory.

Most of these national policy developments, unlike those in local physical planning, are quite recent. Despite the difficulty of assigning dates to policy innovations which are introduced gradually and in bits and pieces, the literature suggests that industrial investment controls only became locationally specific in 1963; that a formal regional policy, including government relocation incentives, dates from 1965; that the political decision to control Stockholm's growth was only made in 1969; and the decision to relocate government offices in 1971 and to adopt an urban-oriented regional structure strategy in 1973. This is not to belittle Swedish achievements, but to indicate that national action on urban systems is just beginning and that an assessment of the consequences of such actions is premature.

Policy objectives have shifted in concert with the changing area of interest. For example, there has been a shift in emphasis, as in Britain, from capital to employment accumulation in assisting problem regions, and from physical to social infrastructure in regional allocation decisions. More specifically there has been a change in orientation from one which encouraged interregional migration, through long-standing practices for improved labour mobility, most of which then went to the metropolitan centres, to a co-ordinated programme of contained intraregional migration.[15] The selected destinations for this migration, while not called by the universal term growth centres, are no doubt points for growth-inducement. And they are identified in terms of accessibility to services. This constitutes a reversal of the usual emphasis on basic employment in traditional regional planning and is indicative of the direction of policy thinking. Similarly, Sweden has recently attempted to employ more direct means of generating balanced employment opportunities and an equitable geography of investment through the physical relocation of central government services and employment from Stockholm.

Any objective observer would have to conclude that Swedish efforts at regional development, as well as the regulation of urban growth at the

[15] The variability of foreign immigration adds a degree of uncertainty to this policy. It may not be widely known outside the country that Sweden has had a net balance in immigration since 1930. The average annual net in-flow during the post-war years has varied between 10,000 and 20,000 (mostly from Finland and the rest of Scandinavia) but has fluctuated widely depending on employment conditions. Stockholm has been most strongly affected.

local level, have been relatively successful.[16] The Stockholm planning experience, now widely documented, has built its success on a long-standing practice of public land ownership, the integration of land use, transport, and public utilities planning, and extensive government-initiated housing construction (Strong, 1971; Adams, 1973). Similar imaginative efforts, although less widely known, have also been made in some smaller centres. This success derives in part from the fact that Swedish cities have fewer and less severe problems, and more freedom to make policy mistakes, than most of the rest of urban Europe—and more scope for introducing social planning controls than either Canada or Australia in terms of prevailing public attitudes. But it also reflects a prevailing social philosophy not duplicated elsewhere. Extending these controls to inter-urban planning problems, however, has not proved to be easy. Urban growth regulation, while long a local strength, has only recently taken on a national perspective.

Even so, all is not ideal. The national and spatial economy is still largely unregulated, dominated by increasingly large corporations,[17] by competition from continental markets, and by the growing pressures of a technological society (Hancock, 1972). Regional policy has been insufficient. Although regional imbalances have declined, they are still considerable (Peters, 1973). The difficult trade-offs between the goals of regulating an urban system and societal pressures for maintaining economic growth have only been marginally discussed and assessed. Local municipalities and countries, which hold a virtual monopoly on urban planning and development decisions, still compete for new employment and tax-producing industries in the North American tradition. Controls on residential location (housing) are strong, but those on job location (industry and offices) remain relatively weak. Regional and national power groups add their weight to maintenance of the *status quo* in the processes of urbanization. And not all the plans and frameworks proposed are likely (or intended) to be realized. But slowly, the issues of public control and regulation of a national urban economy,

[16] The size of these programmes is also relatively large. It has been estimated that labour market and regional policy investments in Sweden accounted for roughly 5 per cent of central government budgetary expenditures in 1970–1 (Vinde, 1971, p. 69). In comparison and recognizing that definitions of policy budgets differ, a figure of about 2 per cent of total government expenditure has been quoted for regional policy in Britain (Kan and Rhodes, 1972, p. 163).

[17] Most multi-national corporations operating in Sweden are Swedish-owned. One problem of concern deriving from the operation of these corporations, besides their obvious political power within Sweden, is that the bases of their operations, and therefore new investments and employment, have recently been shifting increasingly outside the country.

set in an urban system context and responsive to social and environmental criteria, are surfacing. Other countries in the western world should watch these developments with interest.

# Evolving Urban Systems: Australia and Canada

AUSTRALIA and Canada, as emerging urban nations, offer an unusual basis for cross-national comparison. Like the United States, with which they are often grouped, both are federal political systems, encompassing vast areas of immense geographical diversity. Both are typified by resource-based economies and by relatively short urban histories and policy experience. As western, predominantly English-speaking, and capitalist societies, they also share a number of conservative philosophical views and societal values which while having many other consequences also reduce the relative scale and effectiveness of governmental regulation in most social and economic sectors.

The distribution of public administrative power, and of executive decision-making, is diffuse as well as spatially and hierarchically decentralized in both countries. This introduces uncertainty and further complexity into any attempt to achieve comprehensive public policy action or consensus. Clearly then, any interpretation of recent directions of urban policy thinking in Australia and Canada must be set against the specific background of prevailing value systems and political structures. Equally important, the existence of fundamental differences between such federal systems and the more centralized political systems of Britain and Sweden must also be kept in mind when assessing comparative policy experience.

For Australia and Canada, discussion of central (federal) government involvement in regulating urban development may now be of secondary importance to an evaluation of state and provincial actions. Cities in these countries are the creatures of the state or provincial governments, in terms of both constitutional and financial powers, although the explicit relationships differ somewhat. The historical antecedents of a fragmented political organization have also encouraged a high degree of autonomy in sub-national or regional economic systems, and therefore the predominance until recently of regional over national urban policy initiatives. For these reasons, considerable attention is given in this section of the book to urban and locational policies deriving from the state and provincial government levels. Often these policies are more directly parallel, in the geographic scale of application at least, to those introduced in Britain and Sweden.

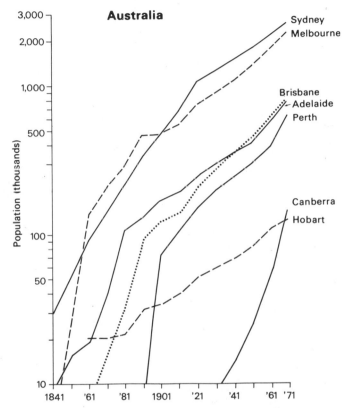

FIG. 5.1. Historical Population Growth of Major Urban Areas in Australia, 1841–1971.

Even so, the principal focus here on urbanization strategies at the national level is not inappropriate. Australia and Canada have both recently and rather dramatically entered the forum of debate on national urban strategies and each has created new institutional forms to define what these strategies should or can be. Both can benefit by each other's experience. Some comparative research has been attempted in fields such as macro-economic policy (Perkins, 1972), agricultural policies

(James, 1971), and in specific planning practices (Miles, 1972); and the two federal governments have recently undertaken a programme of exchanging information on urban research and policy experience.

One obvious reason for this comparative interest is the existence of direct parallels in the historical paths urbanization has taken in both

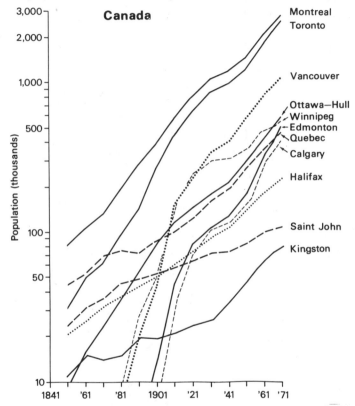

FIG. 5.2. Historical Population Growth of (Selected) Metropolitan Areas in Canada, 1851–1971.

countries (Figures 5.1 and 5.2). A modest introduction to identifying such parallels has been made elsewhere (Bourne, 1974b). While parallels do exist, possibly more relevant to the following policy discussions are the differences and contrasts in urban history. Two points are worth brief mention here: the contrasting evolution of settlement patterns during the initial period of development; and the differential openness of both economies to external influences. Both are reflected in the contemporary character of cities, in the spatial geometry of the two urban systems, and in the background ingredients for current attempts at policy formulation.

Australian urban history, as the saying goes, was written on the waterfront. A remote and vast continent with few navigable rivers and an unhospitable interior, urban Australia developed from series of small settlements around the coast. Most were established at about the same time, many in competition with each other. Each then carved out a rural hinterland but its service functions remained concentrated on the initial port of entry. Subsequent growth followed the progression of continued economic dominance by the colonial capitals (ports)—except possibly Hobart—which Vance (1970) and Johnston (1974), for example, have already described in more general terms. One consequence of this pattern was the evolution of spatially concentrated and geographically isolated (almost independent) regional economic (and political) systems, centred on a few urban nodes. Each node was of relatively similar age. Each historically controlled much of its own transportation network (thus, the varying rail gauges and tariffs), and each performed markedly similar functions for its hinterland. When some centres began to take on 'national' functions they were often in limited and largely complementary sectors. Federal policies in the past have in fact tended to encourage such regional independence (Robinson, 1963) based on individual states.

In contrast, Canadian urbanization was and is a continental phenomenon, unfolding in a progression from east to west. As colonial settlement densities increased and agricultural margins shifted westward, new urban centres arose to market staple products and to serve local needs (see Simmons and Simmons, 1974). Their hinterlands were carved out of the margins of existing hinterlands previously linked to older settlements in the east. Transportation also played an enormously critical role—pushing the margin of settlement westward, and northward from the U.S. border—but unlike Australia it accelerated national integration. External competitive pressures from U.S. cities in fact forced an early political linking of Canadian cities into a system along an east–west axis, but as such probably discouraged the subsequent maturing of those cities into a nationally integrated system. Consequently, the urban system in Canada is more variable than the Australian. Urban areas differ more widely in age, economic base, occupational structure, cultural diversity, service roles, and in the degree of interdependence within the national urban system.

The relative openness of both urban systems to external influence is due largely to their heavily resource-based and branch-plant economies. This means a highly fluid and vulnerable basis for growth within the system, particularly in the peripheral areas based on resource exploitation and in those major urban centres which manage those resources. International monetary influences and the operations of externally controlled multinational corporations are additional sources of uncertainty. In Canada these factors have another dimension—through proximity to the U.S.—an influence which effectively reduces Canadian freedom in national policy-making.

These considerations, combined with those of geography and settlement history, are the principal reasons why this section of the book is titled 'evolving urban systems' rather than possibly the more appropriate label of unplanned or unregulated. Evolving implies both the limited state of functional integration among the cities in each urban system and the early stage of national urban policy experience. Whatever the reasons and titles, however, it is clear that the Australian and Canadian urban systems are more highly regionalized, less economically stable, more sensitive to exogenous events, and therefore in theory at least may be less susceptible to change by public policy than either of the two case studies discussed above. The relative importance of such factors can be seen in the following urban policy reviews of Australia and Canada.

## 5.1. URBAN AUSTRALIA

The well-established literary image of Australia is one of a bustling frontier society marked by strong individualism and suspicion of central authority, and in which national planning is virtually non-existent. While still applicable to the Australian mentality, conditions and attitudes are changing this image. Burgess Cameron (1971), for example, concluded his review of Australia's economic policies by commenting that '. . . economic management is now an established fact—even if planning is still a dirty word.' Further, Professor R. C. Gates optimistically concluded at the 1972 annual meeting of the Australian Institute of Urban Studies in Canberra that: 'A new urban philosophy is now in the making in Australia which should lead to an improvement in the quality of urban life.'[1] What is this philosophy? What is its background and potential contribution to the control of urban growth?

[1] Because of their timing, the reports and proceedings of these meetings provide an excellent documentation on what history may show to be a turning-point in Australian urban policy and in politics in general (See Australian Institute of Urban Studies, 1972a, 1972b, and 1972c; and Department of Urban and Regional Development, First Annual Report, 1973).

## 5.1.1. BACKGROUND: REGIONAL INDEPENDENCE

The unique geography and urban history of Australia make it a fascinating case study of attitudes to planning the character, rate, and spatial expression of urbanization (Figure 5.3). While much has been written on Australian social history (Greenwood, 1965; Blainey, 1966;

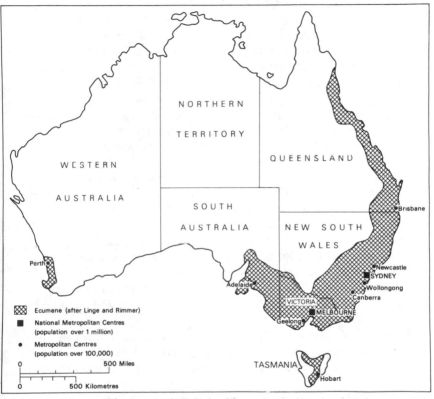

FIG. 5.3. The Settlement Geometry of Urban Australia: Metropolitan Centres and the Developed Ecumene.

Preston, 1969; Abbot and Nairn, 1969; Stretton, 1970) and economic development (Foster, 1970; Linge and Rimmer, 1970; Downing, 1973), much less is known about the growth and operation of the national urban system (Robinson, 1962; G. Clarke, 1970; Neutze, 1971; Rose, 1972; Burnley, 1974; Bourne, 1974b). In the latter context we clearly have less systematic research on national and regional problems to draw on than in any of the other three countries under study. Further documentation will have to wait for release of ongoing urban research—such as that commissioned by the new federal urban affairs department.

The particular path that the urban policy debate has taken in Australia follows directly from the unique urbanization history outlined briefly above, and of course reflects the prevailing societal value systems and, through those systems, perceptions of the country's urban and regional problems. The reasons for the rather late emergence of urban problems are varied.[2] By international standards these problems are probably not relatively serious, either in degree or in extent. Australia does not have the massive and technologically outdated industrial areas of Britain, nor the socially disadvantaged peripheral regions such as those of the U.S. and Canada. Consequently social pressures for change have been less, and the political scope for benign neglect of existing urban and regional problems has been that much greater. What is disturbing is that present practices may be sowing the seeds of much more serious problems in the future.

Effective central government action on urban development has also been hindered as in Canada by intense regional and state rivalries. These rivalries, a long-standing political fact, have led, among other things, to competition among states for economic growth, usually manufacturing investment and particularly that deriving from overseas, but also competition for central government employment and services. It is frequently claimed that if one state places controls on, for example, industrial location (Lonsdale, 1972) or commercial office redevelopment in city centres (Uren, 1973), that investment will simply go elsewhere—usually to another state capital—where the terms are better. Melbourne and Sydney, for example, still maintain their historical competition for economic growth and national influence, much as Toronto and Montreal have done in Canada. This competition often involves explicit pressures in both countries to maintain the urban system *status quo*, or least not to disturb the urban hierarchy in terms of either city size or the functional dominance of cities in specific sectors. The existing and largely unplanned size distribution of centres in the urban system can in itself become a normative construct for the future design of that system.

---

[2] Particularly interesting here is that while urban problems have only recently emerged as important political problems, Australia has been an urban nation (defined as a majority of its population resident in cities) almost since its initial settlement. Ryan (1969) and G. Clarke (1970) provide useful overviews of this historical context.

5.1.2. THE ISSUES: PRESENT AND ANTICIPATED

A recent study by the Commonwealth Bureau of Roads (1972) estimated that by the end of this century nearly nine million persons will be added to Australia's present national population of thirteen million. Of these over seven million will be located in the five major mainland urban centres—Sydney, Melbourne, Brisbane, Adelaide, and Perth. The national metropolises, Sydney and Melbourne, are expected to have between four and five million inhabitants each. The Australian Bureau of Statistics also reported at about the same time that during the last decade the proportion of Australians living in these same five centres increased sharply from 52 to nearly 60 per cent, and it is still increasing. On a more local level, and revealing of the country's historical attitude to urban planning, the present prime minister recently noted that only in the last few years has the house he lived in as a child and as an adult been connected to a sewage system.

These facts summarize several of the prevailing images of the problems of urban Australia: (1) rapid growth, (2) the increasing concentration of national population in a few major centres, and (3) widespread urban sprawl and inadequate local suburban services. All of these problems are highly interdependent, and clearly cannot be solved in isolation. In addition to rapid national population growth (at a rate of about 2 per cent per annum, but now declining) which in itself poses numerous problems, the question of most interest to the urban systems theme of this study is the geographic expression of urban population concentration in the size distribution of cities and the implications of that distribution for future urban policies. Some of the research implications are explored more fully in parallel papers by Rose (1972), Neutze (1973), Holmes (1973), and Bourne (1974b), and the interested reader is referred to these papers for elaboration.

It is well known that Australia is one of the most highly urbanized nations in the world (Table 5.1 and Table 1.1). In fact it may be one of the first countries to approach an equilibrium level in terms of an urban and non-urban population balance. More significant perhaps is the increasing concentration in the larger metropolitan areas. Over 90 per cent of national population growth within the last decade has been in the ten metropolitan centres with populations over 100,000 (see Table 2.4), and nearly 75 per cent in the five mainland state capitals (Table 5.2). Within each state, population is also highly concentrated in the capital city (Table 5.3). Only in Tasmania and Queensland is the

## TABLE 5.1

### POPULATION GROWTH AND DIFFERENCES IN POPULATION URBANIZED AND INCOME, BY STATE, 1971

| State or Territory | Population (a) (in thousands) 1966 | 1971 | Percentage Growth 1966–71 | Percent Urban (b) 1971 | Index of Average Income/Earnings Per Capita (c) |
|---|---|---|---|---|---|
| New South Wales | 4,237·9 | 4,601·2 | 8·6 | 88·6 | 103 |
| Victoria | 3,220·2 | 3,502·4 | 8·8 | 87·7 | 100 |
| Queensland | 1,674·3 | 1,827·1 | 9·1 | 79·3 | 93 |
| South Australia | 1,095·0 | 1,173·7 | 7·2 | 84·6 | 91 |
| Western Australia | 848·1 | 1,030·5 | 21·5 | 81·5 | 104 |
| Tasmania | 371·4 | 390·4 | 5·1 | 74·2 | 90 |
| Northern Territory | 56·5 | 86·4 | 52·9 | 64·1 | 120 |
| Aust. Capital Territory | 96·0 | 144·1 | 50·0 | 97·8 | 105 |
| Australia | 11,599·5 | 12,755·6 | 10·0 | 85·6 | 100 |

(a) Includes Aborigines.
(b) Defined as percentage in urban centres of one thousand or more population.
(c) Estimated by the author using 1969 data.

Source: *1973 Year Book*, Australian Bureau of Statistics.

**TABLE 5.2**

SHARE OF THE FIVE MAINLAND CAPITALS
IN THE NATIONAL POPULATION
AND ITS GROWTH: 1933–71

| Year | Five Mainland Capitals (a) | Australia | Percentage of Population | Percentage of Population Growth |
|------|------|------|------|------|
| 1933 | 3,255,491 | 6,629,839 | 49·1 | 85·8 |
| 1947 | 4,070,165 | 7,579,358 | 53·7 | 64·7 |
| 1954 | 4,979,874 | 8,986,530 | 55·4 | 74·6 |
| 1961 | 6,115,457 | 10,508,186 | 58·2 | 73·3 |
| 1966 | 6,879,557 | 11,550,462 | 59·6 | 70·2 |
| 1971 (b) | 7,724,954 | 12,755,638 | 60·6 | |

(a)  Refers to Statistical Divisions as defined for the 1971 Census.
(b)  Includes Aborigines.

Source: *1973 Year Book,* Australian Bureau of Statistics.

**TABLE 5.3**

URBAN CONCENTRATION IN AUSTRALIA,
BY STATE, 1911–71

| State | Capital City | Proportion of State's Population resident in capital cities | | | | | |
|-------|------|------|------|------|------|------|------|
| | | 1911 | 1933 | 1954 | 1961 | 1966 | 1971 |
| South Australia | Adelaide | 45·0 | 53·8 | 60·7 | 60·7 | 66·6 | 69·1 |
| Victoria | Melbourne | 45·1 | 54·5 | 62·5 | 65·3 | 65·5 | 68·3 |
| West Australia | Perth | 38·0 | 38·8 | 54·5 | 57·0 | 59·8 | 62·3 |
| New South Wales | Sydney | 42·1 | 51·1 | 54·4 | 55·7 | 57·7 | 59·0 |
| Queensland | Brisbane | 23·3 | 32·0 | 39·5 | 40·9 | 40·9 | 44·9 |
| Tasmania | Hobart | 21·0 | 26·9 | 30·9 | 33·1 | 33·1 | 33·4 |

Sources:  Ryan (1969), 204 for 1961 and earlier figures; subsequent calculations
by the author. Time series may not be completely compatible.

proportion of the total state population resident in the capital city (metropolitan) area less than 50 per cent. Moreover, the degree of concentration has been generally increasing over time in all states as well as nationally.

The image of concentration is even more intense when one considers the spatial distribution of major urban centres (see Figure 5.1). Aside

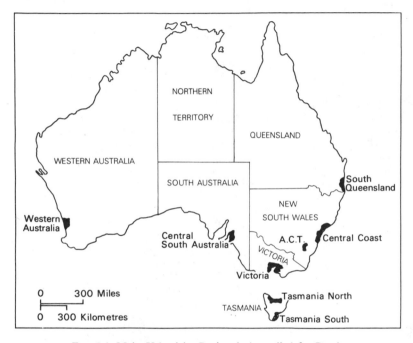

FIG. 5.4. Major Urbanizing Regions in Australia (after Rose).

from the obvious coastal location of all such centres, several large conurbations are developing through the proximity of two or more major centres: notably Newcastle–Sydney–Wollongong, Melbourne–Geelong, Brisbane–Gold Coast, and Perth–Fremantle; suggesting a degree of population concentration typical of urban Western Europe and North America. Rose's (1971) map of future urbanizing regions in Australia (Figure 5.4) illustrates both the potential extent of this concentration and the seeds of future urban problems noted above.

Given the small population base, such extreme concentration in a few major urban nodes has produced a sharply truncated distribution of population by city sizes in Australia (see Figure 2.4 and Section II). In direct comparison to Canada for instance (Table 5.4), there are few cities in the middle-size population range. While a lot could be read into these differences, it will suffice here to note that centres of this size range have frequently served in other countries as the most plausible alternative growth centres to the large metropolitan areas. Such alternatives are relatively few in Australia.

Concentration is as expected even more severe in certain economic sectors than in terms of population. In one example, that of management of the national economy, Johnston (1966) has estimated that Sydney and Melbourne controlled no less than 93 per cent of the total assets of Australia's 887 largest corporations in 1963 (Table 5.5). And their respective areas of influence are largely complementary rather than competitive. Even the other mainland state capitals harboured fewer corporate assets than their populations would suggest.

This rather extreme urban system structure has had several continuing consequences. It has fascinated politicians and researchers in Australia for some time and has as a subject of analysis dominated the urban literature (Robinson, 1962; Rose, 1966 and 1972; Johnston, 1967; Scott, 1968; G. Clarke, 1970; Holmes, 1973). Equally important, the widespread public image of extreme geographic concentration, and its inferred (and often exaggerated) social costs, have permeated political thinking on urban-related policy formulation at both the state and commonwealth government levels. The extensive interest in decentralization is an obvious case in point. Add to this image the politicians mental map of the nation as consisting of vast empty spaces in the continental interior, particularly the north—and the inevitable desire to fill those spaces—and one has a broad picture of most sources of energy in the traditional political debate.

Other urban-related issues have appeared at different times and in varying combinations with that of the concentration of national population. Questions of housing quality, services, and poverty, as in Canada, have been subjects of considerable recent interest (Jones, 1972), but they have only been linked in passing to the operation of the urban system (see J. Paterson, 1971). Interestingly, there does not appear to be the same emphasis on regional poverty problems in Australia as there is in most other developed countries. Regional inequalities do exist, but they appear to be localized within rather than between major regions and states (except possibly between the mainland and Tasmania) and are more limited in number and in spatial scale than those, say, between

**TABLE 5.4**

NUMBER OF URBAN CENTRES BY SIZE, AUSTRALIA AND CANADA, 1971

| Population Size | AUSTRALIA | | | | CANADA | | | |
|---|---|---|---|---|---|---|---|---|
| | No. of Centres | % | Cum. No. of Centres | Cum. % | No. of Centres | % | Cum. No. of Centres | Cum. % |
| 500,000 and over | 5 | 3·6 | 5 | 3·6 | 5 | 2·2 | 5 | 2·2 |
| 250,000–499,999 | — | — | 5 | 3·6 | 7 | 3·1 | 12 | 5·3 |
| 100,000–249,999 | 5 | 3·6 | 10 | 7·2 | 11 | 4·8 | 23 | 10·1 |
| 50,000– 99,999 | 5 | 3·6 | 15 | 10·8 | 11 | 4·8 | 34 | 14·9 |
| 25,000– 49,999 | 12 | 8·6 | 27 | 19·4 | 20 | 8·8 | 54 | 23·7 |
| 10,000– 24,999 | 46 | 33·1 | 73 | 52·5 | 72 | 31·6 | 126 | 55·3 |
| 5,000–  9,999 | 66 | 47·5 | 139 | 100·0 | 102 | 44·7 | 228 | 100·0 |

regions in Canada or the U.S.,[3] although empirical documentation here is difficult (see Table 5.1). Poverty problems do exist within states, and there are serious concentrations within most urban centres and in native population districts. The point here is one of the relative importance of regional differences in Australia between the states and between metropolitan areas.

One possible reason for this pattern is that Australia never did have a large rural or export staple-based population left behind in relatively isolated locations by technological and social change (G. Clarke, 1970). Another reason is that the ports and areas of initial settlement in Australia, unlike say in the Maritimes in Canada, are still the centres of national economic life (again with the possible exception of Hobart and Tasmania). Furthermore, transport systems in Australia historically have been poorly integrated and not particularly efficient. When these factors are added to the extreme distances involved the resulting costs and inconveniences of locating any industrial and service activities outside of the major urban centres become almost prohibitive. Research has also shown that economic-occupational differences between the capital cities, except for Canberra, are relatively small (Smith, 1965; Ryan, 1969; G. Clarke, 1970; Kerr, 1970). Similarly, functional linkages between cities which facilitate the working out of economic fluctuations tend to be relatively fluid (Jeffery and Webb, 1972). In other words, there seem to be few time lags in the distribution of economic growth between metropolitan areas in the urban system. In any case, the absence of extreme inequalities between major regions and the larger cities has meant less pressure on the national government to intercede in shaping the spatial organization of the nation space economy.

Related to these issues are those (perceived as) deriving from rapid growth and extreme concentration in the urban size hierarchy. First, there is the continued low-density sprawl of the metropolitan centres, notably of Sydney and Melbourne, but equally of Brisbane, Adelaide, and Perth, and the appended problems of environmental pollution and social service provision. Of particular concern are the very high costs of building and servicing resulting from Sydney's relatively rugged topography, limited water-supply, rapid growth, and fragmented civic

[3] One standard measure of regional inequality shows that average wage rates between states vary at most in an approximate ratio of 100 : 85, compared to 100 : 50 for provinces in Canada. In part the relatively low level of disparity in Australia is due to Commonwealth employment legislation which tends to equalize average wages in a number of critical sectors across the country. While other measures of poverty or inequality show greater variation between states, they are still considerably less than similar measures taken for provinces in Canada.

**TABLE 5.5**

URBAN ECONOMIC CONCENTRATION: HEAD OFFICE LOCATION OF COMPANIES
BY STATE CAPITAL CITIES, AUSTRALIA, 1963

| Location of Company Head Office | Total Company Assets Controlled (in millions A£) | (1) Proportion of Australian Population % | (2) Proportion of Australian Assets Controlled % | (2)/(1) Location Quotients % | Proportion State Factories Controlled from Capital % |
|---|---|---|---|---|---|
| Sydney | 7,150 | 20·8 | 49·72 | 2·39 | 69·9 |
| Melbourne | 6,223 | 18·2 | 43·28 | 2·38 | 74·8 |
| Brisbane | 203 | 5·9 | 1·42 | 0·24 | 15·8 |
| Adelaide | 394 | 5·6 | 2·74 | 0·49 | 28·4 |
| Perth | 118 | 4·0 | 0·83 | 0·21 | 29·0 |
| Hobart | 44 | 1·1 | 0·31 | 0·28 | 6·9 |
| Other Australian cities | 244 | 44·4 | 1·70 | 0·04 | — |

Source: Adapted from Johnston (1966), 49.

administration. Sydney's combination of problems has provided much of the encouragement and empirical evidence for new national urban policy innovations. Not surprisingly this has led some critical observers to argue that politicians tend to equate Sydney's and Melbourne's problems with national issues and those of other cities with local or state issues. At the other extreme is the problem of the stagnation of small inland towns and rural areas from which migration to the coastal metropolises has been most pronounced and most damaging to those left behind. These two problem areas at opposite ends of the size scale, while treated separately in earlier policy statements, have now been brought together into a more comprehensive view of national economic development by the federal government.

### 5.1.3. THE POLICY RESPONSE

Traditionally, urban planning in Australia has been largely confined to state and municipal levels of government. At the local level these activities date back to the 1920s, and at least since the 1940s the states have taken an active interest (Commonwealth Ministry of Post-War Reconstruction, 1949). Despite a prevailing feeling that such efforts have been unsuccessful (Harrison, 1966), there are numerous examples of good planning at the local level. Most of the subsequent legislative planning guide-lines adopted derive from the British town and country planning movement, with a time lag of about a decade in their revision and eventual implementation. These developments have generally taken two forms: the creation of specific strategic plans for part or all of the state capitals, such as for Cumberland County (New South Wales, 1967) and Port Phillip Bay (Melbourne and Metropolitan Board of Works, 1971), and attempts at regional planning through the framework of regional development committees and decentralization policies. The latter, because of their importance in the Australian context, are discussed more fully in a later section. The former, local planning initiatives, are not discussed in detail here.

Any interpretation of the national policy response to urbanization in Australia must be set in the framework of Commonwealth–State relations in constitutional and financial matters. While it is not the purpose of this section to define such relations, it should be noted that the Commonwealth government holds most of the nation's purse strings, more so than for either the Canadian or U.S. federal governments. The Commonwealth's control of public finance—of all grants to the states since 1910 and of all important national taxes since 1942—is well documented (Parker and Troy, 1972). Yet the states tend to hold the principal responsibility for urban planning, and until very recently have been faced with the financial burden of decentralization.

The recent activities of the individual states in the urban policy field have varied widely, partly complicated by the almost one-to-one relationship of population, government, and power between capital city and state. This correspondence renders policy innovations both more and less difficult at the same time. Urban governments tend to be weak, if the state is strong, and vice versa. Or city and state in some minds are equated. The state of Victoria, for example, now views itself as committed to a strategy of regulating urban growth through regional planning—which of course means essentially controlling Melbourne's expansion. It has proposed a three-tier planning system—state, region, and local municipality. Regional authorities are being established, although in a painfully slow fashion, with planning responsibilities over local urban governments.[4] The definitional basis of each is to create economically efficient regions with a sufficiently diverse employment base and a minimum population of 100,000. What effect if any this strategy will have on urban development on a regional scale has yet to be seen.

The debate on a direct federal role in urbanization blossomed into full political view in the national election in late 1972. Prior to that, Commonwealth government interest in urbanization had been slight and sporadic. During the 1972 campaign the Prime Minister of the long-ruling and rural-based Liberal-Country Party coalition, responding to the emergence of urban issues in the campaign, hastily announced the creation of a new National Urban and Regional Development Authority (NURDA). It was described as a means of co-ordinating Commonwealth activities which impinge directly on urban areas and an opportunity for improving joint Commonwealth–State planning and regulatory activities. This co-ordination was to be enhanced by a cabinet-level Commonwealth–State Ministerial Council. Like most election campaign promises, this one also proposed increased financial aid to the cities, but with few specific guide-lines.

The election of 1972 brought the more urban-based Labour Party to

---

[4] In the Melbourne region, for example, three such authorities have been proposed: (1) Melbourne itself, covering 2,000 square miles and 54 local municipalities; (2) Geelong, covering 1,000 square miles and 8 municipalities; and (3) Westernport, also embracing 1,000 square miles and 6 municipalities.

power.[5] One of Labour's initial platforms in 1972 was the need to control urbanization (Australian Labour Party, 1971). While no one would claim that the urban affairs question was a decisive factor in the election, it no doubt contributed to the sinking fortunes of the Liberal-Country Party coalition.[6] Increased Labour support came principally from the booming metropolitan suburbs—from Sydney and Melbourne—despite the continued imbalance in the electoral map of Australia. One immediate consequence of the victory was a major reorganization of ministerial and departmental responsibilities in January 1973 including a new Ministry for Urban and Regional Development. The former authority (NURDA) was retained but under a new name, the Cities Commission. Its function is now one of co-ordination between the new Ministry and state governments.[7]

The rationale for Australian government involvement in urban areas is couched in the same terms as those used in the Swedish example above. 'Increasingly, a citizen's real standard of living, . . . his access to employment opportunities, his ability to enjoy his Nation's resources . . ., are determined not by his income, not by the hours he works, but by where he lives' (DURD, release S73/36, 18 October 1973). The new Labour government argued its approach on the basis of two themes: (1) that practically every major national problem relates to cities; and (2) that in many ways the government is already a significant force in urban affairs, and these ways need to be identified and co-ordinated. The Ministry for Urban and Regional Development was established as the principal vehicle for achieving this co-ordination.

Given the Ministry's dramatic introduction, potential importance, and the fact that it did not emerge out of an existing department, it might be useful at this point briefly to summarize its organization and objectives. Figure 5.5 outlines the structure of the Ministry and, within that, of the Department of Urban and Regional Development. Under the secretary of the Department, Figure 5.5 also identifies the Ministry's principal responsibilities in terms of functions and reporting agencies.

The Department, which the Ministry's publicity describes as the

[5] The Labour government was returned to power in the May 1974 elections, but with a slightly reduced majority.

[6] *The Times*, London, 19 December 1972.

[7] The 'Cities Commission' has recently assumed an increasingly active role in Commonwealth–State relations, particularly as an instrument for encouraging joint action in urban development. The government indicates that it has three important functions: (1) a professional urban consultative service for federal agencies and state governments; (2) a co-ordinating body to work with the states during the establishment of the new town development corporations; and (3) an agency to prosecute the state's interest in urban matters at the federal level.

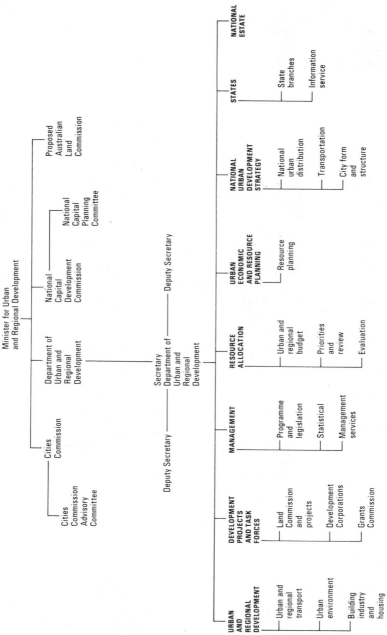

FIG. 5.5. Organization of the Ministry for Urban and Regional Development.

Source: DURD, Annual Report, 1973.

major urban policy arm of the Commonwealth government, has been assigned ten principal responsibilities (Department of Urban and Regional Development, 1973). Six are most important in the present context: (1) the formulation and implementation of a national urban and regional development strategy for Australia; (2) the monitoring of urban and regional budget programmes within the Commonwealth government to improve the allocation of national resources; (3) the development of a capacity for undertaking urban-economic and long-term planning; (4) the co-ordination of federal activities in the urban development field; (5) supervision of the activities of the State land commissions and the proposed Commonwealth land commission; and (6) administration of the evolving new cities programme.[8] More will be said on these and other specific functions later.

The recommendations to establish land commissions, and to give them some power and financial backing, may be potentially among the most influential policies to emerge in the process of setting up the new Department. The federal government is encouraging, and is willing to finance the states to establish land commissions or equivalent bodies, to improve the supply and lower the cost of urban land. These goals might be achieved through land bank purchases, increased co-ordination in land development planning practices, outright subsidies, and subsequently land price stabilization.[9] One of the obvious uses of the commissions, in addition to ameliorating some of the consequences of urban sprawl, is to expedite the planning and construction of new towns. The federal government is to act as over-all co-ordinator and as a resource body for state government activities and agencies. Several states, at the time of writing, have passed enabling legislation to establish such commissions. The strength of this legislation, as might be expected, has varied considerably between states.

## 5.1.4. DECENTRALIZATION

Before elaborating further on these policies we might return briefly to the single issue which has dominated the debate on urban problems and

[8] Among the other responsibilities assigned to the Department are the following: (1) to initiate and co-ordinate urban and regional research; (2) to assess national transportation needs in conjunction with the Department of Transport; (3) to provide assistance to state and local governments to undertake local area and regional planning; (4) to develop a national estate programme for historical land and building preservation.

[9] The land commissions would in effect act as intermediaries between the private sector and the public, and would purchase and release land as local conditions warranted. In those instances where large tracts of land were involved, such as in the case of new towns and expanded cities, development corporations might be established on British lines.

policy in Australia—that of geographic decentralization. It has already been noted that this issue is important here not only because it is still socially sensitive, but also it neatly captures the uniqueness of the Australian urban political situation while at the same time providing the most likely historical platform from which future urban system policies may emerge.

Concern with decentralization in Australia is not recent. H. Mortimer Franklyn, writing in 1880, argued that the future of the country depended on its ability '. . . to promote the decentralization and distribution of those huge aggregations of men and women which are now to be met within all metropolitan centres . . .' Not unexpectedly, the concern about population concentration was permeated by an open preference for the virtues supposedly inherent in a rural way of life, and more generally, in a rural society. Franklyn went on to state the need '. . . to encourage the growth of a feeling in favour of rural life, of the pursuits of husbandry, and of country sports and pastimes'. This attitude, in essence but not exclusively an anti-urban sentiment, has its historical roots in the countryside preoccupation of the élite in Victorian England. In the Australian context of course such attitudes appear even more out of place.

Institutional recognition of the decentralization question came almost exclusively from the states (Woolmington, 1970; Woolmington, Pigram, and Hobbs, 1971). New South Wales and Victoria, the states with the most apparent problems of concentration, led the way. Near the end of World War II a New South Wales boundaries commission established a subdivision of the state into 17 regions (later raised to 20) for purposes of regional planning. Each region, except Sydney, was under a Regional Development Committee consisting of local and senior government officials. The committees had no explicit statutory power and thus were largely ineffective—except for regional inventories and, as Woolmington (1971) notes, through their effect on increasing public awareness of the issues involved. This situation did not change until the 1960s, when '. . . effective revival of decentralization activity took place subsequent to the acquisition of power by the Liberal-Country Party coalition in 1965'. One consequence was the creation of a new state ministry, the Department of Decentralization and Development, which also took over responsibility for the Regional Committees.[10] At about

---

[10] In 1963 New South Wales set up a State Planning Authority as successor to the County of Cumberland Planning Authority for the Sydney region. Because of the way they were set up, the

the same time, the state of Victoria set up a Decentralization Advisory Committee and undertook a similar regionalization programme of its own for regional planning purposes. In both states decentralization and urban planning activities are responsible to different divisions of government, and are generally considered to be different problems.

Both New South Wales and Victoria have had formal and explicit policies to encourage decentralization since 1965. Most such efforts (at least those falling under the label of decentralization) have attempted to influence new industrial location (New South Wales, Development Corporation, 1969), many have been highly 'promotional' rather than substantive in character, not unlike the typical chamber-of-commerce approach in North America, and there is an overtone of competition in seeking new investments to stimulate decentralization.

The specific policy measures and incentives employed are difficult to summarize. They vary markedly between the states over time, and differ depending on which agencies or organizations within the states have the responsibility for decentralization. Many instruments which the authorities would probably consider as regional policy incentives are buried in an array of related legislation. Nevertheless, other than those for transport tariffs and subsidies, the incentives in most states emphasize the capital costs of establishing new (or expanding existing) manufacturing plants and related services in non-metropolitan areas. The incentive payments for industries have been of the traditional kind: loans or guarantees of loans for plant construction, subsidies for supporting industrial services and tax write-downs for the costs of land or factory space. The extent of subsidy, while seldom explicit, is generally based on the costs of operating similar establishments in the major metropolitan areas and therefore is designed to equalize direct financial expenditure by the investor in different locations within the state.

Transport policies in most states have also been used as traditional instruments of location policy. Victoria for example has set road and rail tariffs to assist industries and businesses to move or expand outside the state capital especially in the north of the state. Interestingly, independent state control of most transport systems, as noted earlier, has tended to discourage a closer integration of the national economy and thus to limit the possibilities for decentralization within the national urban system, as well as within the states.

---

decentralization and planning functions of the state government, despite their obvious interdependence, were assigned to different ministers: the former to the Ministry for Decentralization and Development; the latter to the Minister for Local Government.

While assessing the consequences of such varied policies is inherently difficult, it is generally agreed that decentralization efforts in Australia have been largely unsuccessful (Lonsdale, 1972; Stilwell and Hardwick, 1973). As in Canada sporadic resource developments have achieved more than planned efforts at decentralization. Within the states policies have often been conflicting and administrative procedures unclear. Location incentives have been weak, financial expenditures have been limited (Table 5.6), and location controls on developments in the major

### TABLE 5.6

ESTIMATED EXPENDITURES ON DECENTRALIZATION
INCENTIVES, SELECTED STATES, AUSTRALIA, 1969–70

| State | Estimated Expenditures on Decentralization Incentives (A$m.) | Total Expenditures from State Budget (A$m.) | Percentage spent on Decentralization Incentives |
|---|---|---|---|
| New South Wales | 5·0 | 855·8 | 0·6 |
| Victoria | 5·0 | 623·3 | 0·8 |
| Queensland | 1·5 | 340·7 | 0·4 |

Source: Kan and Rhodes (1972).

metropolitan areas either non-existent or easily altered. In those few cases in which specific locations for decentralization and for stimulated economic growth have been identified, such as in Victoria's 1967 report (Victoria, Department of State Development, 1967), the process has virtually ceased. In this example, an advisory committee selected five urban centres as new growth points: Ballarat, Bendigo, Wodonga, Portland, and a complex of small centres in the La Trobe Valley east of Melbourne. Unfortunately little or no action has subsequently been taken. The result of identifying these centres without following through may be more deleterious in terms of social planning than doing nothing in the first place. The parallels with the Canadian provincial experience (Section 5.25) will be obvious.

One of the difficulties hindering effective decentralization efforts in Australia has been the confusion resulting from a multiplicity of goals.

Among the various interpretations of decentralization objectives which appear in the literature are the following:

(1) *regional balance:* to encourage the growth of the less prosperous states relative to the national average.

(2) *urban containment:* to restrict the physical growth of the major metropolitan areas, notably Sydney and Melbourne.

(3) *rural preservation:* to hold the line on the existing level of population (and thus, the number of voters) in rural areas and country towns.

(4) *urban dispersal:* to direct new secondary industries to settle outside the state capitals and thereby to reduce the proportion of the state's population and economic growth in those capital cities.

(5) *local urban concentration:* to encourage the decentralization of population and economic activity to selected centres outside the state capital, eventually providing alternative growth centres to those cities.

(6) *pollution and congestion:* to reduce the perceived increase in the social and economic costs of pollution and traffic congestion attributable to rapid metropolitan growth.

(7) *territorial integrity:* this view holds that commonwealth as well as state interests will be served by a more uniform (or space-filling) development of the national political territory.

These objectives are not necessarily in conflict. All to a certain extent are relevant to a comprehensive strategy of population redistribution in the Australian context. The problem is that each objective varies in importance from state to state and over time from one government to another. Historically they have also been considered a secondary policy priority in the political process (Woolmington, Pigram, and Hobbs, 1971). More critically perhaps, each of the above objectives taken in isolation suggests a piecemeal concern with patterns of economic development and with the redistribution mechanisms operating through national and regional urban systems. Until these objectives converge and attitudes change, existing and future urban policy measures will be largely ineffective if not counter-effective.

### 5.1.5. COMPARATIVE COSTS AND BENEFITS OF CITY SIZE

The arguments for and against decentralization have depended very much on the calculation of the relative benefits and costs of urban growth and spatial concentration. The evidence has varied widely. In concluding a recent and extensive evaluation of the decentralization question, a joint Committee of Commonwealth/State Officials (1972) noted that their studies '. . . have not produced clear evidence of an overriding economic advantage or disadvantage from the national viewpoint arising from continuing centralization of population and economic activity in the major coastal cities' (p. 62).

Hard facts on the relative merits of large and small cities are notoriously difficult to come by. Probably the most systematic economic evidence, for the Australian context, has come from Max Neutze's (1965, 1971, and 1973) and John Paterson's (1971) work on the advantages and disadvantages of different city sizes. Neutze, for example, while rejecting the concept of a single optimal size, has asked more specific questions '. . . about the advantages of further growth of particular cities at particular points of time'. As advantages of large cities, he cites: (1) the economies of large labour markets, (2) economies of scale and agglomeration in both industrial and service activities, (3) savings in transport and communication costs, and (4) minimizing the extent of uncertainty in location decisions. These are of course common factors in the agglomeration process generally, as noted in Section II, but in Australia they take on even greater importance, Neutze argues, because of the small national market, vast distances, large industrial conglomerates (Sheridan, 1968), and the usual instabilities of a resource-based economy. Some of the disadvantages of large cities are given as: (1) higher labour turnover, (2) congestion and increasing costs for internal movements, (3) scarcity of local natural resources (water, recreation) and environmental problems (pollution), (4) higher land and building costs, and (5) more rapid inflation (see Stilwell, 1972; Stilwell and Hardwick, 1973). On balance, the conclusion is, in the Australian context, that the disadvantages outweigh the advantages.

Attempts to attach quantitative values to this balance have also been made. Neutze, for example, has attempted to estimate the *per capita* costs of increased urban growth in terms of selective social services, personal activity systems, and congestion, for existing centres of varying size. One rather extreme estimate suggests that each new resident would impose an annual increase in congestion costs on existing residents of nearly A$64 in metropolitan Sydney, compared to only A$4 in urban Wollongong (population 186,000) and just A$0·20 in the smaller centre of Wagga Wagga (population 27,600). More realistically, the total development costs of adding one serviced residential lot and

**TABLE 5.7**

RELATIVE COST ESTIMATES FOR PUBLIC SERVICES TO ACCOMMODATE
DECENTRALIZED GROWTH FROM SYDNEY INTO SMALL TOWNS, NEW SOUTH WALES*

| Country Towns Receiving Decentralized Population | Summary of Costs for Country Towns (in A$ millions) | | | | | | Cost per Capita of Additional Population |
| --- | --- | --- | --- | --- | --- | --- | --- |
| | Water-Supply | Sewerage | Road and Bridges | Public Transport | Flood Control | Totals | |
| Dubbo | 17·2 | 18·0 | 28·6 | 1·6 | — | 65·4 | 654·0 |
| Grafton | 20·7 | 17·2 | 25·6 | 1·6 | 1·5 | 66·6 | 666·0 |
| Nowra | 19·0 | 16·7 | 28·7 | 1·6 | 1·0 | 67·0 | 670·0 |
| Orange | 27·9 | 18·4 | 21·9 | 1·6 | — | 69·8 | 698·0 |
| Wagga Wagga | 15·8 | 18·2 | 26·6 | 1·6 | 1·0 | 67·1 | 671·0 |
| Totals | 42·2 | 58·4 | 88·5 | 8·0 | 3·5 | 335·9 | — |
| Summary of Expenditures Deferred in Sydney | | | | | | | |
| | 97·0 | 195·7 | 151·5 | 11·6 | — | 455·8 | 912·0 |

* Based on a decentralized population total of 500,000, with 100,000 allocated to each of the five country towns for purposes of deriving cost figures. The five towns were selected to be representative of different environments in the state.

Source: Adapted from Committee of Commonwealth/State Officials (1972), and New South Wales, Department of Decentralization and Development (1970).

related social facilities for one new household have been estimated by Lansdown (1966) at A$10,000 for Sydney and about A$7,000 for a medium-size regional centre. Another study argues that public savings of over A$120 millions could be achieved by diverting 500,000 new residents from Sydney to country towns (Table 5.7). While it is recognized that costs are only one side of the coin, there has not in most studies been a parallel assignment of the benefits deriving from urban agglomeration, for either existing or new residents, which would allow decision-makers to make a more balanced assessment of net social returns from urban growth (Alonso, 1972; Wingo, 1973).

Day (1972) has argued that the evidence from sociological studies also favours small to medium-size cities over larger centres, particularly in amenities and community stability, adding some weight to the above cost-based arguments encouraging decentralization measures. The Committee of Commonwealth/State Officials (1972) quoted previously reached similar conclusions on social factors but left open the relative importance to be attached to economic and technological factors.[11]

### 5.1.6. NEW CITIES PROGRAMMES

The most recent expression of the decentralization debate is the proposal for 'multi-nodal' decentralization, or new town development. The opportunity to create 'new cities in the bush' has fascinated Australian politicians for many years, no doubt partly as a consequence of the apparent success of Canberra and of satellite urban centres such as Elizabeth near Adelaide.[12] Proposals for new cities have taken several forms. Some have argued for the creating the need for new 'Canberra-type' capitals by simply carving new states out of the old—for example, in north-west New South Wales and in northern Queensland. Other observers, following the British experience, have argued for the development of overspill towns for each of the mainland state capitals.

The most detailed, and possibly the most influential recommen-

[11] There were numerous dissenters from this report. New South Wales objected to many of the conclusions and in a minority report argued a much stronger case for the benefits of decentralized urban development. Again, this no doubt mirrors the very serious development problems facing the Sydney metropolitan area (see Report of the Committee of Commonwealth/State Officials on Decentralization, 1972; and Australian Institute of Urban Studies, 1972c), and the historically strong regional independence movements within the state, which have taken much of their energy from the lack of economic growth in most rural regions. The substantive arguments in the report were largely based on cost considerations facing further development in Sydney (see Table 5.7).

[12] Elizabeth, although widely cited, is an integral part of the Adelaide metropolitan area and is therefore not an appropriate example of the regional redistribution of population (i.e. decentralization) through new town construction.

dations for new town construction were contained in a task force report on new cities prepared by the Australian Institute of Urban Studies (1972b and 1972c). The report proposed that three types of centres were needed in Australia, the first two being entirely new on the ground.

(1) *regional cities:* centres located far enough from existing centres to be independent or 'self-contained' in terms of housing and job opportunities and for which a minimum size of 100,000–150,000 population is envisaged.

(2) *system cities:* centres situated closer to and within the spheres of influence or 'urban fields' of existing metropolitan areas, again with a minimum size of 150,000 but more likely with an eventual target population of 250,000. These centres would form part of a new 'multi-centred' metropolitan region.

(3) *the renewed metropolis:* involving the massive rejuvenation of the existing inner city cores of the present metropolises.

The first type, regional cities, are viewed as more than alternative growth points; they would also become major regional service centres designed to improve the quality of services available to existing rural and small town populations. The growth of such centres could not, however, be either rapid or extensive—as is evident in the suggested long-term target of 150,000 population—because of limits imposed by geographic isolation and relatively high costs of construction.[13] System-cities, on the other hand, would offer both political and cost advantages through larger size and more rapid development because they would benefit from close proximity to the existing service infrastructure, employment opportunities, and construction facilities of the central cities, while serving both as counter-magnets to those cities and as checks on urban sprawl. It is argued in the report that the system-cities concept recognizes and in fact attempts to capitalize on the trend toward increasingly large urban complexes and the growing attractiveness for employers and households of large and diversified labour markets. In total, the report projects the need for as many as sixteen new cities in Australia by the year 2010, nine of which would have between 100,000 and 250,000 population and seven would have between 250,000 and 500,000 population, designed to accommodate an aggregate population of between 3 and 4 millions. Surprisingly, for the third type of centre, the 'renewed' metropolis, large-scale public action is not recommended as a top priority in the report, at least at the present time.

[13] This intentionally low target population figure was proposed in part to ensure, for political reasons, more rapid attainment of the initial objective. A considerably greater population was hoped for once the initial objective was reached (see Australian Institute of Urban Studies, 1972b).

Numerous other proposals for new cities have been made in Australia (Winston, 1966; Stretton, 1970; Robinson, 1972). Many include variants of the British new town movement, notably the expansion of existing urban centres, while others involve new satellite centres around the metropolitan areas and limited extensions to those areas along major interregional transport corridors. One interesting point in these proposals is the extent to which they are dependent on the notion of territorial extension—the filling-in of empty spaces.

Such new cities proposals, while the conventional political wisdom and the standard planning solution for decreasing urban concentration in nearly all countries, are not totally without merit in the Australian context (Neutze, 1973; Payne and Mills, 1973). The Australian urban system, as previously noted, is extremely truncated in the lower size range. While there are five metropolitan centres (and ten cities with populations over 100,000), all are located in a narrow coastal strip and all are growing at rates above the national average. There are very few centres in the middle size range and none located in the interior. Any plan that envisages more widespread development of the national territory, although subject to debate and criticism, must involve urban development outside of the present urban regions. And, given the substantial increase in urban population forecast by the end of the century, the opportunity exists for some reordering of the national urban system on the part of government, without relocating existing urban residents on a massive scale. Further, enormous resource development projects, both emerging and anticipated, such as at Pilbara in Western Australia, necessitate plans for controlled and sustained urbanization, again on a modest scale, but which ideally should be linked to a new city system strategy.

In addition to confusing terminology, the above proposals are none the less open to wide criticism on several grounds (Australian Institute of Urban Studies, 1972c). The so-called 'system cities' are anything but that. While possibly separate in physical design, they will by definition become integral functioning parts of metropolitan economies within whose areas of influence or urban field they are located. As such, they will have next to no effect on the redistribution of growth nationally or even within regional urban sub-systems. One recalls Alonso's (1972) premiss on planning for decentralized new town development: 'nearer the smaller, farther the bigger'. Moreover, if the British experience in encouraging office relocation from London to provincial cities is any guide-line, as satellites the system-cities may sap the growth of the smaller and more distant regional cities. Therefore, as a decentralization measure *per se*, system-cities are likely to be neutral in effect if not negative. They represent an important but essentially local reordering of the existing urban form of a metropolitan region, and require different policy instruments and regulation strategies from those necessary for generating new regional centres. The latter are additional nodes in the national (or regional) urban system, and must be seen in that context.

The most likely outcome of these proposals is to reinforce and possibly redirect commonwealth and state government efforts at decentralization. Each state, with the possible exception of Tasmania where capital-city population concentration is relatively low, has at times proposed its own new cities or alternative growth centres. New South Wales (Department of Decentralization and Development, 1970) has identified a number of possible centres, such as the Bathurst–Orange area; Western Australia has discussed the feasibility of encouraging sustained urban growth around the gold-mining community of Kalgoorlie as well as at Pilbara in the north-west; Victoria has proposed a system of 'regional capitals', initially including Ballarat and Bendigo, as future expanded centres and alternatives to Melbourne; and South Australia has plans to develop a new growth centre at Murray Bridge to encourage decentralization from Adelaide. Finally, the federal government has announced its intention to assist the states in the development of several major growth centres, including expansion of the twin towns of Albury–Wodonga which straddle the New South Wales–Victoria state boundary. The latter is the most interesting proposal since it is an obvious attempt to secure the agreement of the two most powerful states to participate in the expanded cities programme.

In most of these examples the emphasis is on increasing existing centres to a minimum size of from 100,000 to 200,000 population, rather than the creation of 'new' cities *per se*. Although the economic studies which have been done in Australia seem to tip the scales in favour of completely new cities (Neutze, 1973), the more pragmatic strategy of stimulating the growth of selected slow-growing country centres—in the light of limited national resources and political realities—may be the most likely outcome. On the other hand, one unfortunate consequence of the new cities movement, in the eyes of some observers, is that it has shifted public attention from the problems of the coastal metropolitan core areas—where most Australians live and will continue to live in the future.

5.1.7. CANBERRA: A MODEL FOR DECENTRALIZATION?

Undoubtedly the single best-known example of national urban planning in Australia is the development of Canberra and the Australian Capital Territory (ACT). An enormous literature has appeared describing the impressive physical design, municipal organization, and execution of the neighbourhood 'cities' which make up the Canberra urban area (NCDC, 1972). Evaluations and criticisms have been widely voiced (Harrison, 1971 and 1973; Robinson, 1972 and 1973). For present purposes, however, the Canberra experience is most useful in terms of what it reveals about Australian attitudes to decentralization and what these attitudes imply about future possibilities for manipulating the national urban system. These links are not as tenuous as one might think since Canberra is often held up as a model of new town development and as proof that urban decentralization will work in Australia (Lansdown, 1971).

The decision to establish Canberra reflects a political compromise of historical state rivalries over national political jurisdiction. In fact the need to create a new capital was written into the constitution for the federation of the Australian Commonwealth in 1901. Its location was also roughly specified in the constitution—it was to be in New South Wales but not closer than 100 miles to Sydney. The present site was selected a decade later and a master plan for the city was subsequently drawn up by Walter Burley Griffin in 1915. Despite the constitutional incentive, and the threat of secession by New South Wales, little or nothing was done with the site until 1942 when the need to centralize power in the face of another World War encouraged the Commonwealth government to begin to take the development of political Canberra seriously. Some administrative functions were shifted from the old national capital (Melbourne) during the War, and by 1945 the beginnings of the current federal government office complex began to take shape. Subsequent decisions by the government to develop Canberra as an urban environment and as a 'national monument' led to an accelerated population growth from 26,000 in 1951 to over 160,000 in 1972.

How successful has Canberra been within the context of influencing national urban systems development? Although Canberra was not initially conceived as a decentralized policy, it did, like Brasilia, grow in concept to become a rationale for further new town development. As a physical plan, of course, it has much to commend it. There are, however, serious reservations about the relevance of the Canberra experience, except as a learning situation, to what might eventually be proposed in terms of a national decentralization strategy. Firstly, it represents a scale of public investment and of direct government involvement which is unlikely to be repeated in the near future. Its functions are obviously unique, and it is supported by unusual financing arrangements. Unlike the British new towns, for example, the National Capital Development Commission which administers Canberra and the ACT is directly connected to the Commonwealth treasury and seems to have an almost unlimited potential for financial support with few explicit legislative checks, although this relationship has changed recently.

Canberra's effect on national population distribution has also been relatively minor. Its present population of slightly over 160,000 must be seen within the context of fifty years of planning and development. Even though the bulk of the population movement has taken place in the last decade, when Canberra has been the fastest-growing city in Australia, an equivalent population increment spread over the five major state capitals during a similar period of time would have had only a minor effect if any on the growth rates and the problems of those cities. The future may be different. Within the next three decades, if the population as anticipated rises to over 500,000, the Canberra contribution to urban population decentralization may be more significant. But, as some critics have asked, at what cost (Robinson, 1973)?

What of the local multiplier effects of Canberra's growth on the regional redistribution of economic activity? Although data in this regard are almost non-existent, it is not inappropriate to conclude that Canberra's major contribution in stimulating regional growth has been felt, through the complex network of links which characterize any mature economy, primarily in Sydney and Melbourne. Aside from the growth of Queanbeyan,[14] which provides many of those urban functions conveniently omitted from the Canberra plan, there is little evidence of substantial spin-off effects from Canberra's growth in generating employment opportunities in the immediate region.

As a basis for future new cities, the Canberra model might also be questioned as a means of attaining national social policy objectives. Canberra is almost exclusively a middle-class community in which

[14] Queanbeyan is a small town located immediately outside the boundary of the Australian Capital Territory in New South Wales. It existed as a local agricultural centre prior to Canberra's siting and development and served an important function during the early stages of development. Since then it has expanded its 'unplanned' role as a service centre providing a number of functions for Canberra which the planners zoned out of the capital.

housing and employment for the poor, the socially disadvantaged, and those otherwise afflicted are zoned out. Clearly, it was not intended to contribute to a redistribution of income or social opportunities, either hierarchically by class or spatially by region. Yet it would be difficult to imagine such a massive undertaking today which did not have such egalitarian principles among its objectives, explicitly or implicitly.

Few argue that Canberra as such is a model for other national urban policy decisions, given its unique history, functional composition, and position in the Australian political structure. One possible exception to this conclusion is the application of public landownership practices developed primarily in Canberra to the planning and development of the proposed new cities. Also on the positive side, the political growth of Canberra in itself substantiates the potential role that the Australian government can have directly on spatial patterns of urbanization, through decisions on the location of public sector employment, as well as indirectly through the multiplier effects of government employment on the rapidly increasing tertiary and quarternary sectors of the economy (Smailes, 1971).

## 5.1.8. EVALUATION AND FUTURE POSSIBILITIES

The principal shift in emphasis in the Australian urban policy debate has been from decentralization *per se* to one of selective decentralization, leading to proposals for new city development. These labels may be simply opposite sides of the same coin, although the different attitudes they reflect are fundamentally more important. The decentralization question has in historical terms been underlaid by an almost exclusive focus on rural areas and their depopulation. Its political emergence coincided with rural political dominance of Commonwealth governments augmented by documentation in the popular press of the escalating social and economic costs of continued rapid growth in Sydney and Melbourne. The new city movement has brought a more urban focus to the decentralization issue, recognizing the necessity of influencing the form of the urban system to achieve effective changes in patterns of national growth.

Defining the future role of government, and specifically of the Commonwealth, in a national urban strategy in Australia will be difficult. Assessing the consequences of such roles is equally difficult. Yet there is little doubt that the present political climate in Australia is more conducive to increased regulatory powers than has been true in the recent past. Although there was some previous interest in the 'national' urban system some fifteen years ago, interest which subsequently dissipated, the present government's strong convictions in this area should produce some concrete action. Such action will clearly have to be a co-ordinated effort with the states, in which the latter would do most of the detailed physical planning and the former would provide strategic guide-lines. This will not be easy as the states are still extremely jealous of their independence.[15] The principal argument for Commonwealth involvement, in the view of many of the states at least, is the need for basic 'priming' decisions and of course financial assistance. As one state official put it to the author, 'All we [the states] need from Canberra is money and good will.' These conditions are necessary, but are not sufficient, for effectively regulating national or even regional urban systems.

It is much too early to attempt to evaluate the impact of recent national urban policy directions in Australia. The new Ministry for Urban and Regional Development had at the time of writing only just begun to formulate specific guide-lines for a national urban strategy and policy reorganization. But in more general terms, attitudes and values are changing. Continued rapid economic and population growth and metropolitan concentration are being questioned openly. For instance, Commonwealth policies relating to one of the major components of urban growth, foreign immigration, are now under careful scrutiny.[16] The day of the massive search for new settlers in Australia may be drawing to a close. The possibilities of more direct government involvement in shaping national development patterns, and in the reordering of urban development are no longer immediately dismissed as unrealistic and inappropriate.

The government's energetic plans for decentralization face several difficulties. Proposals for major regional centres away from the coast have dubious prospects—rural settlement densities are extremely low and, therefore, such areas will provide little in the way of a service population or economic base for a new town. Development costs, par-

---

[15] This independence often goes to the extreme of including discussion of secession from the Commonwealth, most recently by groups in Western Australia (*The Times*, London, 1 March 1973). The arguments parallel those heard from western Canada, for example, and are not unusual in countries of large continental extent and social diversity.

[16] The Australian government has established a National Population Enquiry to review the country's population prospects and policies (see Neutze, 1973, and Harrison, 1973, for examples). Of particular concern is the long-standing practice of encouraging rapid population growth through high intakes of foreign immigration. This intake, which has already been deliberately reduced, and will probably be further reduced in the future, has its greatest impact on Sydney and Melbourne.

ticularly for water-supply, but also for transportation, are likely to be much higher away from the coast and amenity values are clearly lower. Moreover, most Australians—if one believes the popular press—do not want to be decentralized from the attractions of the coastal environment. Even if these reservations are incorrect, the numbers of people involved will be relatively small, at least in the short run. Most suggestions for decentralized urban development are in fact proposals to be realized in the 1980s if not later. The present generation of British new towns, for instance, have about a twenty-year development horizon, and there the population sources which could be drawn on for relocation purposes were obviously substantially greater. Another difficulty, relating to constitutional and power-sharing questions, is the degree to which federal decentralization efforts are dependent on, or are seen to be dependent on, a redistribution of responsibilities for urban affairs away from the state governments. This issue alone may determine the fate of the current urban policy debate.

There is little evidence at present that the government or its urban ministry will take the urban system as its perspective for co-ordinated national policy planning and resource allocation. This may seem somewhat surprising since the government has already committed itself to the direct support and encouragement of new town development and, as mentioned earlier, it has agreed to the selection of at least two new towns (one at Albury-Wodonga) as locations for a major effort at decentralization. The identification of these specific towns, while partly a political compromise to the wishes of the states, does at least implicitly recognize the existence of an integrated regional urban system in southeastern Australia, if not of the entire nation (Brotchie, 1971). Such locational choices for new and expanded towns are, in effect, attempts to redistribute growth within the urban system, that is to alter the spatial and hierarchical structure of that system toward some specified goals.

What, then, are the prospects for urban Australia? The most probable actions which will have positive benefits in controlling the consequences of rapid urbanization at the national (and urban system) level are twofold. The real and urgent problems lie not in establishing free-standing regional cities away from the existing metropolitan areas, but in more effective control and planning of the growth of the major centres, and in the redistribution and rearrangement of population on a local or regional scale. On the one hand, we might expect to see greater co-ordination between different levels of government in reducing the social costs of congestion and sprawl in the state capitals through local decentralization. Second, closer integration of emerging urbanization policies with resource and economic development plans, possibly through the Cities Commission, and with land-use planning, possibly through state land commissions, could go a long way toward improving the quality of urban life both in the cities and in the interior.

## 5.2. URBAN CANADA

Canada is a mosaic of cultures, economies, and politics. The search for national identity, the polarization of provincial interests, the multiplicity of regional goals and objectives, have all complicated attempts to formulate comprehensive policies for a more orderly spatial distribution of urban and regional development. Further, there is a significant body of conservative opinion, not all of it misdirected, which argues that such attempts are inappropriate and unconstitutional, if not positively dangerous to the continued existence of Canada as a nation. These factors have led to a particular state of urban policy thinking which in Canada has been characterized by conceptual vagueness, political rivalries, and legislative inconsistency over time. Yet there are signs that the situation is changing and that a sharper focus for the urban policy debate is beginning to emerge.

This chapter examines recent directions of urban policy evolution in Canada in two broad areas: urban development and location-sensitive regional policies. The principal emphasis, as in preceding sections, is on prevailing urban issues and on the apparent strategies underlying policy responses generated by these issues. Because of the political diversity and policy inconsistencies noted above, the discussion could not treat the specific ingredients of urban and regional planning legislation at the federal level and in each of the ten provinces, but instead is selective of both levels of activity.

This review builds on an extensive and rapidly expanding literature on the aggregate spatial aspects of Canadian urbanization (Stone, 1967; Maxwell, 1967; Simmons and Simmons, 1969; Lithwick, 1970; Economic Council of Canada, 1971; MacNeill, 1971; Bourne and MacKinnon, 1972; Yeates, 1974; Simmons, 1974). Consequently, much of the burden of describing urbanization trends is lifted from this paper (see Section II Figure 2.4, and Figures 5.2 and 5.6). Although useful descriptively, much of the available research is unfortunately not oriented to the kinds of analyses which contribute directly to the identification of policy problems and alternatives (Jackson, 1971; Kaplan,

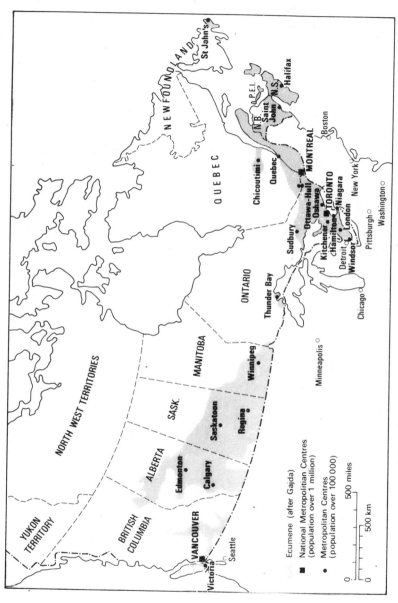

FIG. 5.6. The Settlement Geometry of Urban Canada: Metropolitan Centres and the Developed Ecumene.

1972; Ritchie, 1972). Unlike the Swedish situation (Section 4.2), for example, there has been little assessment of the types of processes and multiplier effects which geographically spread the benefits of urban and economic growth (Simmons, 1974). Nor has there been a systematic treatment of variations in welfare and quality of life indices such as social service provision which arise through urban concentration. To some extent the weakness of the latter research mirrors, as in Australia, poor data sources and more important the absence of explicit goals and concepts of what are the desired urban futures which could guide research on urban and social policy.

## 5.2.1. BACKGROUND: NATIONAL DUALITY AND DEPENDENCE

Any attempt to influence the evolving social and economic geography of Canada faces at least two fundamental realities. First, the innovator is faced by extreme political fragmentation—principally the size and economic strength of the ten provinces and the constitutional powers they inherited from the British North America Act (Lithwick, 1970; Gertler, 1972). In practice these powers often question the very need for and the continued existence of federalism in Canada (Meekison, 1969). Superimposed on this political pattern is the territorial dominance of the two original cultural groups—English- and French-speaking —which are differentiated by location and life style as well as by language and history (Wade, 1960). The convergence in the province of Quebec of the cultural fact with the political fact has tended to entrench regional differences, and to strengthen provincial independence in matters of urban importance throughout the country. Even issues with obvious national implications, such as the Canadian response to the world energy crisis, often become translated into narrow provincial perspectives, and are assessed against different provincial goals and priorities.

The second reality is Canada's obvious external dependence on the United States. The resulting questions of foreign ownership, economic independence, and the preservation of national identity are now major social issues (Rotstein and Lax, 1972), as is the question of attempting to 'buy back' the national economy. No perspective on social and economic problems can ignore the impact of urban conditions and policy experiences in the U.S. Nor can Canadian urban development be understood or its future course be plotted without direct reference to changes in the U.S. national urban system and its various regional subsystems. The urban systems of the two countries are highly interdependent in terms of growth-generating factors (Wonnacott and Wonnacott, 1967), capital flows (Caves and Reuber, 1969), industrial location (Ray, 1972d), and organizational links (Simmons, 1974). The Canadian urban system appears as a collection of highly regionalized sub-systems, almost regional branch-plant economies, each one closely interrelated with neighbouring American regions (in the west, Great Lakes, and Atlantic regions), but loosely linked with each other (Lithwick and Paquet, 1968). Analogies have frequently been drawn with Scotland's economic dependence on England.

Equally important, attempts to shape patterns of urbanization in Canada have been and will continue to be influenced by the prevailing philosophy on regulating national development in the U.S. This influence takes two forms: one indirect in terms of defending the prevailing arguments of supporters of 'privatism' and of limited or even decreasing government intervention in the processes of Canadian economic development; and the other direct through interregional and interurban competition in new employment opportunities and therefore in urban and economic growth. While these external effects are present everywhere, for example, in co-ordinating British policies within the enlarged EEC (Section 4.16), the degree and strongly unbalanced direction of the relationship in Canada are unique. Although no specific parallels of policy evolution in the U.S. and Canada are included in this study—in part because the U.S. situation is now so widely publicized (Moynihan, 1970; Feldman, 1971; Strong, 1971; U.S. Domestic Council, 1972; Hansen, 1972; Clawson and Hall, 1973; Berry, 1973b and c), reference will be made in this and subsequent chapters to the American urban experience and to its effects on Canadian urban policy.

5.2.2. THE ISSUES: THE REGIONAL MOSAIC

Each of us has his own list of urban issues. Most such lists, however, contain a number of common denominators. One is poverty. In its fifth annual review published in 1968, the Economic Council of Canada concluded: 'Poverty in Canada is real. Its numbers are not in the thousands, but in the millions' (p. 103). This striking conclusion, while applicable to most western countries, is of particular importance in Canada. Poverty is a serious problem in its own right, but it also underlies much of the debate on regional and urban policies and on national economic policy. In terms of the importance attached to structural maladjustments in the economy as well as to social and locational inequalities, they are politically explosive. Both have a profound regional expression (Department of Forestry and Rural Development, 1966; Podoluk, 1968; Comeau, 1969; Shapiro, 1970; Green, 1971; Drummond, 1972). Combined with poverty in numerous and complex ways are the inevitable political issues of housing, the concentration of economic development in (and the rapid growth in population of) the largest metropolitan areas, and the persistence of high unemployment and low incomes in the peripheral areas and in the inner cities. These are the same bread-and-butter issues as in most other countries, but in Canada they take an unusual form.

In an earlier section we summarized the most common goals of urbanization strategies as being threefold: (1) reducing the negative consequences of an over-concentration of population and economic activity in the largest metropolitan centres; (2) ensuring a minimum level of living standards and reducing social inequalities throughout the country; and (3) maximizing aggregate economic and employment growth. These three offer a simple framework around which to organize a discussion of the Canadian policy situation. The issues lying behind these goals, while not part of a formal national or provincial development strategy, are real and perceived issues in Canada.

The apparent over-concentration of population and wealth in the three major metropolitan areas—Montreal, Toronto, and Vancouver—has only recently become an open political argument. Over a third of all Canadians live in these rapidly growing urban complexes and the proportion is increasing (Table 5.8). The initial review of the role of the federal government in urban development (Lithwick, 1970) was commissioned in an atmosphere of apprehensiveness concerning the impending 'big-city' problem. The Lithwick report itself further stimulated this concern by forecasting massive population increases in these same urban regions by the end of the century. Although the consequences of this concentration have never been effectively documented, the debate has continued (Lithwick, 1972c; Miles *et al.*, 1973; Ray and Villeneuve, 1974; Blumenfeld, 1974). There have as well been discussions on limiting or slowing the growth of Toronto, Vancouver, and even Edmonton and Calgary, and at one time of Montreal. In fact, the federal government has now committed itself to the principle of limiting the growth of the largest centres and to the redistribution of that growth to about a dozen medium-size centres across the country. It is as yet unclear, however, if and how these intentions might crystallize into effective policy action based on city size and balanced urban

TABLE 5.8

THE URBAN HIERARCHY AND METROPOLITAN
CONCENTRATION IN CANADA, 1871–1971

| | 1871 | 1901 | 1921 | 1941 | 1961 | 1971 |
|---|---|---|---|---|---|---|
| 1. No. of centres with populations: | | | | | | |
| 100,000 and over | 1 | 2 | 7 | 8 | 18 | 23[a] |
| 30,000–99,999 | 2 | 8 | 11 | 19 | 28 | 35 |
| 5,000–29,999 | 16 | 43 | 70 | 85 | 147 | 170 |
| Total centres over 5,000 population | 19 | 53 | 88 | 112 | 193 | 228 |
| 2. Per cent population urbanized | 18·3 | 34·9 | 47·4 | 55·7 | 69·7 | 76·1 |
| 3. Per cent population in three national metro areas* | 5·3 | 13·3 | 18·8 | 22·2 | 35·0 | 39·3 |
| 4. Total population in three national metro areas (in thousands) | 197 | 717 | 1,651 | 2,551 | 4,725 | 6,453 |
| 5. Per cent population in all metropolitan areas** | — | 26·0 | 35·4 | 40·2 | 48·3 | 55·4 |

* Montreal, Toronto, Vancouver: Census Metropolitan Areas (CMA).

** Prior to 1961 using Stone's (1967) definition of 'principal regions of metropolitan development'; for 1961 and 1971 using the census defined metropolitan areas.

[a] The census bureau, Statistics Canada, recognized only 22 metropolitan centres in 1971. The additional centre included here is Oshawa–Whitby which has a population of 120,000, and a core area population over 50,000, and therefore would seem to qualify as a metropolitan area.

Sources: Figures for 1961 and earlier dates adapted from Stone (1967). Those for 1971 are preliminary census figures.

growth, as in Sweden, except possibly in the special case of Toronto. Pressures for economic growth generally overrule serious implementation of such policies, at least when they are applied on a uniform national basis.

Provincial politics, combined with the desire for increased rates of regional growth, adds to the complexity of the urban growth issue. Any attempt to limit or slow the growth of Montreal, for example, will probably be resisted in Quebec. The recent decline in Montreal's population growth rate has if anything stimulated provincial government requests for increased federal assistance to urban economic development in Quebec. In part this pressure reflects an implicit goal of preventing Montreal from losing its historically pre-eminent position in relation to Toronto within the Canadian urban hierarchy (Kerr, 1968; Simmons, 1974), and the relatively high unemployment levels in Quebec; and in part it is a reflection of the traditional federal–provincial money game. Fresh rethinking on city size and growth is hardly likely in this context of overt regional interests in maintaining the *status quo* of the urban system and in maximizing regional growth.

The issue is even more complicated than this reference suggests. Raynauld (1971) for instance has argued that economic development in Quebec depends on a strong and expanding economy in metropolitan Montreal. The assumption is that few other growth centres exist in the province. Even the capital, Quebec City, is at a locational disadvantage with respect to the spatial structure of the provincial economy. The best that can be hoped for in improving equity in economic well-being throughout urban Quebec is to encourage the hierarchical diffusion process in spreading opportunities outward from Montreal. Although the Montreal area's share of total industrial production in Quebec has remained relatively constant, it has generated 'super-multiplier' effects (Raynauld, Martin, and Higgins, 1970; Higgins, 1972) throughout the province.

Other expressions of spatial and sectoral concentration within the Canadian urban system are more difficult to document. Many are a function of the relatively rapid growth of Canada's population in the last two decades, and some have already been identified in comparisons with other national systems (as in Section III. See also Hodge, 1971; Ray and Murdie, 1972; Simmons, 1974; and Bourne, 1974). However, while important and increasing in scale, population concentration is not yet nearly as severe in Canada as it is in Australia, Britain, or in most Western European countries. Canada has a relatively extensive urban system, given its small population base and limited settled area. Although there is a dominant urban-transportation corridor from Windsor to Quebec City, there are growing centres outside this corridor. Concentration has severe consequences at the local and microregional levels, around Toronto and Vancouver in particular, but less so at the national or regional urban system level. There is less evidence to support the creation of new nodes (i.e. new towns) in the system at the national level. The problem of redistribution at these levels is one of reducing the variance in benefits from growth within the existing urban system.

This issue of regional and urban inequalities, the second underlying the three initial objectives outlined above, also exhibits several complex patterns.[1] The principal spatial dimensions of inequalities in Canada, as in most countries, tend to be along the rural–urban continuum and between national centre and periphery. But in Canada there are other dimensions (Ray, 1971 and 1972b; Yeates, 1974). The dominant pattern in Canada, as in Australia, is rural–urban. While in Australia this dimension is essentially intra-urban and regional in expression, and therefore is largely contained within each state, in Canada the micro-scale urban and rural differential is overlain by a macro-scale difference of regional and provincial inequality, much as in the United States or other countries of vast geographic area.[2] Unlike the U.S., however, these inequalities seem to be increasing over time. Furthermore, the disadvantaged regions, the Maritimes and eastern Quebec, the agricultural fringe stretching across mid-Canada and the north, represent quite different mixes of social, structural, and locational inequalities—outdated industrial complexes, depleted resource areas, and areas which should never have been settled. Each region itself also contains similar micro-scale variations. A further and highly sensitive pattern superimposed on the regional one is the differential in living standards between French- and English-speaking Canadians (Officer and Smith, 1970). The 'white niggers' analogy drawn by the Quebecois (although not a very meaningful analogy) is all too well known. One obvious inference from this complex pattern is that as the processes and the problems of inequalities differ between rural and urban areas, and between levels of the urban hierarchy, so the policy responses must differ in both design and application. Generally they have not.

The degree of regional disparities in Canada is difficult to document empirically (Table 5.9). Income and employment levels, the standard measures, are only symptoms of more basic problems and they tell us little or nothing of individual well-being and of differences in personal

[1] Ray (1969, 1971, and 1972b), for example, identified four major spatial dimensions to regionalism in Canada: (1) rural–urban; (2) heartland–periphery, that is the Windsor to Quebec corridor contrasted with the rest of the country; (3) east–west contrasts, essentially following the direction of initial settlement; and (4) French–English contrasts. Each of these four clearly overlaps to some extent, and each is reflected in the evolving pattern of urban population distribution (Ray and Villeneuve, 1974).

[2] Clearly such indices of concentration and disparity should be interpreted with caution. They are heavily dependent on the scale of aggregation employed in the analysis, and on the size and diversity of the territory over which the indices are defined.

## TABLE 5.9

### SELECTED MEASURES OF REGIONAL, URBAN, AND ECONOMIC DISPARITIES IN CANADA

| Province | Population (in thousands) 1971 | % Population Percentage Change 1966–71 | Number of urban centres >100,000 | % urban 1971 | Poverty Measures/Income % families below poverty line* Total families | Incidence % | Index Income/Capita |
|---|---|---|---|---|---|---|---|
| Newfoundland | 522·1 | 5·8 | 1 | 57·2 | 5·0 | 55·7 | 55 |
| Prince Edward I. | 112·6 | 2·9 | 0 | 38·3 | 0·8 | 49·2 | 63 |
| Nova Scotia | 788·9 | 4·4 | 1 | 56·7 | 6·3 | 40·3 | 78 |
| New Brunswick | 634·6 | 2·9 | 1 | 56·9 | 5·2 | 43·5 | 71 |
| Quebec | 6,027·8 | 4·3 | 3 | 80·6 | 30·1 | 27·9 | 90 |
| Ontario | 7,703·1 | 10·7 | 10 | 82·4 | 27·7 | 18·6 | 115 |
| Manitoba | 988·2 | 2·6 | 1 | 69·5 | 5·0 | 26·1 | 100 |
| Saskatchewan | 926·2 | −3·0 | 2 | 53·0 | 5·4 | 34·8 | 90 |
| Alberta | 1,627·9 | 11·3 | 2 | 73·5 | 6·0 | 22·9 | 99 |
| British Columbia | 2,184·6 | 16·6 | 2 | 75·7 | 8·6 | 21·3 | 107 |
| National Totals | 21,568·3 | 7·8 | 23 | 76·1 | 100·0 | 25·3 | 100 |

* Defined as an annual income of $3,500 per household of four persons.

Source: Economic Council of Canada (1968); Brewis (1969); Bourne et al. (1974). Reprinted by permission of Information Canada.

living conditions. Nevertheless, they are important measures in themselves, in part because they represent sectors over which national governments traditionally have direct influence. They also help to identify the objectives of locationally sensitive public policy in Canada. It has been demonstrated that average incomes rise with each larger city size group (Podoluk, 1968; Economic Council of Canada, 1968)—although the increase is not particularly consistent by region. However, incomes in metropolitan areas are nearly 50 per cent higher than in predominantly rural areas and over 30 per cent higher than in smaller urban areas. More significant, income differentials vary by as much as 100 per cent between regions and provinces (Green, 1971), and are highly correlated with the degree of urbanization and the rate of urban growth in each region. These differentials therefore, Ray (1974) argues, are unlikely to be reduced unless disparities in urban growth rates can be reduced.

Ethnic and cultural differentials, predominantly between French and English, are estimated to be of a similar order of magnitude to those between regions.[3] These dimensions (city-size, urban–rural, interprovincial, and ethnic) have also been shown to be interrelated in various and complex ways with occupational inequalities.[4] While the size of these income inequalities in relation to international averages is interesting, and could be further elaborated here, the more important point is not that they are necessarily greater in Canada than elsewhere but that they are viewed as severe enough to warrant extensive governmental activity in regional development and to have contributed to a long history of federal-provincial financial transfer payments favouring the poorer provinces.

The third universal policy objective, maximizing aggregate economic growth, has been a particularly crucial issue in Canadian context. Not only is the growth ethic as strong here as elsewhere in North America, but the need to maintain high levels of economic growth is further emphasized by extremely rapid expansion of the labour force (recently the highest in the western world) and, as noted above, by the persistence

[3] Higgins (1972), for example, has calculated the coefficient of variation of average income in Canada (excluding Prince Edward Island and the Jewish population which, because of their small size, distort the over-all figures), as 15·1 and 13·1 per cent for provinces and ethnic groups respectively.

[4] The ratio of income differences between the richest and poorest regions (provinces) in Canada of approximately 2 : 1 is of the same order of magnitude as that found in the larger Western European countries—Germany, France, and Italy (*The Economist*, 14 April 1973). It is, however, significantly higher than that of Britain and Sweden (see Section IV) and of Australia.

of structural and regional unemployment. The scale of the unemployment problem, in cyclical and regional terms, is staggering (Economic Council of Canada, 1971). And recent estimates suggest that the problem will persist for some time in the future (Economic Council of Canada, 1973) despite recent successes in job formation. Unemployment overrides all but the national unity question in terms of expenditures of political energy, and has been the dominant issue in terms of public opinion for over a decade. Both of course are intimately interrelated, and most recently both have been exacerbated by inflation.

The extent of the problem is amply demonstrated by examining temporal and spatial variations in unemployment (Brewis, 1970). In an economic recession the curve of unemployment in the Maritime provinces begins its upward turn (from a higher initial base) months before the industrial heartland of central Canada, rises to more than twice the national average, and then persists for several months longer before the downturn begins. During the 1960s unemployment levels reached as high as 20 per cent in parts of the Maritimes (Atlantic Economic Council, 1971). Similar temporal trends, although slightly less pronounced, have been documented for Quebec and the prairie provinces. While recognized elsewhere, the major instrument in a policy of regional equality in Canada would be a reduction in aggregate levels of unemployment through more rapid economic growth, possibly combined with manpower retraining and restrictions on immigration. Thus any policy suggestions for the more orderly development of urban Canada must square with the dominant political emphasis given to maintaining economic growth. Canadians have not yet demonstrated the need or willingness to accept a trade-off between growth and urban containment as their British counterparts seem to have done.

5.2.3. THE POLICY RESPONSE: INSTITUTIONAL FORMS

Historically, urban planning in Canada, as in most British parliamentary democracies, has been primarily a local responsibility. Municipalities have been vested with the greater part of statutory physical planning powers (Gertler, 1968 and 1972). The provinces, which hold constitutional authority over local governments, have recently begun to exert more direct influence over the planning functions of those governments and some have initiated efforts to shape the evolving pattern of urban development through regional policies and planning. Federal government interest and formal involvement in urban policy-making are even more recent. For political reasons neither the provinces nor Ottawa have in the past been keen to see this involvement increase. The parallel with the Australian political climate discussed previously, and the U.S. experience throughout the 1960s, is clear.

Given the increasing role of provincial and national governments, the diverse functions and objectives of both must be recognized. In Canada this means two policy areas: urban affairs and regional planning and economic development. Reference to provincial activities in this essay will draw heavily on the experience of two provinces, Ontario and Quebec, particularly the former, with which the author is most familiar.

The traditional distribution of functions to each level of government sets the stage for the current policy debate. The provinces have been the consultative body for local planning agencies and the initiators of system-wide standards of urban physical development. Some provinces, Ontario, Alberta, and Saskatchewan for example, have developed elaborate legislative guide-lines for the local planning process, some now reaching absurd levels of complexity.[5] In each case there have also been sporadic attempts at devising comprehensive strategies for urban development within the boundaries of the province, but none of these at the time of writing has been formally adopted. There have, of course, been innovative planning developments at the local level, such as in the Lower Mainland of British Columbia, in Edmonton, Saskatoon, and Winnipeg, and in the Toronto region (Ontario Economic Council, 1972; Hodge, 1974). While these are in detail beyond the scope of the present review, they do suggest that a diversity of regulatory strategies have appeared in Canada and will probably continue to appear in the future. The question is whether these strategies have any relevance to the national urban perspective.

Federal government involvement in cities has traditionally been in-direct in Canada, largely because of the limitations of constitutional powers. Housing, as in most other countries, has been the dominant focus of policy activity at the national level since 1945, but it could hard-ly be described as showing an urban or locationally sensitive perspec-tive. Nevertheless, through housing practices, combined with man-power and mobility programmes, transport policies, immigration, rail and air tariff regulations, harbour and airport location, and civil service

[5] While a continuing source of conflict in all democracies, in the province of Ontario proposals for urban development may have to surmount as many as 90 legislative checks and approvals before they are completed which may take two to five years. This is bureaucracy, not planning, and is clearly a primary source of the rapid increase in the costs of urban land and building space.

## TABLE 5.10

### INDICES OF FEDERAL GOVERNMENT INVOLVEMENT IN SELECTED URBAN AREAS IN CANADA*

| Urban Area | Federal Employees (in thousands) | Payroll ($ millions) | Land Owned (acres) | Grants Paid in Lieu of Municipal Taxes ($ millions) | Per cent Population Foreign Born (1971) | Population 1971 (in thousands) |
|---|---|---|---|---|---|---|
| 1 Montreal, Que. | 26·3 | 17·2 | 744·6 | 20·9 | 14·8 | 2,743 |
| 2 Toronto, Ont. | 19·4 | 16·1 | 49·8 | 5·0 | 34·0 | 2,628 |
| 3 Vancouver, B.C. | 11·3 | 5·6 | 1,141·2 | 2·4 | 26·5 | 1,082 |
| 4 Ottawa–Hull, Ont./Que. | 57·4 | 32·6 | 5,112·5 | 12·0 | 4·2 | 603 |
| 5 Winnipeg, Man. | 6·7 | 4·6 | 357·9 | 2·5 | 14·9 | 540 |
| 6 Hamilton, Ont. | 1·5 | 0·7 | 21·1 | 0·4 | 26·7 | 499 |
| 7 Edmonton, Alta. | 5·4 | 2·6 | 115·7 | 0·7 | 18·3 | 496 |
| 8 Quebec City, Que. | 5·0 | 2·6 | 320·0 | 1·3 | 3·1 | 481 |
| 9 Calgary, Alta. | 3·4 | 1·6 | 263·7 | 0·8 | 20·5 | 403 |
| 10 London, Ont. | 4·8 | 2·4 | 535·9 | 1·3 | 20·0 | 286 |
| 11 Windsor, Ont. | 1·7 | 0·7 | 26·9 | 0·3 | 21·5 | 259 |
| 12 Halifax, N.S. | 9·7 | 4·4 | 381·9 | 3·3 | — | 223 |
| 13 Regina, Sask. | 1·7 | 0·8 | 1,322·8 | 0·4 | — | 141 |
| Totals** | 154·5 | 91·8 | 10,393·8 | 51·3 | 17·3*** | — |

\* Dates of surveys vary, 1968 to 1971.

\*\* Small differences due to rounding.

\*\*\* Average for all cities over 1,000 population.

Source: Statistics Canada, Lithwick (1970), Science Council (1971); by permission of Information Canada.

employment distribution, the federal influence on urban development in Canada has been substantial (Table 5.10). But it has been in the past un-coordinated, unimaginative, almost unconscious, and often counter-productive.

Formal recognition of the unity of urban issues was ignored at the federal level until the establishment of the Ministry of State for Urban Affairs in 1970 (Lithwick, 1972d). The general purpose of the Ministry was to begin a process leading to an integrated federal approach to ur-ban problems. It was to emphasize the role of programme co-ordination rather than programme generation, and it was to be active in both policy planning and research. How it was to achieve policy integration, however, was not clear. What was clear was the intention to avoid es-tablishing yet another on-line programme-oriented government depart-ment, as the U.S. had done previously in setting up the Department of Housing and Urban Development (HUD). Unlike the U.S. on the other hand, the new Ministry's portfolio encompassed a relatively vast and well-established housing agency—the Central Mortgage and Housing Corporation (CMHC)—with its own organizational structure and priorities. Watching this evolution with interest, the Australian govern-ment (Section 5.1) elected instead to create an entirely new department for urban affairs and to combine it with regional development responsibilities. In Canada regional policies remained separate.

Several factors converged in convincing the Canadian federal govern-ment to take these steps. There was a feeling, deriving primarily but not exclusively from the metropolitan areas, of a heightened public awareness of and sensitivity to urban problems. Formal pressures from the cities, and from the growing numbers of city-based federal politicians (thanks to redistricting) for increased financial aid and senior government policy and programme co-ordination, added to the incen-tive. At about the same time, a number of important commission and council reports were released—the Economic Council of Canada (1964, 1967, 1968), the Science Council (1968), the Hellyer Task Force on Housing and Urban Development (1969), the Lithwick (1970) report, and a Privy Council study assessing the state of environmental manage-ment in Canada (MacNeill, 1971). These gave considerable prominence to problems of urban environments and controlling urban growth, and combined to bring urban issues to the centre of the political stage. The initial response to these pressures was a typical bureaucratic one, first to create a new institution and then to look for policies and strategies (Dennis and Fish, 1972). Despite the vagueness of its initial objectives

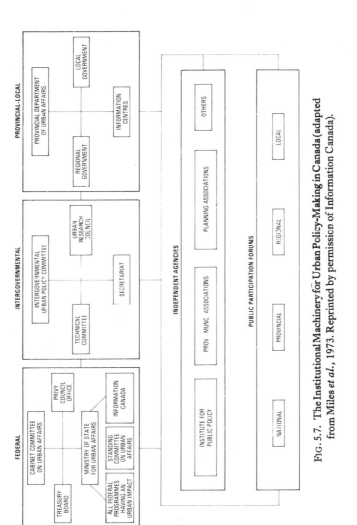

FIG. 5.7. The Institutional Machinery for Urban Policy-Making in Canada (adapted from Miles *et al.*, 1973. Reprinted by permission of Information Canada).

the establishment of the Ministry did at least represent an important commitment by the government to take a direct interest and involvement in the nation's urban affairs.

Concern with the direction the new Ministry has taken since its inception has been frequently voiced (Lithwick, 1972a, 1972b, 1972c, 1972d; Cameron, 1972; Blumenfeld, 1974). Without programmes, and lacking a strong constitutional and financial base, its power and influence have been limited. But it is clearly too early to assess success or failure. All that can be said at present is that the new Ministry does not yet have the necessary machinery to ensure much success in a policy co-ordinating capacity, although it does have a potentially important policy research role. Given the complex legislative process for urban policy formulation in Canada (Figure 5.7; Sayeed, 1973; and Lithwick, 1972a), the essence of success lies in co-operation and persuasion, and particularly in encouraging other federal agencies to assess the urban impacts of their own programmes.

### 5.2.4. REGIONAL ECONOMIC DEVELOPMENT: A POLITICAL OR LEARNING PROCESS?

Without doubt the dominant area of macro-spatial planning in Canada has been regional economic development. Given the enormous problems of regional imbalances in economic growth cited earlier this orientation is not surprising. The relevance of this policy area to the present review, in addition to its scale and predominant political position, derives from the increasing urban focus of its objectives. Moreover, if a future urban system strategy is to be effective, it must be co-ordinated if not fully integrated with regional planning efforts.

Regional development programmes and policies in Canada have been the subject of a considerable literature (Brewis, 1968, 1969, and 1970; Gertler, 1968; Officer and Smith, 1970; Economic Council of Canada, 1968, 1971; Mathias, 1971; Higgins, 1972). Much of it has not been enthusiastic. There has been a welter of policy developments, revisions, and repeals at both federal and provincial levels since World War II, and primarily since the early 1960s. To chronicle all of these would be time-consuming and not particularly productive. Instead stress should be given to examples of the dominant themes and policies and their relationship to urban issues.

Earlier federal policies derived largely from the problems of a rural economy. These policies were primarily concerned with the plight of impoverished rural farmers—initially by improving agricultural land capability and farming practices; and later by encouraging rural emigration and farm abandonment (Buckley and Tihanyi, 1967). These concerns culminated in the Agricultural Rehabilitation and Development Act (ARDA) in 1961. This was later supplemented by the Agricultural and Rural Development Act, reflecting a broadening of programme emphasis. Other components of the regional problem—unemployment and industrial stagnation—were incorporated into the policy context through creation of the Area Development Agency (ADA) in 1963. ADA was supposed to encourage employment growth in designated development areas, as had become the standard practice in other countries, by providing tax incentives on capital investment in manufacturing. Areas were designated primarily on the basis of relative unemployment rates, although some attempt was made later to co-ordinate the distribution of capital incentives with related federal activities such as manpower retraining programmes. These acts were followed in 1966 by the creation of the Fund for Rural Economic Development (FRED) and finally in 1968 by the Department of Regional Economic Expansion (DREE). The latter was charged with over-all responsibility for '. . . planning and co-ordinating action for regional development'.[6]

Probably the dominant impression from a review of regional development programmes in Canada is one of continual revisions of, and lack of

| | Type of Project/Grant | |
| --- | --- | --- |
| Location | Modernization or Expansion | New Plant or New Product Expansion |
| Region A (Atlantic Provinces) | 30% of eligible capital costs | 35% of capital cost plus $7000 per eligible direct job created. |
| Region B (Standard Designated Regions) | 20% of eligible capital costs | 25% of capital cost plus $5000 per eligible direct job created. |
| Region C* (Special Designated Region—South-western Quebec and South-eastern Ontario) | | *Incentive grants ceased to be available at the end of 1973. |

[6] In terms of specific federal policy, the Regional Development Incentives Act and the Department of Regional Economic Expansion Act make provision for incentives in support of the establishment, modernization, or expansion of manufacturing and other types of facilities. The maximum available grant depends both on location (see Figure 5.8), and type of project, as shown in the following table:

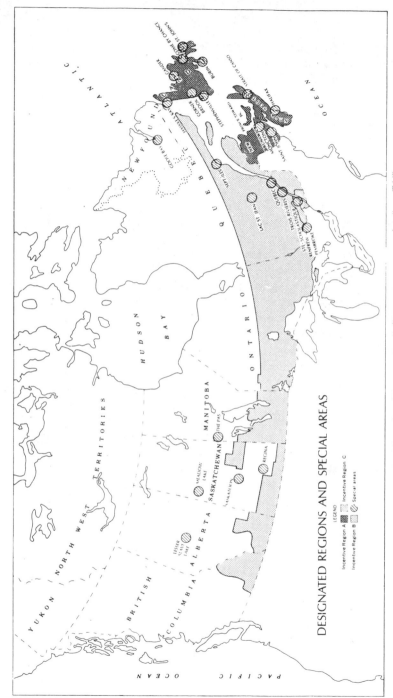

DESIGNATED REGIONS AND SPECIAL AREAS

LEGEND

Incentive Region A  Incentive Region C
Incentive Region B  Special areas

Fig. 5.8. A Locational Strategy. Regional Development Areas in Canada (after Department of Regional Economic Expansion 1973).

clarity in, policy objectives. This may be a reflection of the political realities and attitudes noted above or it may simply represent part of what Dunn (1971) refers to as a developmental learning process. No doubt it is both. In any case it has meant a history of repeated shifts in strategy and in regional policy legislation, which has discouraged long-range planning and sustained social investment in the development regions.

The diffuse nature of regional objectives (other than reducing high levels of unemployment) is also reflected in the enormous area of the country included in the incentives scheme. The same criticism has of course been directed at British regional policy, but in Canada the scale of the problem is much greater. Geographically, the area encompassed by current DREE programmes includes the vast majority of the Maritimes, eastern Quebec, the mid-central Canada forest, and the northern fringe agricultural belt (Figure 5.8). Presumably only jurisdictional limits prevented it from encompassing all of northern Canada. Obviously this is much too large an area to serve as a realistic framework for distributing growth incentives. It may identify problem areas but it is not a strategy for attacking those problems.

For these and parallel reasons Canadian efforts in regional economic development, at both national and provincial levels, have been largely unsuccessful. The Department of Regional Economic Expansion has, since its establishment in 1968, contributed enormous grants for industrial expansion, which it estimates had created about 90,000 jobs by the spring of 1973 (DREE, 1973). This might on the surface be favourably compared with a figure of 50,000 jobs a year created by regional policy in Britain. But this comparison is misleading. In critically reviewing the regional impact of their own programmes during the last few years, DREE concluded that the effect of their subsidies had been minimal except in small areas on the margin of the nation's heartland—such as in south-eastern Ontario or near Georgian Bay north of Toronto (Yeates and Lloyd, 1970). Further away, in northern Ontario for example, little new growth has been generated and employment losses from existing industries continue apace (Davies, 1973).

This result is not unique to Canada, and the explanation is relatively obvious. Many industries assisted in moving to peripheral areas have failed outright, or at best have not generated the range or quantity of local multiplier effects that was hoped for. Failure to appreciate the benefits of concentration and the extensive network of interorganizational and interregional linkages, which Pred (1973a) has argued are necessary for sustained growth, has been one cause. Another is that the locational strategy employed is not sufficiently explicit nor its designated areas sufficiently and realistically concentrated. Equally important, most subsidies are inadequate to cover the 'true' costs of relocation and decentralization, particularly in the light of what might appear to be continued government subsidy of the economic heartland. Consequently, many of the industries attracted have been new, often originating abroad, and landed with generous and often excessive subsidies and tax benefits. In other cases industries have set up branch plants in assisted areas and then subsequently closed their old plants. A number of these plants have been in the battered inner cities where employment opportunities for operatives and the poorly skilled are limited. The structural problem remains but it has simply shifted location—and at great social cost. These difficulties are well known in other countries, and in Canada are compounded by the traditional lack of co-ordination between provincial and federal regional development agencies, and between these agencies and those responsible for transport, housing, and trade.

### 5.2.5. PROVINCIAL PLANS AND STRATEGIES

Some of the most interesting developments in urban and regional planning strategies have taken place at the provincial level. While many of these changes have been purely administrative in nature, as at the federal level there are signs of more substantive policies emerging. Quebec for instance has taken one route toward comprehensive planning for urban and regional development (Raynauld, Martin, and Higgins, 1970). The province has made it known that the federal role is one of review and approval, with both political and design incentives coming from the provincial government. In 1963 Quebec passed its own ARDA legislation, shortly after it had established an investment corporation (GIC) to encourage industrial development. Additional financial incentives to stimulate growth in designated regions have been added in recent years. Now all of the inhabited area of the province is included in one designed area or another. Not unexpectedly, the locational strategy which has underlain these programmes is very similar to earlier thinking in French regional policy (Perroux, 1950; Hansen, 1968). This strategy has depended heavily on the 'growth pole' concept and on a recognition of the benefits of metropolitan concentration. It also reflects an attempt to redirect the spatial pattern of development through the province's economic structure rather than, as is more commonly the case, through its physical structure (Higgins, 1972). While at present there is only one region (*territoire-pilote*) of intensive regional planning activity in Quebec, the eastern Gaspé Bay, it is intended that a province-wide framework will follow based on the experience of this region.

Ontario has taken quite a different route. Again, not surprisingly, much of the stimulus for planning innovation in the province has come from the British regional planning movement. Since most of the steps on the route have been outlined elsewhere (Thoman, 1971; Gertler, 1972; Tindall, 1973; Hodge, 1974), only a brief mention need be made here. Since 1966 at least, Ontario has been formally concerned with the 'orderly development of the province'. This was, in an inherently conservative and prosperous province, a small but significant step to take. It has led to the creation of an impressive administrative machinery —an Ontario development corporation (ODC), the Ontario Planning and Development Act passed in 1973, regional development councils, and particularly innovative regional government units (Price, 1971). But as yet little in the way of specific policies, or a single unified development strategy, has emerged.[7]

The *Design for Development* statements published in 1966, 1968, and 1972 are the key indicators of future strategies. These resulted in the creation of a system of ten economic regions for planning purposes, each with a regional development advisory council.[8] These regions have since been reduced to five in number, partly because of the experience of attaining agreement and implementing proposals for the largest region—the Toronto-centred region (1970)—and partly because of the need for more realistic 'functional' regions. It is not clear to what extent these new regions will coincide with the new system of regional government units (Tindall, 1973).

The contrast in regional strategy between these two provinces is symptomatic of the diversity of strategies in spatial planning which is likely to be increasingly typical in Canada in the future. While neither province has attempted to regulate development through its urban system, or even to set its planning mechanism in an explicitly urban context, both use urban growth centres as tools in regional develop-

[7] Formal authority for review of municipal planning in Ontario is vested in the province. The Planning Act of 1973 assumed a wider range of development controls than in the past.

[8] Ontario's original ten economic regions were apparently delineated by the federal government for statistical purposes, and were 'never intended to be the territorial basis for implementing regional plans' (Government of Ontario, Design for Development, Phase Three, 1972, p. 18). The advisory councils established for each region, the Regional Development Councils, are similar in form to the British Regional Planning Councils (Thoman, 1971).

ment. Both use capital incentives to attract industries to designated centres, but neither has any effective controls on location in the more
prosperous regions. Consequently these programmes lose much of their
meaning. Ontario has hinted at limiting the future growth of the Toronto region and has proposed the spatial reordering of allowable growth
within that region (Thoman, 1971; Hodge, 1974). Quebec, on the other
hand, apparently has no intention of limiting Montreal's economic and
physical growth.[9] Neither province has been willing to accept emigration from peripheral regions as a development strategy. Instead, the
objective, as in eastern Quebec, is to maintain the existing population
base while increasing both absolute and relative living standards. At the
same time both provinces have accepted the need for a more rational
distribution of public, and presumably private investment by selecting
urban nodes for development which offer locational, site, and environmental advantages.[10] There is, however, little resemblance to the
more formal Swedish regional location strategy (see Section 4.2).

### 5.2.6. NORTHERN VISIONS

One of the prominent but seldom stated arguments underlying
economic development policy and spatial planning in Canada, and in
Sweden and Australia as well, has been a concern for filling-in national
territory. In fact one of the few identifiable and persistent national goals
in each instance has been the desire to extend the settled ecumene (see
Figure 5.6). The pre-eminence in national policy discussions of the
decentralization issue in Australia, and of northern development in
Canada, are examples (Acres, 1969; Davies, 1973).

Settlement of the north, as in the case of the American frontier,
became part of the Canadian national dream. Why this desire should
continue to be so strong is not immediately obvious. At one time it was
encouraged for defence purposes, but this condition no longer applies.
Or the argument was based on access to the north's resource potential,
but exploiting such resources does not now require extensive permanent

[9] Despite Montreal's recognized social and environmental problems, it is argued by some
authorities in the province that the city is still not large enough to compete with nearby U.S.
metropolitan centres in the race for economic growth (Higgins, 1972).

[10] See Thoman (1971) for details. As an example, in north-west Ontario the government
designated fourteen 'centres of opportunity', classified on the basis of past growth performance and
present structural characteristics, in the following hierarchy: (1) primate: a centre with a high level
of services and the best growth prospects; (2) strategic centre A: a resource-oriented urban centre
with a mixed economic base and one which holds some promise of expansion in both resources industries and services; and (3) strategic centre B: a centre based on a single industry possessing
some service functions (but often these are inadequate for the local population) (see Davies, 1973).

settlements. Probably the soundest interpretation was given to the author during a conversation with Professor Torsten Hägerstrand in Lund, Sweden. He remarked that he knew of no country in the world which, having inherited a particular piece of geographic territory, did not undertake to develop all of that territory, regardless of difficulties and costs, or the logical design of that territory as an economic unit, for reasons of international prestige and national fulfilment.

There is increasing support for the argument that in Canada this territorial preoccupation has shifted public interest and energy away from the more critical problem areas on the periphery of the ecumene and most notably in the metropolitan cores. In viewing the national space economy in its entirety it could be argued that the geographic extent of the settled area should be reduced rather than expanded. The case could most easily be made on economic grounds, but also increasingly in terms of social and ecological costs. Space is Canada's and Australia's greatest asset as well as their greatest liability. Yet while resource exploitation and scattered urban settlement based on that exploitation will continue in the Canadian north, it remains to be seen whether these are integrated into a national development strategy which balances current urban needs and northern visions.

### 5.2.7. NEW TOWNS AND OLD CITIES

The resource-based towns, scattered across mid-Canada and the north, form part of a long Canadian history of new town development and new city recommendations (Robinson, 1963). While considerable in number, most are small in total population. Few have reached 20,000 (i.e. the present size of Thompson, Manitoba) and most are less than 5,000. Many are impermanent and most, as single enterprise communities, are highly vulnerable to economic cycles and international trade variances. Recently, attempts have been made to co-ordinate these developments with government policy for northern development (and for native peoples), to decrease economic instability, and to improve the range and quality of local services provided by both public and private sectors. With the possible exception of Inuvik in the North West Territories, however, none has been wedded to a national or even regional development strategy, to which the urban system concept would be particularly appropriate.

In contrast, recommendations for new cities rather than resource towns have come from many sources, but without success.[11] While Canada has no 'new urban towns' in the European or Canberra sense (Ottawa is an 'expanded' town), it does have examples of new communities built on the fringes of metropolitan areas. Important as these may be in ordering intraregional patterns of urban growth, they are at present largely privately financed and simply represent metropolitan extensions and dormitory suburbs. They have as yet contributed little or nothing to regional development, population redistribution, or even to the containment of urban sprawl.

Equally important is the role that recent recommendations for major new cities have had and will have in determining future urban policy directions. It is not too difficult to assess the reason for this growing preoccupation in Canada with new cities. It derives from the same strain of planning philosophy as that of British new towns and more recently of new city proposals in Australia. While it has not generated the same political interest in Canada as in Australia, suggestions for major new city efforts have recently been given formal government sanction. Lithwick (1970), in his review of the state and needs of Urban Canada prepared for the former Minister of Housing (now the Minister of State for Urban Affairs), concluded that in his view a national urban policy for Canada should have as one of its principal objectives: '. . . to allocate national growth in an optimal manner, . . . the strategy being . . . basically a *new communities programme* with associated programmes to deal with the extant urban system'. Taking the Stockholm experience as his example, particularly the Vallingby model, Lithwick went even further.[12] He proposed that three new cities of at least half a million population be built between Montreal and Toronto as a counter-magnet to the growth of these centres.[13]

---

[11] The provincial government in Ontario for instance has proposed two new cities in the last year, one to be built at the site of the proposed second Toronto airport at Pickering and the second at Nanticoke on Lake Erie to house the population needed for extensive industrial development, primarily the relocation of a steel complex from Hamilton. Both centres are planned to have over 100,000 population, but both remain highly tenuous at the time of writing. Only the latter represents a potential contribution to urban population redistribution, and in this case the initiative was from the private sector.

[12] Blumenfeld (1974) has already commented on the lack of supporting evidence for new cities in Canada and, in particular, the inappropriateness of this reference to Swedish new towns such as Vallingby. The latter are highly successful, given their initial objectives—that is as satellite boroughs and dormitory communities for Stockholm—but they are not independent new towns or cities in the British sense (see Schaffer, 1972).

[13] An opportunity to achieve part of this proposal was lost when the decision was taken, for obvious political reasons, to build new international airports at both Montreal and Toronto, rather than for instance a joint facility midway between.

New town proposals of course have a certain attraction for governments. It is a relatively easy policy position to take since it does not involve selecting priorities for immediate action from among the existing urban centres, and thus alienating the voters they represent. On the other hand it is immensely more difficult to implement such strategies. Given the degree of institutional co-operation necessary for such massive undertakings, and the weakness of locational controls on private investment in Canada, significant advances in new town construction outside the metropolitan regions are unlikely.[14]

The rationale for new and 'free-standing' cities, as opposed to satellite centres, is also less convincing in Canada than in either Australia or Britain. As is the case in Sweden, there are a number of existing towns, even major cities, in Canada which are economically depressed, eager to attract growth despite the recent increase in anti-growth feeling, and for which political pressures to improve their share of national growth are substantial. Even if it can be proved to be more economical to build entirely new cities on 'green fields' than to house equivalent employment and population aggregates in existing medium-size centres, the social costs of doing so may be too great for any government to bear. New cities would probably be located in the peripheral regions and would therefore suffer from locational disadvantages similar to those of existing centres. There is just not sufficient expansion in the economic system to accommodate the wishes for growth of the existing centres as well as to create totally new entries in the national urban system.

## 5.2.8. FUTURE DIRECTIONS

This brief discussion has testified to the relative complexity and regional diversity of urban and locational planning in Canada. Locational decision-making on the part of government has for a long

[14] The potential importance of new satellite communities located within the major metropolitan regions in improving the quality of urban environments should not be obscured by this conclusion. Among the many proposals for such communities in Canada the Toronto-Centred Region (TCR) plan is one of the most extensive and innovative (Thoman, 1971; Government of Ontario, 1970). It contains ingredients of both the British green-belt concept (Thomas, 1970) and the Stockholm design of dormitory suburbs at varying distances from the metropolitan core (Strong, 1971), and is not unlike earlier proposals for the Sydney region (New South Wales, State Planning Authority, 1970), and to a lesser extent those put forward more recently for Melbourne (Melbourne Board of Works, 1971). The questions that have not been resolved in Canada are how seriously provincial and local governments will take these proposals, whether sufficient control mechanisms will be provided, and to what extent the objectives of guiding, if not slowing, growth in such areas can be incorporated into those national policies which impinge on urban growth in total.

time been sensitive to the regional make-up of the country. Urban issues have tended therefore to take a backseat to the overriding regional and national economic development question. As a result it has not been possible in this review to identify a single direction of policy evolution designed to influence the shape of urban Canada, at either federal or provincial level. The provinces have carried what little recent initiative there has been in attempting to regulate urbanization, but this has been largely indirect through regional development strategies. Even these in-itiatives have varied widely between provinces and have tended to emphasize institutional reorganization rather than strategic policy plan-ning. Consequently, the urbanization process and its expressions in diverse regional urban systems have remained largely unregulated.

Nevertheless, there are signs that more effective policy frameworks may emerge. What directions these will take is difficult to say. There is some disposition in both research and policy planning toward a com-prehensive national and integrated systems approach (Brewis, 1970; Science Council of Canada, 1971), as defined earlier in this volume, but the task remains uncompleted.[15] What is certain is that there will not be a single national urban policy in Canada for obvious reasons (Miles, 1972; Boothroyd and Marlyn, 1972; Lang, 1972; Blumenfeld, 1966 and 1974; Miles *et al.*, 1973). Virtually no one now subscribes to the objec-tive of a single and uniformally applied national policy. Instead, what may emerge is a set of urban development strategies which recognize the essential presence of regional variations within the country and which in fact encourage regional urban systems to develop in a manner most suited to their needs. For instance, urban decentralization in Australian terms might have some support in southern Ontario, Alber-ta, and in the lower mainland and Gulf Islands of British Columbia (provinces prosperous enough to accept experimentation and the short-term costs of decentralization), but has little support in Quebec and none at all in the Maritimes and most of the prairies. Clearly, federal and provincial policies will have to be co-ordinated, with the former taking a flexible and long-term attitude to planning the national system and the latter being more explicit in terms of responsibilities and more specific in geographically implementing such plans. In Canada, given an extensive land mass, diverse regional economies, and large ethnic blocks, con-siderable independence of regional policy action and implementation is

---

[15] The Ministry of State for Urban Affairs has undertaken a major modelling effort on urbaniza-tion in Canada based on systems concepts (Major, 1972; Ulrich, 1972), and designed to provide a means for assessing the present and possible impacts of government policies and practices.

both necessary and preferable. The urgent problem is to find a more correct balance of political and financial centralization and decentralization than exists at present and to match this with appropriate policy responsibilities (possibly in the manner discussed in Section III).

One of the most encouraging signs in an otherwise discouraging picture is the increasing public demand for intergovernmental and interdepartmental co-ordination. Several provinces, Alberta and Ontario for instance, have reorganized ministerial responsibilities on urban matters to facilitate contacts among government departments and between the three levels of government in the Canadian federal system. Federal agencies such as the Ministry of State for Urban Affairs and DREE are seeking closer integration with provincial, urban, and regional development programmes; and tri-level councils involving federal, provincial, and city authorities have recently been initiated to focus attention on the specific problems of the major urban areas.[16] Strong pressures also exist for a revised national transport policy, an essential ingredient in any development strategy particularly in a large country such as Canada in which transport costs play a major role in distributing economic growth, and for integrating this policy with a strategy for urban development.

These efforts would, of course, be immensely facilitated by the existence of strategic policy frameworks to guide assessments of social needs and decisions on the evaluation of alternatives. If the national unity question is at least temporarily relaxed, there may be more public scope for defining these frameworks. While most of the urban policy discussions to date have involved debates on the distribution of constitutional and taxation powers, other issues are now entering the debates which will directly affect the future of urban Canada.

---

[16] The tri-level urban councils, administered by the federal Ministry of State for Urban Affairs, provide an interesting model for such co-ordination ventures. They have taken either of two forms, provincial and urban. Provincial councils bring together urban affairs representatives from federal and provincial governments, with the municipalities in that province present as observers. In the second case councils have been established for several individual cities (e.g. Winnipeg) with that city government participating directly in the discussions with provincial and federal authorities. Needless to say, provincial authorities, jealous of their political control over municipalities, prefer the former type of council while the municipalities usually argue for the latter.

# Comparative Evaluation of Recent Policy Directions: A Convergence of Interests?

NONE of the four countries under review here has a national urbanization strategy or an integrated set of strategies. Few countries, in fact, have the necessary administrative apparatus in existence to establish systematic frameworks for regulating urbanization and its spatial consequences. In Europe generally, Holland and Sweden might be considered exceptions to this statement. Nor do most have the machinery at hand or the political will effectively to implement such frameworks. What many countries do have, on the other hand, is a complex array of policies and legislative guide-lines, sometimes conflicting, which have both responded to and shaped the processes of urbanization. The objectives of these policies, their form and execution, as well as the emerging directions of thinking which underlie recent policy debates, vary widely between countries. Yet there is a sense of movement within the policy debate in most western countries toward acceptance of the importance of a national urban perspective and the need for national urban planning. The four countries studied here present four quite different examples of this debate.

The present section poses a number of simple questions for discussion in concluding the review. What have been the generative factors stimulating an interest in national urban strategies? What has been the comparative experience of the four countries under examination? What are (or should be) the goals of national strategies? Has there been a convergence of interest within national planning and development policies which is both urban and spatial in focus? What lessons are to be learned from the relatively long experience of Britain and Sweden in urban planning? Are there any advantages to be derived from the experiences of decentralized federal political systems? Can the multitude of factors influencing the extent of urban policy development be summarized and evaluated? Can policy responsibilities be matched to levels of the urban hierarchy? The organization of this section follows from this sequence of questions, and reflects the learning process identified in the introduction.[1]

## 6.1. THE GENERATIVE FACTORS IN URBAN POLICY

The reasons for the intervention of government in urban development are as varied as the socio-political contexts of the governments themselves. But they are underlaid by a limited number of common premisses. One such premiss, using Emery and Trist's (1972) terms (see Section II), is that the 'auto-regulatory' devices presently operating within the urban system (for both individual cities and aggregates of cities) are inadequate. They are inadequate in both strength and direction to achieve a balance between locations in terms of economic growth and in the distribution of social welfare and opportunities.

In each country there were obviously specific generative factors leading to government recognition of urbanization as a concern for policy. Part of this awareness was a greater knowledge of and sensitivity to what Chisholm and Manners (1971) refer to as the spatial ramifications of urban development and to the inherent 'system' characteristics of that development (Chisholm, 1972). Some of the political generative factors were sharp political crises, others were more subtle and of a longer-term nature. In Britain, for example, extensive war damage to cities—in housing, industrial facilities, and public service infrastructure—necessitated massive involvement in housing construction and urban redevelopment and provided both the need and the opportunity for achieving a consensus obligation to national planning. In Canada the growing housing crisis of the 1960s resulted in substantially increased federal money for private mortgages and public housing construction. At the provincial level in Canada and at the regional level in Britain, urban sprawl and the rapid conversion of rural land created immense pressures for policy action. In Australia, the continued sprawl of Sydney and Melbourne and the escalating costs of providing commensurate services in these areas ensured that a political response was forthcoming. In Sweden the difficult realities of war-time neutrality, continued rural depopulation, and the rapid polarization of employment growth in the three urban areas accelerated the need for a central urban planning function.

---

[1] Many of the responses to these questions could have been placed in the introduction to this volume as guide-lines for interpreting the policy experiences of four diverse countries. They remain in this section to encourage the reader to follow the same lines of reasoning which the author went through in determining those responses.

While these factors in detail are specific to each country, they contain a number of common expressions of the same urbanization problems. These include: (1) the inability to regulate urban growth and its consequences in the metropolitan cores; (2) the necessity to minimize imbalances between urban core and rural periphery; and (3) the difficulty of matching the changing needs and patterns of social and economic development brought on by urbanization with the distribution of national and public resources and responsibilities. If these are in fact 'universal' urban problems they are no doubt in part a reflection of a convergence of problem definition and policy recommendations brought on by the common perceptions of professional planners and administrators.[2] The global village is indeed in existence.

The length of time horizon involved in such generative factors is also important. We may recall from the preceding discussion (Section 4.1) that problems of urban life in Britain were recognized as being of national significance early in the nineteenth century.[3] Regional imbalance was a political and social issue by the early 1930s. In Sweden, the sudden and dramatic transformation of the economy and of life styles from an agricultural to an industrial state in the early decades of this century brought questions of containing the urban consequences of economic growth into the political arena. In contrast, Canada and Australia, with seemingly unlimited space and a dedication to filling in national territory, only grasped the scale and degree of their urbanization during the 1960s. Urban problems were something that occurred in other countries. The specific policy responses in each country bear this mark of time.

The importance of specific political events also cannot be overestimated. Most countries, for example, owe their regional development programmes to the depression of the 1930s and the enormous scale of unemployment and human suffering incurred during that period. Consequently most such policies were (and still are) stop-gap measures designed to smooth over localized economic inequalities rather than to tackle the underlying causes of inequality in the social order. There is nothing wrong with stop-gap methods *per se*, except

[2] The author is indebted to Professor B. J. L. Berry for pointing out how quickly a commonality in the perception of urban problems among professional planners can develop and how influential these ideas can be on national governments.

[3] An entertaining and perceptive review of the causes and problems of rapid urban growth with reference to suburban sprawl in the London of 1811 is contained in the *Monthly Magazine*, 31, 1, February 1811, reprinted under the title 'Economic Base and City-Size: An 1811 Commentary on London', in *Land Economics*, 50, 2, 1974, 202–5.

when they are presented as other than short-term sporadic responses or when they become incorporated institutionally into inflexible long-term planning strategies.

One other major stimulus to government action has been the geographic distribution of political power. It might be argued that the situation most likely to lead to government action is where the spatial distributions of the unemployed or socially disadvantaged coincide with political jurisdictions. The convergence of policies and problems on the Maritime provinces and Quebec in Canada, on Wales, Scotland, and Northern Ireland, and on Norrland and Sweden's rural counties is an illustration. When the poor or the socially disadvantaged are indirectly disenfranchised by political boundaries, such as is common in the inner cities, they have generally been ignored or assigned a low political priority. If this thesis is correct, then it is possible to attribute the late emergence of an urban focus in national policy in part to the absence of a convergence between problem definition and political jurisdiction. Part of this convergence is geographical and part is not—but both are interrelated and self-reinforcing in determining the policy response.

Thus, those countries in which the problems of urban system development and regional inequalities coalesce have been the first and often the most successful in regulating urbanization. Those, for instance, in which the problems can be arrayed against a dominant metropolis (capital) and relatively impoverished periphery (provinces) have the best possibilities for effective urban containment and redistribution at the national level, all other things being equal. Britain is the obvious example. The metropolis, prosperous, overgrown, and congested, may welcome limits on industrial and office employment growth in order to preserve the environment it has. Generally the metropolis knows that the limits will not be so severe as to create undue social and economic stress—particularly for middle- and upper-income groups—although, as in London, stress may take some time to appear. The provinces on the other hand welcome the relocation efforts in most instances because of their need to keep employment opportunities and income levels from lagging too far behind expectations (and the national average). But, in those situations, such as Australia, Canada, and the U.S., in which urban problems are expressed in the context of several dominant cities rather than one, as well as in many smaller centres, scattered across both growing and declining regions and varying political jurisdictions, achieving unitary consensus and action is infinitely more difficult.

Many other factors affecting the rate and distribution of national urban growth are also beyond direct regulation by national and regional governments. Their impact depends on the relative openness of the system under study as well as on the nature and location of origin of the factors involved. The more important of these factors, at least in reference to western capitalistic democracies, include (1) inflation rates and international monetary policy, (2) world economic growth, (3) militarization, (4) international trade flows, (5) emigration and professional mobility, (6) social and technological innovations, and (7) the global diffusion of information and ideas, including, as noted above, common perceptions among professionals as to what are the most important urban problems. Emery and Trist (1972) refer to these kinds of factors as elements of the turbulent environment for social systems.

Each factor has a considerable effect on interregional and on interurban growth patterns in a modern economy and on the problems generated by these patterns. Inflation, for example, has markedly different impacts on prosperous and depressed regions, but is as yet virtually untouched by research (Neutze, 1973). Emigration, whether to and from regions, provinces, or nations, is seldom monitored and even less frequently assessed in terms of social impact or economic benefits. Consequently predictions are difficult. The long-term population estimates made in Britain in 1971 have already been shown to be in considerable error, in part because of incorrect assumptions on emigration (national and regional) rates, added to the inevitable difficulty of projecting changes in fertility.

Although all four countries under review here represent 'open' systems in the classical sense, the extreme dependence of urbanization in Canada on developments in the U.S., and increasingly of Britain within the EEC, offers an obvious example of the role of external turbulent environments. What this condition implies is that urban policy must consider both the external structure of urbanization and the interdependences which link the urban-economic system to its contextual environment.

## 6.2. THE GOALS OF URBANIZATION STRATEGIES

Goal specification is the most difficult aspect of urban policy on which to generalize. As a point of departure we might refer back to the general policy literature. In the broadest possible terms, the application of goals to social systems may be broken down into three types: (1) survival considerations, (2) boundary conditions, and (3) targets. All three are relevant to urbanization strategies. The first is commonly contained in the language of continued national economic growth and prosperity in the face of international competition; and the second in the external dependences noted above (see Section III). The third, targets, can be redefined to include most of the distribution questions and policy goals raised in the national urban context.

The goals to which urban and locational policies have traditionally been directed tend to be diffuse, and inconsistent, and to vary widely between political systems. The two preceding sections have demonstrated these attributes in relation to the importance of: (1) locational balance and social welfare as goals in Swedish policy (and research); (2) urban containment, rural preservation, and regional balance as goals in British planning; (3) regional equality in income and employment in Canada; and (4) decentralization in Australia. The essential differences are not simply that these goals differ in content, or that they are more diffuse and more highly localized in the latter two countries, but that the goals which do exist are of a lower order of generality and are less operational in a policy context than in Sweden and Britain. The first set of goals above (i.e. Sweden) in fact subsumes the latter three sets, almost in a hierarchical fashion. Clearly this is suggestive of the greater degree of articulation of national social and planning goals in Sweden and Britain as compared to Australia and Canada.

What then should the goals of an urbanization strategy be? This question obviously can only be answered in reference to conditions prevailing in any given country or region, even though most countries have, as previously noted, agreed to at least three general goals. These goals are: (1) reducing the negative consequences of population over-concentration in the metropolitan core areas; (2) achieving a geographic balance of both social and economic opportunities across their national territory; and (3) maintaining the rate of national economic growth and thus of effective increases in standards of living. The first goal is almost universally interpreted by politicians and planners alike as a problem of excessive city size. The concern with increasing city size is most frequently rephrased in terms of greater congestion costs, higher levels of pollution, and mounting diseconomies in the public sector. The second goal, clearly interdependent on the first and the third, is the explicitly stated objective of most regional policy measures, although what is meant by balance is seldom clearly defined or justified with hard facts. The third objective has two dimensions: one relates indirectly to the operating efficiency of the urban system, while the other refers directly to the problem of co-ordinating goals for aggregate economic growth with those for the geographic and social distribution of the fruits of that growth. Lasuén (1973), for example, argues that since the former dimension (urbanization) is less dependent than the latter (economic development) on influences external to each country, urban development policies have a much higher probability of attaining their respective national goals than do economic policies. This is an interesting point worthy of further debate.

To some observers national urban policy is primarily big-city policy. Richardson (1972), for instance, describes the practice of promoting growth centres in depressed areas as regional policy rather than urban policy. More central to the national policy debate, he argues, '. . . is what if anything can be done about a nation's large cities'. This is too restrictive an interpretation of national urban problems, not just in reference to the strategy of growth centres, but in terms of the entire spectrum of developmental problems in both urban and rural regions. As one illustration, growth centres will only work, as Hansen (1972) suggests, if they are viewed as part of a national system of growth centres—a system which is predominantly urban. Further, undue emphasis on the largest centre tends to mitigate against reducing the problems of small centres by diverting public interest and resources.

More broadly, the issue demonstrates that regional and urban policy, even as traditionally defined, cannot logically be divorced. Their goals and policy areas overlap in much the same way as the spatial systems they are dealing with overlap. The integration of policy goals and procedures at different levels is critical. For instance, new towns in Britain were greatly assisted in attracting private capital through regional planning limits on development in nearby existing towns which might have offered competition to the new towns for jobs, shopping, and services. Britain also has attempted to link central city relocation and redevelopment with policies directed at regional decentralization. Few other countries have done so.

Similar goals may also be expressed in seemingly conflicting policies. One example is Sweden's wide-ranging efforts at improving the quality of the work environment. Subsidies for labour mobility are available to encourage workers to move to better positions often involving relocation from the north to the south. At the same time, regional policy attempts to maintain and improve a diversified employment base in the north and other peripheral regions through location and employment subsidies. Some Swedish authorities argue that this apparent conflict is in fact necessary and desirable since the two policies are dealing with different streams of migrants who are responding to different needs and opportunities. Both sets of migrants and both regions should be better-off.

Given this diversity of opinion and need, it is not surprising that the identification of explicit goals often turns into a debate on the relative merits of virtue and sin. Yet it is clear from the experience of the four countries under review that goals have to be explicit and broadly representative if strategic planning for national urban development is to succeed. They must include the difficult and often conflicting issues of stability, equity, efficiency, and diversity, such as Lithwick (1970) and Simmons (1974) have discussed in the Canadian context. They have to be more responsive to social rather than production or technological criteria, to local and regional desires for self-determination, and to spatial as well as sectoral considerations, than they have been in the past. Whatever the definition of goals, the experience of the four countries reviewed in this study is that the most difficult hurdle is achieving a consensus on the matching and trading-off of differing sets and levels of goals. These sets and levels may, in the urban context, include possible conflicts between federal–provincial, local–regional, sectoral–geographical, or short- and long-term goals.

What, given these potential conflicts, is the role of goal-specific urban policies in the future. Despite initial pessimism on the part of most observers, there is some evidence that such policies can be successful. In concluding his recent review of the social consequences of twentieth-century urbanization, Berry (1973a) argues that '. . . the most important fact of the past quarter-century has been the realization that . . . sought-after futures can be made to come true', and that . . . 'Images of the desired (urban) future are becoming major determinants of that future in societies that are able to achieve closure between means and ends'. In other words, politically motivated and intentionally goal-directed efforts have themselves become much more important components in shaping the urbanization process. This convergence is probably most widely demonstrated in north-western Europe and in the Socialist-bloc countries. The critical and obvious rider to this statement is that societies must be able to achieve closure between available means and desired ends. Sweden and Britain have been able to achieve such closure on selected national problems, although only the former has done so in terms of the national urban system.

## 6.3.   RECENT POLICY DIRECTIONS: A COMPARATIVE ASSESSMENT

Goals must of course be realistic, in both a political and a logistical sense. For this reason urban strategies in most countries have tended to develop out of limited areas in which previous policy development has been modestly successful. There seem to be two of these areas from which efforts at urban policy formulation at the national (and provincial) level have derived: (1) regional economic development policy, particularly those policies directed at industrial location, job mobility, and subsidies for social infrastructure support in depressed regions; and (2) urban land use and environmental planning including the often less explicit strategy of containing the physical expansion of the major metropolitan areas, which in Europe is principally the national metropolis.

Both of these streams have evolved considerably over the last two decades in all four countries under study. Regional policy has moved, in most countries at least, from a narrow concern for rural redevelopment and industrial employment subsidies applied in rather limited circumstances, toward a more comprehensive attempt at managing the space economy and the provision of an interrelated package of social services and community infrastructure. One approach has been to concentrate policy efforts on clearly recognizable centres with the greatest growth potential, usually urban centres located in the depressed regions, and on clusters of mutually reinforcing activities and services which may act to attract further growth.

Attempts at influencing the form of metropolitan development through land use and developmental controls have also shifted in both purpose and design. One example of this shift, evident in most countries, has been the expanding focus of urban planning from a concern with the rural-urban fringe of the larger urban areas to a broader strategy of limiting growth at several locations within the national metropolitan regions while at the same time redirecting some of that growth to smaller and more peripheral urban centres. Metropolitan containment in its simplest form has become a strategy of regulating the distribution of growth over a much larger spectrum of the urban size hierarchy. While land-use controls *per se* may still be in the hands of local municipalities, the mechanisms of planning involved are being applied on a larger scale. In Sweden, for instance, land-use controls have recently been extended in a national physical plan covering all aspects of man's use of the natural environment—recreation, forestry, mining, and so forth. In Britain, the combination of various countryside and recreational programmes with green belt restrictions and historical preservation areas has brought more than one quarter of the national territory under some type of land-use regulation.

Numerous other examples of these trends could be cited for each of the four countries studied. In Sweden regional policy traditionally focused on the specific problems of Norrland and the arresting of rural depopulation. Now, regional policy is both national and explicitly urban. British efforts were directed primarily at the aged and depressed industrial concentrations of peripheral regions in the north, Scotland, and Wales, but are now more comprehensive in locational terms and in the activities considered for assistance. Similarly, Canada's regional policies have traditionally emphasized the northern agricultural frontier of mid-Canada, eastern Quebec, and the Maritimes. Australia, with fewer and smaller concentrations of rural disadvantaged, has shown less interest in regional policy *per se*, but has witnessed a change in the long-standing interest of decentralizing urban and economic growth from the coast to the interior, from one which is rural-based to one which is predominantly urban.

## 6.4. A SUMMARY OF POLICY TRENDS

Many of the above directions in urban policy thinking can be conveniently summarized in tabular form. Table 6.1 cites thirteen selective examples of the evolving policy focus in both urban and regional policy, grouped under three broad headings: (a) definitions of the geographic areas and problems of interest; (b) specific policies and implementation procedures; and (c) types of goals and the institutional forms necessary for achieving those goals. The table is in shorthand, and should be interpreted in the following manner. For each of the thirteen examples, column 1 gives a brief description of the criteria used in selecting the specific policy approach included, column 2 lists the traditional focus, while column 3 gives the current or evolving focus for that policy. Between columns 2 and 3 there is an implied shift or transition in policy thinking and application. Columns 4 and 5 provide selected examples of these shifts in the country or countries best illustrating the trend. Take the first point for illustrative purposes. It is argued that regional policy in the four countries under review here has gradually shifted its traditional emphasis in most countries from an interpretation of regions as uniform homogeneous entities (whether agricultural or industrial) to the concept of a region as an organizational entity: a system in its own

## TABLE 6.1

### EVOLUTION OF LOCATIONAL (URBAN AND REGIONAL) STRATEGIES IN THE COMPARISON COUNTRIES: SELECTED EXAMPLES

| Examples of Criteria (1) | Previous (or Existing) Policy Focus (2) from . . . | Evolving (or Anticipated) Policy Focus . . . to (3) | Countries Illustrating Trend (4) | Examples of Policies in (4) (5) |
|---|---|---|---|---|
| **A. Definitions of Areas and Problems** | | | | |
| 1 type of region | uniform region | functional region | Sweden | Country Plan |
| | | | Britain | SE. Region Plan |
| 2 type of economy | localized regional economies | national space economy | Sweden | National Land Use Plan |
| 3 types of problems | isolated problem areas: rural and industrial | tier of problem areas and types | Britain | Development Areas |
| | | | Sweden | Regional framework |
| 4 spatial units | individual cities and regions | systems of cities and regions | Sweden | Regional Structure Plan |
| | | | Canada | Research strategy (MSUA) |
| 5 Types of urban problems | big-city problem | problems of systems of cities | Sweden | Equitable urban structure |
| **B. Policies and Implementation Practices** | | | | |
| 6 range of policy instruments | limited location controls and incentives | array of location controls and incentives | Britain | IDCs, REPs, ODPs |
| | | | Sweden | Decentralization subsidies |
| 7 sectors affected | primarily industrial (re)location | integration of industrial, tertiary, and public service (re)location | Britain | Location of offices |
| | | | Sweden | Public service infrastructure subsidies |

| 8 | treatment of location | blanket areal incentive schemes | spatially concentrated schemes | Sweden | Norrland centres |
|---|---|---|---|---|---|
| | | | | Britain | Growth centres |
| | | | | Canada (Quebec) | Development poles |
| 9 | urban proposals | small new garden towns and suburbs | new major and expanded cities | Britain | Milton Keynes |
| | | | | Sweden | Norrköping |
| | | | | Australia | Albury–Wodonga |

*C. Goals and Institutional Forms*

| 10 | national emphasis | economic growth | social development | Sweden | Social renewal |
|---|---|---|---|---|---|
| 11 | distribution goals | maximum economic efficiency | regional balance and equality | Sweden | Regional welfare |
| 12 | planning strategy | limitation: rural preservation | initiation: urban redistribution and national conservation | Britain | Regional policy |
| | | | | Britain | Green belts |
| | | | | Sweden | Satellites |
| 13 | decision-making prcess | institutional independence | institutional reorganization and co-ordination | Britain | Dept. of Environment |
| | | | | Canada (Quebec) | Super ministries |
| | | | | Sweden | National boards |

right with a nucleus (usually an urban centre or centres) and an explicit spatial structure oriented about that nucleus. In the former context, problems tended to be viewed as spatially uniform and blanket policies were applied accordingly—of course with differing results. Under the latter concept, policies have had to be of multiple forms applied with varying intensities to different locations. The South-East Region Strategy Plan (1970) is an excellent example of the case in point.

Similarly, at a more macro-level, the preceding review has demonstrated a shift in regional policy from treating problem areas as localized economic structures (criterion 2, in column 1), isolated from the rest of the nation (criterion 3), to a recognition of a range or tier of different problem areas (criterion 2, in column 2). A parallel movement toward more comprehensive, integrative thinking has taken place in formulating urban policy. This has involved a focus on cities as functioning parts of a national system of cities (criterion 4), as well as a shift from a preoccupation with the primate city or cities to an awareness of the range of problems facing cities of varying size and character. The Swedish view of the nation's urban system structure is again the best illustration.

Under the second heading, policies and implementation practices, the increasing diversity and scale of government activity are demonstrated by four indicators. These four are: the range of development controls and incentives (6), the types of economic sectors involved (7), the spatial pattern of application of these controls, that is their treatment of locational differences (8), all of which relate to traditional regional policy; and in the case of urban policy, the well-documented evolution of new town schemes (9) from an emphasis on small essentially suburban towns to one of expanding existing cities as growth centres.

Broader and possibly more significant changes have taken place in the area of goal specification, planning strategies, and institutional behaviour. Social development, or what the Swedish literature calls social 'renewal', has grown in importance as a national goal in relation to and in some instances at the expense of simple economic growth. Distributional goals, when they are applied, are now less heavily weighted toward maximizing operating efficiency in various economic sectors and more toward regional and urban equality (criterion 11). Planning strategies have become more normative and innovative and less responsive and negative (that is, based strictly on formal limitations on development) in content and design. Finally, all of the above changes have been paralleled by pressures for increased policy co-ordination among those public agencies whose decisions impinge on urban and regional growth.

While each example in the table is highly generalized and each could be considerably expanded in this review, the point to be stressed is that between columns 2 and 3 is an assumed transition through which policy has evolved or may evolve. Not every reader, however, will agree that these transitions are present in each of the countries studied, or even if present, that these are the most important and relevant trends. The author's reply to these criticisms is that within the limited objectives and detail of this study these capture most of the major discernible trends in locational strategies. Clearly, the position of each country will vary on the continuum between present and evolving policy focus (in some instances the categories only marginally apply), and the specific meaning of each criterion must be interpreted in its own socio-political context.

Not everyone would agree either that all of these trends are to be welcomed. The apparent (or perceived) movements in both urban and regional policy thinking listed above have negative attributes. The shift to comprehensiveness in planning design, to gigantism in project execution, and to spatial concentration in terms of regional strategies will concern those in particular who value incrementalism in policy formulation, smallness, and local area option. But need these two sets of preferences, and the objectives they represent, be conflicting? Or is it in part a matter of restructuring the policy and institutional apparatus to separate out the different political-spatial levels at which certain strategies are relevant? If the present review stimulates further thinking on these questions, this book will have achieved one of its primary purposes.

## 6.5. A CONVERGENCE OF POLICY INTEREST?

The observer of these developments might be inclined to speculate on a convergence in the recent evolutionary paths of these two major policy areas. That is, regional policy in its shift to greater spatial and sectoral comprehensiveness now includes a wider range of socio-economic criteria and is more explicitly urban-centred. Similarly, the metropolitan (or big-city) containment strategy, typical primarily of Sweden and Britain rather than Canada or Australia, has expanded its area of interest in two directions. One is to include reference to the problems of other large and rapidly growing cities in the national urban system. The other is to consider the impact of specific containment policies on the areas which receive the redirected growth in population and employment. This means at a minimum that decisions to stop, slow, or modify growth in one area must be integrated with attempts to redirect growth elsewhere, particularly in encouraging the relocation of such growth to depressed regions through various incentives and subsidies, regions which may or may not be able to accommodate such growth. Policy makers are beginning to see this need. Clearly such integration can only adequately be achieved within the context of an integrated system of cities or regions and by linking urban and regional policies.

Only in Sweden has this convergence been publicly recognized in a policy context. The crude urban system classification scheme outlined in Section 4.27 illustrates one version of this growing linkage, in approach and in practice, between regional and urban policy areas. In Britain, various small links have been made between regional policies and other spatially sensitive policy sectors—new town planning, housing, office decentralization, and transport, for example, but as yet no formal integrated strategy has emerged. There is still considerable reluctance in Britain to view cities or economic regions as interacting systems and to devise policies accordingly. Australia has recognized this interdependence in policy responsibility by the creation in 1972 of a new federal ministry of urban *and* regional development. Canada, given its long-standing regional programmes at both federal and provincial levels, still maintains separate urban and regional portfolios at the federal level although in some provinces the two functions have been combined or formally co-ordinated under a senior government minister.

## 6.6. SPECIFIC EXPERIENCES FROM REGULATED AND UNREGULATED URBAN SYSTEMS

In reading the extensive national urban policy literature a cynic might get the distinct impression that most urban problems could be solved overnight if all cities were to be instantly transformed (by divine edict or otherwise) into uniform medium-size metropolitan centres. Each centre could then be assured equal growth rates (not too fast or too slow—but all above the national average), by assigning each a proportionate share of growth-inducing, income-producing, or export-multiplying manufacturing and service activities. In a more serious vein, there is a widespread belief that altering the size structure of national urban systems will substantially improve the quality and equality of urban life. Whether this belief is valid or not is debatable. Nevertheless, the belief exists and it continues to influence the urban policy discussions in most countries.

While no one has seriously proposed such a uniform system, some of the idealized constructs of an equitable urban system currently in vogue come remarkably close to it (Hägerstrand, 1972; EFTA, 1973). The extensive adjustments which would be necessary to the national space economy in order to achieve such a situation would no doubt reduce the analytical difficulties in undertaking research on urban system growth, but would not touch many of the more serious problems of social and economic inequality deriving from that growth (Pahl, 1971; Mills, 1972; Alonso, 1972 and 1973; Wingo, 1972). In more practical terms, of course, there is simply not enough investment capital, employment activities, or human resources to stretch that far, even if the goal itself were desirable.

The latter point may represent one of the more important lessons to be gained from the present review. That is, urbanization strategies in general, and urban system policies in particular, necessitate explicit decisions on the allocation of scarce resources to competing locations and thereby to different economic and social groups. As was argued in the discussion of regional development policy in Canada (Section 5.24), although the same point applies elsewhere, such as in Britain (Section 4.15) and Sweden (Section 4.25), there are far too many locations for current urban and regional strategies to succeed in their present form.

Another point is the importance of understanding the socio-political system toward which public intervention is directed and from which problems derive. Assuming that urbanization in Canada and Australia, for example, has developed in a largely unregulated *laissez-faire* environment, one might ask how this environment is reflected in the way their respective urban systems have developed? In other words, what differences in structure arise through the absence of planning influence at the national scale and what others mirror contemporary processes of development viewed at different times in the evolution of an economic system? And what are the consequences of tight planning controls at one level (for example, the local level) with little or no regulation of urbanization at other levels (i.e. national)?

Are there lessons here for the more centralized planning authorities in Britain and Sweden? Clawson and Hall (1973), in their comparison of the English megalopolis (see Section 4.1) and that of the north-east seaboard in the United States, do draw some advantages out of the American experience which have relevance to Britain's planning systems. Among the latter are the benefits of a wider choice in housing, workplace, and living styles, that is except for the bottom third of the population, and lower densities typical of suburban developments in the U.S. Similarly, urban decentralization, which British planning has actively encouraged, has in some regards progressed further and faster in Canada and Australia (as in the U.S.) without the benefits of formal land-use controls and decentralization policies. Urban densities tend to be lower and private space consumption higher in the latter countries, monopoly profits in urban services may be lower, and the spatial distribution of industry has been more responsive to rapidly changing residential patterns. The number and quality of consumer services also tend to be higher in the U.S. suburban context. But what are the relative balances of benefits and costs? Who benefits and who pays?

One also cannot overlook the importance of institutional forms in describing, let alone understanding, differences in the evolution of urban policy in different countries. While this study has not given special emphasis to political, legal, or administrative forms, their importance lies behind all of the preceding discussion. In the broad sense used here, institutions encompass those public sector agencies, government bodies and crown corporations which directly or indirectly set public policy. Some institutions, and the political and territorial power they represent, are of interest here in two regards: (1) in terms of the scope they provide (or do not provide) for urban policy development, and (2) in the institutional or organizational forms this development eventually takes. A few brief examples will suffice. Britain has benefited immensely from formal institutionalization of the garden cities movement and the creation of the Town and Country Planning Association. The new town development corporations have been a considerable success as an administrative means to a given end. Without the autonomy, cohesion, and financial backing given to these corporations, it is unlikely that the new towns would have had the success they obviously have had. Australia, in exploring the outlines of a new cities programme, has proposed similar types of administrative bodies.

There are on the other hand many examples in which institutional forms may be political tactics first and policy vehicles second. Even more serious, institutions often become inhibiting factors in attempting to solve social problems by taking on an existence of their own quite apart from their policy objectives. The Canadian and Australian governments have responded to pressures deriving from their own urban problems firstly by creating new institutional forms and then by launching policy inquiries. Sweden in contrast has no government body which is explicitly urban (aside from local government) but has depended more on co-operation among departments and special purpose boards. This co-operation, as noted earlier, has been greatly facilitated by the unique structure and relatively small size of the Swedish ministerial body.

Thus the institutional 'syndromes' which have fascinated political scientists for some time have a great deal to do not only with the shape that urban policies take but whether those policies succeed or not. Friedmann (1968a, 1972b, and 1973) has probably developed this line of argument as far as anyone and the interested reader is referred to his work as well as to the growing literature on American efforts at organizing national planning.[4] What emerges from these studies is that no one institutional form for administering urban affairs will guarantee success. Nor does the absence of such forms necessarily preclude success. The concluding point is the necessity of considering institutional (and political) structures as part of the necessary organization for national urban strategies.

Before returning to the question of institutional forms, the obvious point should be made: comparative lessons may also appear in a negative way. British planning efforts, despite their long history, innovativeness, and wide publicity, have recently come under considerable criticism, as has the Swedish approach. Few observers would doubt the over-all success of these efforts, with reference to the objectives set out in the British planning acts of the immediate war-time years, but there has not been an effective process of evaluation of the initial objectives and of the unintended side-effects of the policy actions taken. There is also some question as to whose values the various planning systems have responded to, and who benefits accordingly. Clawson and Hall (1973) are particularly critical on both accounts. Urban planning in Britain has, in their terms, produced . . . 'an urban structure few among the public can be said to have chosen and few would want if they were given a choice'. While this comment applies specifically to the policies of urban containment and the higher-density suburbs they may have produced, it is revealing of one of the difficulties facing countries attempting to regulate urban growth. That is, simply, how can a broad

---

[4] Excellent reviews of the U.S. experience are also provided in: Wendt (1962), Moynihan (1970), U.S. National Goals Staff (1970), Wholey (1970), American Society of Planning Officials (1971), Beckman (1971), Mydral (1971), Beckman and Langdon (1972), Derthick (1972), Wingo (1972), Hockman and Paterson (1974), and Berry and Horton (1974).

spectrum of social values and aspirations be accommodated within a comprehensive national planning strategy? Needless to say this study does not solve or attempt to solve that problem.

In summary, what specifically has the much longer experience of British and Swedish planning demonstrated about the conceptual bases, operating rules, and possible side-effects of national (and regional) urbanization policies? In capsule form, among the most important lessons from the preceding review the following stand out:

(1) *planning integration:* planning at the local level, that is of the internal organization of urban areas and metropolitan regions, cannot be effective without regulating trends in the broader urban systems of which these regions are integral parts.

(2) *spatial integration:* intraregional policies operating entirely on their own can have considerable negative effects on national policy objectives for both urban and regional development.

(3) *existing instruments:* governments at all levels already have an effective measure of influence over the pattern of urban development simply through their own decisions on the location of government employment and the distribution of public investments and services.

(4) *no policy option:* misdirected and contradictory policies may lead to more serious consequences than having no explicit policies at all.

(5) *balancing carrots and sticks:* location incentives applied to urban development without parallel controls are usually a waste of public money and effort.

(6) *land and capital:* the essence of location control mechanisms in urban policy is the regulation of land use at the micro- (urban area) level, and of investment decisions at the macro- (urban system) level.

(7) *sectoral imbalance:* a concentration in urban growth strategies on the manufacturing sector is likely to be self-defeating in the long run and in the short run it is not likely to alter existing inequalities in either interurban or interregional occupational and social structures.

(8) *sectoral co-ordination:* specific urban policy objectives, relating, for example, to the redistribution of population and employment, cannot be attained independently of allocation decisions in other government sectors, principally in housing and transport, but also in fields such as manpower training and education.

(9) *goal specification:* urban goals must be simple, explicit, and appear to be feasible if there is to be any degree of closure between available means and desired ends.

(10) *goal stability:* a continuous process of reassessment and revision of goals and objectives is necessary. Goals are fluid and highly elastic.

(11) *images:* the success or failure of urban policies depends to a considerable extent on the presence or absence of common images of what the urban environment should look like and the degree to which those images are articulated in ongoing research and through political debates in the public forum.

(12) *political reorganization:* for the regulation of urban development to be effective in the long term requires a reorganization of government and administrative responsibilities and the creation of a new system of political and administrative units.

While none of these points is entirely self-explanatory, and in terms of past experience in all of the four countries studied exceptions could be found for each, they will be left in this shorthand form as similar conclusions have been reached in most comparative studies. The last point, however, the necessity of governmental reorganization in urban affairs, warrants further elaboration. If, for example, the political fascination with excessive city size continues, Thompson (1972) argues that the important policy problem may be to create a more optimal system of governments rather than to find an optimal size distribution of city sizes. While this argument has been made previously, it does suggest at this point the need to consider a matching, more explicitly than in the past, of the distribution of problems to that of administrative responsibilities within the urban system. Part of this matching is a hierarchy of urbanization strategies. Certainly in a modern and complex society a single unitary set of strategies uniformly applied across a country is unlikely to be effective and may in fact be counter-productive.

## 6.7. POLICY RESPONSIBILITIES AND THE URBAN HIERARCHY: A FRAMEWORK

Proposals as to what such reorganized administrative systems for planning should look like are many and varied (Cooper *et al.*, 1971). But there have been few attempts to integrate the various possible levels of urban policy in a national planning context. None of the four countries under review has faced this issue head-on, although all have recently undertaken extensive reorganizations of local government boundaries (Sweden, England, Ontario, and New South Wales, for instance) and planning duties. Table 6.2 is a highly experimental attempt to identify some of the types of policy interest in a theoretical hierarchy of urban and regional systems, and to relate these to examples of (1) the type of regulatory strategies involved, (2) goals, (3) examples of specific policy instruments, and (4) the nature of the application of these instruments, which together might constitute a comprehensive framework for national urban policy. The table was prepared with no single country in mind although clearly it reflects the greater elaboration of hierarchical responsibilities necessary in a federal political system.

Four such levels of urban systems are recognized: (1) the international urban-economic system, of which economic development and urbanization in any nation are integral parts; (2) the national urban system, which comprises the operating mechanisms of national social and economic life, set in a spatial context; (3) major regional urban systems, such as the South-East, Wales, and Scotland in Britain, the Canadian provinces and Australian states, and to a lesser extent the Swedish regions; and (4) the individual urban (city) region, the daily urban system. Clearly there is overlap in each level and the table intentionally does not elaborate on the role of level 5, planning at the local community level. In non-federal political systems levels 2 and 3 would be merged, but with some policy responsibilities in level 3 taken up by individual urban municipalities.

The essence of the proposed framework in Table 6.2 is not the hierarchy but the nesting of problem sources and urban policy responsibilities. The concept of the urban system (or systems) is the integrating device. The vertical arrows in column 1 are meant to apply both as directives for policy responsibility (i.e. from national to regional levels) as well as for flows of information and ideas on setting out policy goals and defining strategies (i.e. from local communities and neighbourhoods to cities and regional levels). The two-way process implied is not unlike that operating in some areas of Swedish planning practice (see Section 4.2), particularly that employed in devising the current regional policy plans for national urban development. The important point in the Swedish planning experience is not so much the instruments used but how they are applied.

Table 6.2 begins with the international context for national urbanization policies (level 1). Another of the obvious lessons from the preceding review is the extent to which urban systems are open to external influence. They are not, as politicians would prefer, closed entities. They cannot be treated independently of their external environment. As described in Sections II and III, social systems are inevitably open 'learning' systems which continually derive a part of their energy and character from that environment. It is the obvious responsibility of the national government to monitor changes in the global (urban-economic) environment and to contain or minimize the negative impact of these changes on patterns of national development (column 3). Examples of available policy instruments to achieve these goals (column 4) include tariff, business, and population policies. The final column (5) for level 1 argues that, while such policies may be explicit in form, their usefulness depends to a considerable extent on persuasion and on bartering with competing interests and policies in other countries.

The national urban system (level 2), the principal policy focus of national governments, is the bridge between the international context and the growth of regional systems of cities and of individual cities. The policy emphasis at this level is obviously more macro in concept, of longer-term design, and more normative in purpose than is usually necessary or possible at the other two system levels. Long-term social investment and equity considerations, as they apply to urban development, are appropriate objectives at this level. The number of potential policy instruments which can be used to influence the shape of urban development is considerable. They range from manipulation of the national economy and interregional fiscal transfer policies to housing policy and locational assistance applied through such programmes as transport, manpower, and regional development. As to the nature and application of these policies, they must be somewhat permissive in terms of implementation by region, but at the same time they must frequently take the initiative and preferably should demonstrate the innovativeness which will attract regional support and inputs. The style of decision-making of course will vary with the political context.

The suggested urban policy responsibilities of the other two levels of government follow from this same line of argument and need not be repeated in detail here. Some readers may wish to revise the ordering of policies and instruments in line with their own experience and in reference to their own national setting. Others may be critical of the entire approach. In any case, note in scanning the lists in the table that examples are drawn from both spatial and traditionally aspatial government activities and that these two are not mutually exclusive activities for any level in this idealized urban hierarchy. Similarly, despite the principal emphasis here on the spatial dimensions of policy questions it is intended that the outline in Table 6.2 refer to the vertical (organizational) distribution of responsibilities as well. Sweden for example has taken a step in the direction of linking the two by defining a set of territorial building blocks as part of their urban system planning

**TABLE 6.2**

SCHEMATIC FRAMEWORK FOR MATCHING URBANIZATION STRATEGIES
AND THE URBAN SYSTEM HIERARCHY

| urban System Level | Spatial Policy Focus (1) | Type of Regulatory Strategies (2) | Policy Goals and Objectives (3) | Selected Examples of Policy Instruments (4) | Nature/Application of Policies (5) |
|---|---|---|---|---|---|
| 1 | International urban/economic system | Containing external pressures, Monitoring consequences of change at boundaries of national system | Survival, Minimize environmental turbulence, Co-ordination of foreign activities with national systems and needs | Tariff and development policies, Monetary reform, Corporation taxes, Immigration and emigration policy | Specific in form but persuasive in application externally |
| 2 | National Urban System | Redistribution of social opportunities, Anticipating futures, National socio-economic and environmental planning, Long-term and goal-directed strategies | Social investment, Equity, Economic growth targets, Social welfare balance, National unity, Continuity and internal stability, Social conservation | National economy, Population policy, Public investment, Fiscal transfers, Taxation, Transport and communication, Housing finance, Employment location, Information distribution, Interregional location assistance | Locationally flexible and permissive by region, Creative and initiating at the national level, Emphasis on co-ordination by sector and region |

| | | | | |
|---|---|---|---|---|
| 3 | Major Regional (provincial/state) urban subsystems | Redesigning and articulating national policy frameworks, Initiating strategic physical and environmental planning | Social services, Intraregional equity. Orderly urban development, Regional viability, Environmental protection, Land-use rationalization | Local government expenditures, Regional public investment, Transport policy, Housing loans and construction, Employment location, Land policy, Educational facilities, Locational assistance | Location specific, Matching national and local needs, Inter-municipal co-ordination, Emphasis on implementation and evaluation |
| 4 | Urban (city) Systems | Redesigning and implementing regional policy frameworks, physical and allocative social services planning, both short and long term | Service delivery Intra-urban equity, Orderly physical development, Containing local externalities, Viability of urban services | Land use, Location of services, Building code enforcement and construction, Traffic planning, Local educational facilities, Site location assistance | Location specific in aggregate, flexible within communities, Matching city and neighbourhood needs |
| 5 | Communities and Neighbourhoods | | | | |

Notes: (1) Arrows in column 1 refer to directions of policy responsibility and flows of information and ideas.
(2) The number of units involved varies with each level: from one national urban system to several regional subsystems to many daily urban (city) systems and neighbourhoods.

which exhausts the populated area of the country. The building blocks are hierarchical and are designed to be the spatial context within which future public location decisions are formulated, implemented, and eventually evaluated.

## 6.8. EXISTING POLICY INSTRUMENTS

One of the additional lessons from this comparative review, particularly from the British and Swedish policy experience, is the extent to which governments already hold the weapons (some of which are enumerated in Table 6.2) that they can wield to influence urban systems development. One set of weapons is the direct impact in generating urban growth through the geography of location decisions regarding public sector employment, investment, purchasing, and services. Sweden is now making considerable use of both government employment and public investment allocations to improve the equitable structure of the Swedish urban system and to encourage more balanced regional development. Britain is following the same path.

A second set of existing instruments operates on the demand side of urbanization by attempting to control the demographic bases of urban growth (Morrison, 1972). This approach, suggested in Lithwick's (1970) study of urban Canada, has at least two major dimensions: (1) regulating population growth through controls on foreign immigration, and (2) managing the resulting space needs of that growth. The latter, as noted in previous sections, has been most strongly pursued in Britain. The first has not been used effectively in any of the four countries as an instrument of urban or locational policy. All four countries, as net importers of population, have numerous controls on immigration, but these restrictions tend to reflect economic conditions rather than social policy needs. The difference between the two strategies, of course, lies in the fact that the former deals with one element in the over-all rate of urban growth, while the latter treats the localized 'spread' effects of this growth. The latter is somewhat easier to control directly through existing policy instruments, but is less directly related to national government planning. The much more difficult task of linking over-all growth rates in population and employment to their distribution at a national scale has not been successfully achieved in any of the examples studied. Without this integration neither approach will be highly effective over the long term.

There are numerous other policy measures which national (and state) governments have and could use to steer spatial patterns of urban development in desired directions. Among these are tariff and pricing policies (as in Sweden), manpower mobility and retraining (as in Canada), transport regulatory rates, industrial development strategies (as in Britain), provision of educational services (as in Sweden and Britain), and housing (as in Britain), to name a few which have both sufficient scale and a strong spatial component. In federal political systems such as Australia and Canada, these measures may emanate from either the national or provincial (state) levels, or both. While more difficult to co-ordinate, this may also allow for the more flexible application of uniform policies to regions with differing needs. Sweden already has considerable regional autonomy within the country administrative structure, while Britain is now debating further policy decentralization involving Scotland, Wales, and the major regions in England.

Housing policy warrants special emphasis. Although national housing policies have not been the subject of discussion in this study, they are of fundamental importance in expanding the present frame of reference for urban policies. Traditionally housing in most countries has not been employed as a means of achieving urban or locational objectives despite its obvious impact on urban development patterns. The reason is not that housing is ignored as an essential social good but rather that it serves other purposes as well. As everyone knows housing construction is one of the major tools of national governments in regulating economic cycles, a practice which in most instances increases housing problems in urban areas. Housing policies *per se* have tended to be production rather than distribution oriented.

Nevertheless, there are examples in which the effectiveness of urban policies has been increased through the spatial allocation of housing. The much greater involvement of the British and Swedish governments in the provision of housing—through actual construction and direct financing—compared to Canada and Australia (and the U.S.) has proved to be a powerful policy device. For instance, controls on the allocation of housing supply, particularly public housing, have been of immense importance in the success of the British new towns and in achieving modest decentralization from the major cities in Sweden to satellite communities. Combined with a policy of widespread public land acquisition (nearly two-thirds of Swedish housing is now built on publicly owned land), public authorities have been able to shape the form of urban growth through housing investment at least at local and regional levels. Both Australia and Canada could make much more effective use of their limited but growing public housing sectors to achieve urban goals without of course infringing the basic 'shelter' objectives of adequate housing for all.

## 6.9. ACHIEVING CONSENSUS AND ACTION

Throughout this study the inherent difficulties of setting national goals and defining national planning strategies in pluralistic and capitalistic societies particularly, have been stressed repeatedly. The factors which define the degree of difficulty are many and varied. Each one takes a somewhat different form in any given country and each has a variable influence on setting the preconditions and determining the feasibility of formulating national strategies for regulating urban growth. While most are evident in the preceding discussion, it might be revealing in summary to attempt a qualitative assessment in tabular form of their relative importance in the four countries under study. Table 6.3 is such an attempt.

Recall from Section I Rodwin's (1970) summary of those preconditions he argues are necessary for national governments to formulate urban strategies. The two most important are: (1) that urban problems must be perceived as national problems; and (2) that these problems must appear capable of solution through political means. To these, Berry (1973a) added the will to plan and the ability to plan through achieving a closure of means and ends in policy formulation. The following factors are elaborations and additions to these preconditions. They deal largely with the socio-economic, cultural, and political backgrounds which are hypothesized to influence the ability of a country to formulate and implement explicit national policies for regulating urbanization.

The following criteria are proposed as a basis for comparing the four countries under study:

(1) the degree of *social-cultural homogeneity:* which implies that the higher the degree of national heterogeneity or pluralism, *ceteris paribus*, the more difficult it is to achieve a consensus on national priorities and policies.

(2) the degree of cultural and *political polarization:* as a corollary of point (1) the heterogeneity factor generally becomes accentuated if it is also geographically pronounced and politically organized in discrete territorial units (i.e. counties, provinces and states).

(3) the historical inheritance of a *political and social consensus* on the need to define objectives for social policy. Clearly an ability to achieve agreement on

overt national government action in general will set bounds on the feasibility of regulating urbanization.

(4) historical *inertia*, and *institutional rigidity* to social change, inhibit efforts to accommodate new modes of decision-making necessary for planning policy implementation.

(5) degree of *economic regionalization:* the extent to which local economies are integrated into a national urban-economic system influences both the perceived need and the power of central governments to plan development at the national level.

(6) level of *structural imbalances* in the national economy such as outmoded industrial or resource sectors, imbalances which dictate major government efforts at economic growth and therefore allow less scope for policies directed at income redistribution, regional balance, and economic relocation.

(7) level of *unemployment:* although often a short-term phenomenon as in (6) above, high levels of unemployment also demand a strong priority be given to maximizing economic growth but in particular growth which is labour intensive.

(8) the *level of dependence* of the urban-economic system in each country on external influences. High levels of interdependence almost invariably reduce the ability of governments to shape their own urban futures, most especially at the national level.

(9) *degree of localization* of the external dependence noted under (8) above further inhibits the scope for national planning since the consequences of altering that dependence have a differential impact by region.

(10) present and anticipated *rates of urban growth.* For countries in which the rate of urban population growth is relatively high, the emphasis given to short-term ameliorative solutions to immediate urban problems will outweigh that given to long-range strategies—a necessary perspective in regulating urban system development.

(11) anticipated rates of national *economic growth.* Although somewhat in conflict with the preceding point, and the converse of point (6), the argument here is that very low rates of aggregate economic growth will inhibit the ability of governments to pursue redistribution policies simply by limiting the public resources available.

(12) the degree of consensus on the degree to which problems, as in Rodwin's (1970) terminology, are amenable to *political* solution.

(13) facility for *intergovernmental co-ordination:* an effective national strategy

## TABLE 6.3

### A SUBJECTIVE COMPARISON OF SELECTED PRECONDITIONS FOR FORMULATING NATIONAL URBAN STRATEGIES

| Social Factors | Direction of Influence for Ranking | Relative Rankings for Countries | | | |
|---|---|---|---|---|---|
| | | Britain | Sweden | Australia | Canada |
| 1 Degree of social/cultural homogeneity | positive | high (4) | very high (5) | high (4) | low (2) |
| 2 Territorial polarization: cultural and political | negative | medium (3) | low (4) | very high (1) | very high (1) |
| 3 Existence of political consensus on social objectives | positive | high (4) | high (4) | low (2) | low (2) |
| 4 Historical inertia and institutional rigidity | negative | medium (3) | medium (3) | low (4) | low (4) |
| 5 Degree of economic regionalization | negative | medium (3) | low (4) | high (2) | very high (1) |
| 6 Degree of structural (economic) imbalances | negative | high (2) | low (4) | low (4) | medium (3) |
| 7 Level of unemployment/ necessity for growth | negative | medium (3) | low (4) | low (4) | high (2) |
| 8 External dependence of the urban system | negative | medium (3) | high (2) | very high (1) | very high (1) |
| 9 Degree of localization of external dependence | negative | low (4) | low (4) | medium (3) | high (2) |

| | | | | | | |
|---|---|---|---|---|---|---|
| 10 | Rate of urban growth | negative | low (4) | low (4) | high (2) | high (2) |
| 11 | Scope provided by estimated future economic growth | positive | low (2) | high (4) | high (4) | medium (3) |
| 12 | Consensus on degrees of problem solvability | positive | medium (3) | high (4) | low (2) | low (2) |
| 13 | Extent of intergovern-mental co-ordination | positive | medium (3) | high (4) | very low (1) | low (2) |
| 14 | Degree of goal-directedness in policy | positive | low (2) | medium (3) | very low (1) | very low (1) |
| 15 | Impact of urban policy research | positive | low (2) | high (4) | very low (1) | low (2) |
| | Totals | | 45 | 57 | 36 | 30 |
| | Ranking | | 2 | 1 | 3 | 4 |

for urban growth depends by definition on integration of public sector location policies among levels of government and by sectors of responsibility.

(14) degree of *goal-directedness* in social policy: societies vary widely in the extent to which nationally applied policies can be explicitly directed toward long-term goals, even given a consensus on the need (point (3) above) for such goals.

(15) impact of *policy research:* the influence of ongoing research, both basic and mission-oriented, can have a significant influence on the perception of problem definitions and alternative solutions and, if integrated with policy formulation, can alter the probabilities of success for such policies.

To facilitate a direct comparison of the four countries, each country is assigned a relative weight on each of the above factors using a rather arbitrary ordinal scale of 1 to 5. The weighting is intended to order the countries in terms of the actual (and potential) contribution of each factor in determining the outcome of the debate on national urban strategy formulation. Those factors considered to be positive attributes are scaled from 5 (very high) to 1 (very low), while negative factors are scaled in reverse order.

| Positive factor facilitating national action | Ordinal Scale | Negative factor inhibiting national action |
|:---:|:---:|:---:|
| 5 | very high | 1 |
| 4 | high | 2 |
| 3 | medium | 3 |
| 2 | low | 4 |
| 1 | very low | 5 |

Of course, any number of other weighting scales and measures could be used. The scalings in Table 6.3 are not meant to be universal, but are relative to the four countries themselves with background reference to Western Europe and North America, and to currently prevailing rather than anticipated conditions. The rationale is to focus attention on specific conditioning factors which might define or circumscribe the changes of achieving consensus and action on mechanisms for regulating urbanization, or on any national policies for that matter, and to stimulate further discussion.

Homogeneity, for example, is defined as a positive factor with values assigned from 1 to 5 based on very low (complex pluralism) to very high levels of homogeneity. Sweden is given a value of 5 on this factor while Canada is assigned a value of 2. Australia and Britain are placed in between. The U.S. for instance might be weighted at 2 or 1 on this same scale, depending on one's perspective. It is, of course, possible to counter this specific argument by suggesting that pluralism allows for 'the organized simplification of complexity' which is necessary to achieve political consensus on any complex issue (Dye, 1972; Emery and Trist, 1972), and thus heterogeneity should be considered a positive attribute. Nevertheless, on balance, it is argued here that the inhibiting elements of social heterogeneity, at least at the national level, outweigh this reductionism argument. The same weighting procedure is, then, repeated for each of the other indices. The rankings are summed, but only for illustrative purposes.

The results may be misleading if not interpreted with caution. The factors are not mutually exclusive and most, as in the above example, could be argued in reverse. Several sweeping assumptions are also necessary in the comparison: that the same attribute has generally the same impact on policy in each country; that all factors are subject to the same scaling; and that a single direction of influence can be specified for each factor. Consequently, readers may prefer to set out their own criteria and weights. Nevertheless Table 6.3 summarizes an immensely complex set of preconditions in a form which isolates some of the unique qualities of the policy environment in the four countries. The exercise itself also demonstrates why subsequent policy evolution will follow different paths in each country.

The result of the scaling is almost to be taken for granted. Sweden emerges with far fewer identifiable limitations on attaining a formal regulatory system for urban development. Canada, as a geographically extensive, bicultural federal state, with heavy economic interdependence on another federal state, emerges with much the lowest over-all rating. Australia and Britain are ranked between the other two on most factors, with most advantages given to Britain. This should not, however, be interpreted as saying that Canada and Australia will not in the future produce effective means of guiding urban development at the national level. Instead it argues that these means, if they emerge, will be different, probably less comprehensive in scope and less formal in application, and certainly they will be less centralized in both political and geographical terms than in Britain or Sweden. But this summary also indicates that the task will be substantially more difficult in Australia and Canada and that considerable independence of province and state action in urban policy will be essential. In Britain and Sweden, on the other hand, national urban strategies, because of historical factors, may emerge from different sources and under different institutional titles and labels. In any case, the same preconditions will not necessarily produce the same policy response and as attitudes change these preconditions will themselves change. A better understanding of these preconditions will enable us to chart more effective paths to our national urban goals.

# Commentary:
# Conclusions and Prospects

---

It is idle to talk of limiting the extent or size of the town by law, unless you could prevent colonists, aliens and annuitants from coming to dwell among us.
*(Monthly Magazine, 1811)*

MOST western countries are currently searching for ways and means to regulate urban growth and its spatial consequences at the national scale. Issues of relating economic development to patterns of urbanization and of achieving rates of urban growth which minimize the negative aspects of economic and industrial expansion have also been the subject of wide scrutiny and interest.[1] In particular, the problems of urban population over-concentration and regional imbalance have been the principal focus of spatially sensitive policies.

Some countries, because of social climate, geography, and historical circumstances, have been more successful than others in approaching solutions to these problems. The degree of success in a global perspective, despite the impression given by positive reviews such as Rodwin's (1970), has been limited, and even then is evident primarily at the level of the individual urban region, not at the national level (Richardson, 1972; Blumenfeld, 1974). This is the case not principally because policies have been misdirected or through a failure to understand the full complexity of urbanization—although both of these most certainly apply. Rather the more basic reason is that such policies have seldom been tried. Through political convenience or lack of conviction, national

[1] For additional details the interested reader is referred to a number of recent and excellent reviews on national urban problems and policy. Among these are Beckman and Langdon (1973) on the U.S.; Berry (1973a) on the social consequences of and policy developments on urban planning in selected countries; Cameron and Wingo (1973) on the theory and practice of urban systems and planning; Clawson and Hall (1973) on the comparative experience of U.S. and British planning; EFTA (1973) for a review of urban development policy in EFTA countries, including Britain and Sweden; Friedmann (1973) on the relationship between urbanization and national planning in underdeveloped countries; OECD (1973c) for a detailed review of urban growth policies in Western Europe; Rodwin's (1970) now classic review of urban growth plans and projects in selected countries; and for systems applications in urban research generally see Mesarovic and Reisman (1972).

plans for urban development, in the few cases where they have been formulated, have been narrow in orientation and application and limited in influence. Few countries have developed longer-term strategies and applied these to the national urban system in its appropriate sectoral and geographical complexity.

## 7.1. STUDY OBJECTIVES IN REVIEW

This volume has sought, in a very general and personal way, to document the problems and the recent experiences of four different countries in regulating national urban development in a spatial context. In each country examined—Britain, Sweden, Australia, and Canada—the review looked to two broad areas of innovation in urban and related locational policies: national urban planning and regional policy. Other policy areas which have major impacts on urban areas, and on locational questions generally, but are not explicitly labelled urban or regional, were also considered.

Emphasis was placed on issues and policies at the national or macro-level, but where appropriate (i.e. in federal political systems) reference was made to activity at provincial (state) and regional levels. The specific argument for the inclusion, in a review of urban development, of regional policies, regional development programmes, and regional planning is that in most countries these are the dominant areas of governmental activity in macro-spatial planning. Regional issues are of course intimately related to questions of urban development and there is widespread evidence that regional policy is taking a more formal urban perspective. In fact in some countries national policies for regulating patterns of urbanization may well emerge, if they emerge at all, as direct extensions from regional policy—emanating either from national or sub-national governments, or both.

The four case studies (Sections IV and V) were selected to display different expressions of and approaches to these issues. The author's choice of Canada (Section 5.2) is obvious. Australia (Section 5.1) was selected because it shares many of the same historical and geographical preconditions which underly urban development in Canada. Also it is perceived to have similar kinds of urban problems and growth potentials, set in similar social and political climates. Both offer examples of countries with evolving urban systems, relatively short urban histories, and limited national policy experiences. Equally important, both have recently initiated efforts to establish national urban goals, institutions, and policies. Britain (Section 4.1) and Sweden (Section 4.2), on the other hand, provide a basis for evaluating relatively long histories of attempts to shape national development patterns. They are, as the title of Section IV notes, urban systems which have been under a significant measure of national regulation. Sweden also contains urban and regional problems which parallel those in Australia and Canada, while Britain holds the common cultural and political base. The selection of examples therefore was designed to minimize unnecessary differences while maintaining those contrasts between countries which might contribute to an understanding of urbanization problems and policies in a comparative context.

The discussion in each of the preceding sections is focused on broad strategies of regulating urbanization and its spatial consequences rather than on detailed inventory of policies. The latter obviously could not be ignored since it is by the formulation and execution of policies that strategies are most easily identified and subsequently implemented. However, in a comparative review designed to draw general lessons from the experience of different countries, specific policies are seldom directly transferable. Strategies—that is, the organizing framework of ideas, means, and goals behind the policies—may, with appropriate transformation, be applied elsewhere (see Figure 3.1, Section III).

The other principal focus in the review was on the most recent directions in urban strategies and on the likely course of future policy changes. Detailed historical policy reviews are now plentiful in most countries and need not be repeated here. Sections VI and VII attempt to summarize these recent policy directions and then to speculate on possible trends in and the preconditions of national policy evolution. This approach, however, has dangers. It means that subjective interpretations are more prevalent than they might otherwise have been, and therefore that misjudgements on the part of the author are more likely.

## 7.2. CONSEQUENCES OF FUTURE URBAN GROWTH

Expectations of the future, either in the form of social anticipations (Vickers, 1974) or formal forecasts (Jantsch, 1972), can play two other important roles in achieving consensus and action in urban policy-making. One is that images of future urban development serve as inputs to the process of debating the need and selecting the approaches to solving urban problems. Such images therefore contribute directly to common perceptions of what those problems are. Second, the anticipated rate and character of future urban growth act as boundary constraints on policy decision-making. As such they delimit the freedom which governments have to design future states of the urban system—that is, to undertake normative and goal-oriented planning of the kind outlined in Section III.

One corollary of the second role of anticipations of the future is to ask the question whether the importance of formulating national urbanization strategies depends on the expectation of high rates of future urban growth. Over the last decade, almost all forecasters looking to the future urban environment, and to future patterns of urban development, have projected rapid population growth and the massive geographic extension of urban areas. It now seems that many of these projections err considerably on the high side. Birth-rates have dropped to their lowest levels this century. Rates of natural increase have declined accordingly as death-rates have almost stabilized. Population projections based on post-war trends are now being revised downward aciordingly. Many countries in fact have almost reached zero population growth—the U.S. and most of Western Europe, for example. Their populations are still increasing only because of a demographic structure inflated in the fertile age brackets by the post-war baby boom, or through continued immigration from outside the country.

None of these trends need imply that changes in national urban systems will not be substantial. Far from it. Instead it suggests that change will be of different kinds with differing consequences. Material expectations will continue to expand and social needs will diversify. Less importance need be attached, however, to aggregate population size. As a result, change on the one hand may be more purposeful and possibly more amenable to regulation, but on the other will likely contain greater uncertainty. Even if most western industrial countries should attain zero population growth by the turn of the century, combined with zero (net) rural-to-urban and small-city-to-large-city migration, urban problems will continue if not increase in magnitude. Innovations in communication, changes in organizational structure, and increases in affluence and leisure time will further expand the spatial imprint of urbanization.

Thus, what Thompson (1972), Berry (1972b), Pred (1973b), and others have called 'spread' effects are likely to continue in the future, as the urban system responds to new demands placed on it. Movements of people, goods, and information within and between cities in the urban system will also continue, if not expand in intensity. At the same time continued integration of the national urban system will provide greater scope markedly to affect the diffusion and redistribution of resources within that system. Linkages within and between organizations, particularly the huge multi-nodal and multi-national corporations, add a further dimension of unpredictability to the complex equation of urban growth. Technological change may also accelerate, but possibly will be more conditioned and directed by social checks and balances if not actually spawned by social goals and needs. Social values will become more explicit inputs in the setting of such goals (Vickers, 1971). Thus, anticipated trends in urbanization over the next decade or two provide both opportunities for and difficulties in achieving improved means of regulating urban development at the national level.

This twofold conclusion poses an interesting dilemma. If aggregate population growth is lower than anticipated in the next few decades locational decisions regarding the allocation of public resources will be both more and less difficult. For instance if the present universal preoccupation with economic growth continues, it will be increasingly difficult for governments to realize a more equitable distribution of the benefits of such growth because of lower rates of expansion of the labour force and a rapidly changing population age structure. During the post-war period most western governments could always count on the rapid growth of the national population to diffuse some spill-over effects of economic growth into smaller and more peripheral regions and to soften the immediate impact of relocation measures applied to the more prosperous regions and cities. Sweden has already reached this state. Like other Western European nations Sweden has become increasingly dependent on imported migrant labour (there are estimated to be more than three million in Europe); even heavily populated Britain may find itself in a similar position. Canada and Australia will also find it increasingly difficult to attract skilled immigrants. The luxury of absolute numbers may be over. Obviously a similar argument does not apply to Third World countries.

In contrast, there seems little doubt that the rapid population and technological growth of the post-war period has been one of the principal causes of urban diseconomies and a contributing factor in the current urban *malaise*. Most observers have concluded that these rates of change exceed what might be considered optimal for policy and planning purposes. Thus the anticipated decline in population growth rates may solve one of the planner's major objectives without his trying. Whether this reduced growth aggregate will be more purposeful than in the past is impossible to say. The large random component which has dominated regional and urban development patterns in most western capitalistic countries could decline in importance. New resource discoveries and technological breakthroughs are likely to be more locationally fixed, and although still spectacular (i.e. North Sea oil and gas, Australian iron ore, Arctic oil and gas) they should form a smaller proportion of national income. Other growth sectors, such as public service, recreation, and retirement developments, may be more easily anticipated.

Thus, combined with lower rates of aggregate population growth, the consequences of future trends in urbanization may be more readily predicted. It is in this sense that we suggest that opportunities for directing future urban growth, and therefore for shifting the initiative in designing our urban future from the private to the public sector, may be greater than they have been in the recent past. In contrast, as economic growth will be increasingly directed and managed through national urban systems, adding to and enforcing the historical stability of those systems, the scope for major structural changes at this level may consequently decline.

## 7.3. URBAN SYSTEMS CONCEPTS IN PERSPECTIVE

Precisely because of the rapidity of urban change in the past, and the increasing complexity of modern society, planning and regulatory strategies have been forced to change. Social instability and economic uncertainty have increased as direct consequences of the rapidity of change. New concepts, revised institutional forms, and better policy instruments are needed to meet the challenge. In this context urban systems concepts become of central importance. Interdependence is the definitional backbone of urban systems (Chisholm, 1972). A trend toward even greater interdependence necessitates more integrated and comprehensive policy thinking; that is treating social systems holistically. When social systems were less interdependent, urban policies could be (and most still are) discrete, administered by a host of separate agencies, and locationally specific in application. Increasingly, given the interdependence noted above, these same policies and procedures become correspondingly inappropriate (Chadwick, 1971). At the same time, greater economic uncertainty requires a longer-term, more future-oriented perspective in both urban research and policy. The problem of course is deciding what kind of social system (or systems) urban centres represent and designing strategies accordingly. Do we, for example, use the urban system to facilitate economic growth or to change the existing economic structure?

These attributes, of modern society and advanced economies, and the experience of the four countries under review suggest one of the major conclusions of this study: that urban systems concepts have enormous potential as a 'learning' framework for urban policy. The argument is neatly summarized in the EFTA (1973) report on national settlement strategies in its member countries. It notes that, just as acceptance of the individual city as an interacting social and spatial system is now widely recognized by planners and politicians, so it is essential to consider interactions between cities as constituting a system for decision-making and planning purposes. The sub-title of this volume 'Strategies for Regulation' can itself be interpreted both as a basis against which current policies may be compared and assessed, and as an objective in terms of recommendations for future approaches to national and sub-national urban planning.

This approach, however, does not necessarily imply a specific political philosophy or inclination. For example, national urban planning in general, or the urban systems strategy in particular, does not require that a supporter be a 'centralist' in the political sense, or for that matter a decentralist, or that an increase is necessary in central government powers (the federal role). Rather it requires a different and more effective use of existing public powers. A single 'comprehensive' national plan (in the traditional town planning sense) is not necessary; various plans may well emerge, including consideration of the complementary roles of rural and agricultural areas. Instead, urban systems offer several advantages as a basis for policy formulation. They explicitly recognize the obvious but often overlooked interrelationships between cities and spatial sectors of the national economy; and allow for the decomposition of a national economy, and of a nation's cities, into logical sub-units for purposes of regional administration and regulation. They facilitate the creation of an interface between research and policy planning, since many of the underlying concepts are transferable, and provide one framework for continuous monitoring of urbanization and of the consequences of policy decisions on the spatial and hierarchical structure of national development.

## 7.4. POLITICAL AND SOCIAL CONSIDERATIONS

Most major questions, in debating the merits and form of national urban policies generally, are essentially political. One such question is whether the argument for regulating urbanization in terms of national goals conflicts with recent pressures for greater participation and local

autonomy in planning and policy decision-making? The obvious answer
is that it need not. What is argued here is a strategy—a way of approaching the complexity of contemporary urbanization in terms of
policy at all jurisdictional levels. An urban systems approach need not
involve increased regulation by any level of government (although in
most countries an increase is clearly appropriate); rather it seeks to encourage more effective and co-ordinated regulation directed toward
specified goals.[2] This can be done while allowing for an increase in
freedom of choice, but it will not be easy.

A further and critical social question in national urban policy is
regulation of whom and for whom? If the public sector is positively to
intercede with and shape (if not create) those ongoing processes of
growth and distribution operating within an urban system, more must
be known about the social and behavioural bases of that system. Who
makes the major private investment decisions? Who influences the
allocation of urban public resources? What are the corporate linkages
which transmit impulses of growth and change through the urban
system? What kind of system do people want? Even if it is possible to
identify the critical decision agents and preference patterns and then to
propose effective guide-lines for public policy action, who benefits?
How do we measure what Alonso (1968b), Hägerstrand (1972), and
Harvey (1973) have called 'equity in spatial systems'? Any planning
procedure involves the redistribution of income and opportunities, in
many instances creating further inequities. The latter are usually new in
form and location, but ideally are less severe than those created by the
absence of planning. But this cannot be taken for granted. Clawson and
Hall (1973) and Hall *et al.* (1973), for instance, have noted the enormous
gains which certain sectors of British society derived through the
application and enforcement of the post-war policies of containing urban sprawl. When there are gainers there are generally losers. The
benefits and costs may be exaggerated or inadvertently redirected by in-
competent, inadequate, or inoperative policy responses—but they are
certain to appear in one form or another whatever ideal model or
regulatory system for urban development is devised. While we are not in

---

[2] One obvious political limitation is that urban systems have no voters, no lobby in the corridors
of power, and few active special-interest groups supporting their identification as a problem area
worthy of public attention. Regions have the political power: provinces in Canada; states in
Australia; counties in Sweden; and in Britain, increasingly, Scotland and Wales and to a lesser extent the major regions in England. Yet this factor also gives a positive advantage to political action.
The absence of direct voters means no voters to alienate and, in theory, few vested interests to inhibit the active design of new public decision-making frameworks.

a position totally to eliminate or even fully anticipate these consequences, society must, as Emery and Trist (1972) conclude, be willing to face up to them.

## 7.5. EMERGING URBAN STRATEGIES AND PROSPECTS

In those countries which have achieved some success in guiding national urban development—in Sweden (Section 4.2), the Netherlands (OECD, 1973c), France (Hansen, 1968), or Israel (Schacher, 1971), for example—success has normally followed from a convergence of needs, incentives, and goals in a unique geographical-political setting. Even though these conditions are not commonly present elsewhere, some smaller nations may well serve as important social learning situations for policy applications relevant to the larger and more complex nations. This review of two countries with established urban policies and two others with an emerging interest in urban problems may assist in improving the groundwork for such applications.

While the lessons from this comparative review have been many and varied, few, if any, universal guide-lines have emerged. Each of the four countries exhibits a different approach and each is at a different point in time in the evolution of policy thinking. Only Sweden among the four has made a formal attempt at national urban system planning in an explicitly spatial context. While the guiding framework for local decision-making, the Regional Structure Plan, is very recent and still largely untested, it is, as Pred (1973c) notes, a unique experiment in attempting to design a more equitable spatial structure for a national urban system. Britain has a number of regional urban strategies applied by the central government from which a network of regional urban plans may emerge. How (and if) these are integrated at the national level into a regional urban system perspective is as yet undefined.

Australia and Canada (and by inference other young and vast nations) do not as yet have a national perspective on urban development or even regional urban strategies which add up to a national perspective. Nor do they have explicit national urban goals. Some observers in both countries argue that such perspectives are inappropriate, unconstitutional, unnecessary, or simply infeasible. Berry (1973c) has commented that '... American society is inherently incapable of being goal-oriented for deep-seated ideological reasons.' By inference, roughly the same value structure prevails in Australia and Canada. Similar arguments, of course, have also been made in Britain and in Sweden. Infeasible in political terms they may eventually turn out to be in federal systems, capitalistic economies, and pluralistic societies, but inappropriate they are not.

A number of difficult problems will have to be surmounted if any of these efforts are to succeed. The first is to define realistic urbanization goals. A related issue is the necessity of balancing conflicting goals—between social and economic sectors and within and between regions (provinces/states). This is a continuous process for which there can be no immediate solution. Another problem is the appropriate distribution of urban policy responsibility among various levels of government and territorial units. Such institutional problems are not limited to federal states. Sweden already has considerable regional autonomy in central government functions; Britain does not as yet. Canada and Australia will have to achieve some greater degree of centralized co-ordination in strategic planning while maintaining, if not encouraging, regional independence in policy innovation and implementation.

What are the prospects? While the arguments in support of a more explicit national perspective to planning urban and economic growth are not, as expected, equally shared among the four countries, it is likely that the extent of regulation of urbanization at the national level will increase. The goals will vary between countries as will the means to implement those goals. In Canada and Australia, it is possible that a locational decision-making framework along the Swedish lines will emerge, but with a more complex set of linkages to urban subsystem policies and plans deriving from provincial and state governments. Although no policies (or even frameworks for policies) have emerged, a step has been made in laying the groundwork for those policies. In Britain, with its more effective controls on the spread of 'daily' urban systems and an emerging regional 'system' strategy, the most probable outcome is an increase in co-ordination within regional planning. The importance of the latter, of course, reflects the population size and complexity of economic regions in Britain.

Clearly, in looking at the four countries together, one can hypothesize some convergence of interest and an increasing focus of policy thinking on the national space economy and on the urban systems which organize that economy. What these directions of thinking actually produce in the future in terms of results will be exciting to watch and, more importantly, to participate in.

# References

A. URBAN SYSTEMS RESEARCH AND NATIONAL
URBAN STRATEGIES

ABLER, R., JANELLE, D., PHILBRICK, A., and SOMMER, J., eds. (1974) *Human Geography in a Shrinking World*, Duxbury Press, North Scituate, Mass.

ALONSO, W. (1968a) "Urban and Regional Imbalances in Economic Development", *Economic Development and Cultural Change*, **17**: 1–14.

—— (1968b) "Equity and its Relation to Efficiency in Urbanization", *Working Paper 78*, Center for Planning and Development Research, University of California, Berkeley.

—— (1970a) "What are New Towns For?", *Urban Studies*, **7**: 37–55.

—— (1970b) "The Question of City Size and National Policy", *Working Paper 125*, Center for Planning and Development Research, University of California, Berkeley.

—— (1972) "The Economics of Urban Size", *Papers of the Regional Science Association*, **26**: 67–83.

—— (1973) "Urban Zero Population Growth", in The No-Growth Society, *Daedalus*, **102**, 4: 191–206.

—— and MEDRICH, E. (1971) "Spontaneous Growth Centers in Twentieth Century American Urbanization", *Working Paper 143*, Center for Planning and Development Research, University of California, Berkeley.

—— and MCGUIRE, C. (1972) "Pluralistic New Towns", *Lex et Scientia*, **9**, 3: 74–84.

AMERICAN SOCIETY OF PLANNING OFFICIALS (1971) "The Making of a National Urban Growth Policy", *Planning 1971*, A.S.P.O., Chicago.

ANSOFF, I. (1965) *Corporate Strategy*, McGraw-Hill, New York.

BASSETT, K. A., and HAGGETT, P. (1971) "Towards Short Term Forecasting for Cyclical Behaviour in a Regional System of Cities", in M. Chisholm, *et al.*, eds., *Regional Forecasting*, Butterworths, London, 389–413.

BECKMAN, N. (1971) "Development of a National Urban Growth Policy", *Journal of the American Institute of Planners*, **37**, 3: 146–60.

—— (1974) "National Urban Growth Policy: 1973: Congressional and Executive Action", *Journal of the American Institute of Planners*, **40**, 4: 226–42.

—— and LANGDON, B. (1972) *National Growth Policy: Legislative and Executive Actions*, Urban Land Institute, Washington.

BERGSMAN, J., GREENSTON, P., and HEALEY, R. (1972) "The Agglomeration Process in Urban Growth", *Urban Studies*, **9**, 3: 263–88.

BERRY, B. J. L. (1964) "Cities as Systems within Systems of Cities", *Papers and*

*Proceedings of the Regional Science Association*, **13**:147–63.

—— (1966) *Essays on Commodity Flows and the Spatial Structure of the Indian Economy*, Department of Geography, Research Paper 111, University of Chicago, Chicago.

—— (1967) *Strategies, Models and Economic Theories of Development in Rural Regions*, U.S. Government Printing Office, Washington.

—— (1968) *Metropolitan Area Definition: A Reevaluation of Concept and Statistical Practice*, Working Paper No. 28, U.S. Bureau of the Census, Washington.

——(1971a) "City Size and Economic Development", in L. Jakobson and V. Prakash, eds., *Urbanization and National Development*, Sage Publications, Beverly Hills, Calif., 111–55.

—— (1971b) "The Geography of the United States in the Year 2000", *Ekistics:* 339–51.

—— (1971c) "Contemporary Urbanization Processes", in U.S. National Academy of Sciences, *Geographical Perspectives on Urban Problems*, 94–107.

—— (1972a) "Latent Structure of the American Urban System", in B. J. L. Berry, ed., *City Classification Handbook*, Wiley Interscience, New York.

——(1972b) "Hierarchical Diffusion: The Basis of Developmental Filtering and Spread in a System of Growth Centres", in N. M. Hansen, ed., *Growth Centres in Regional Economic Development*, The Free Press, New York, 108–38.

—— (1973a) *The Human Consequences of Urbanization: Divergent Paths in the Urban Experience of the Twentieth Century*, MacMillan, London.

—— (1973b) *Growth Centers in the American Urban System*, Vol. 1, *Community Development and Regional Growth in the 60's and 70's*, Ballinger, Cambridge, Mass.

—— (1973c) "Deliberate Change in Spatial Systems: Goals, Strategies and Their Evaluation", Department of Geography, University of Chicago (mimeo).

—— and HORTON, F., eds. (1970) *Geographical Perspectives on Urban Systems: Text and Integrated Readings*, Prentice-Hall, Englewood Cliffs, N.J.

—— —— eds. (1974) *Urban Environmental Management: Planning for Pollution Control*, Prentice-Hall, Englewood Cliffs, N.J.

—— *et al.* (1974) *Land Use, Urban Form and Environmental Quality*, Department of Geography, Research Paper 155, University of Chicago, Chicago.

BOULDING, K. (1953) "Toward a General Theory of Growth", *Canadian Journal of Economics and Political Science*, **19**:326–40.

—— (1956) "General Systems Theory: The Skeleton of Science", *Management Science*, **2**:197–208.

—— (1970) *A Primer on Social Dynamics: History as Dialectics and Development,* The Free Press, New York.

BORCHERT, J. (1967) "American Metropolitan Evolution", *Geographical Review,* **57**: 301–22.

—— (1972) "America's Changing Metropolitan Regions", *Annals, Association of American Geographers,* **62**: 352–73.

BOURNE, L. S. (1974a) "Forecasting Urban Systems: Research Design, Alternative Methodologies and Urbanization Trends", *Regional Studies,* **8**: 197–210.

BROADEN, N. (1971) *Urban Policy Making,* Cambridge University Press, Cambridge.

BROWN, L. A. (1974) "Diffusion in a Growth Pole Context", *Discussion Paper 3,* Department of Geography, Ohio State University, Columbus.

BRYCE, H. J. (1973) "Identifying Socio-Economic Differences Between High and Low Income Metropolitan Areas", *Socio-Economic Planning Sciences,* **7**: 161–76.

CAMERON, G. C. (1972) *Regional Economic Development: The Federal Role,* Johns Hopkins University Press, London.

—— and WINGO, L., eds. (1973) *Cities, Regions and Public Policy,* Oliver and Boyd, Edinburgh.

CARSON, J. (1972) "A National Growth Policy", *Urban Land,* **31**, 2–10.

CARTER, H. (1972) *The Study of Urban Geography,* Edward Arnold, London.

CASETTI, E., KING, L. and JEFFREY, D. (1971) "Structural Imbalance in the U.S. Urban-Economic System, 1960–65", *Geographical Analysis,* **3**: 239–55.

CHADWICK, G. (1971) *A Systems View of Planning,* Pergamon Press, Oxford.

CHARNES, A., KOZMETSKY, G., and RUEFLI, T. (1972), "Information Requirements for Urban Systems: A View into the Possible Future", *Management Science,* **19**, 4, Part 2: 7–20.

CHEN, K., ed. (1972) *Urban Dynamics: Extensions and Reflections,* San Francisco Press, San Francisco.

—— et al. (1974) *Growth Policy: Population Environment and Beyond,* University of Michigan Press, Ann Arbor.

CHINOY, E., ed. (1972) *The Urban Future,* Lieber-Atherton, New York.

CHISHOLM, M. (1972) "Macro- and Micro- Approaches to Urban Systems Research", *The Geographical Journal,* **138**, 1: 60–3.

—— and MANNERS, G. (1971) "Geographic Space: A New Dimension of Public Concern and Policy", in M. Chisholm and G. Manners, eds., *Spatial Policy Problems of the British Economy,* Cambridge University Press, Cambridge, 1–23.

CLARK, C. (1967) *Population and Land Use,* MacMillan, London.

CLAWSON, M. (1971) *Suburban Land Conversion in the United States: An Economic and Governmental Process,* Johns Hopkins University Press, Baltimore, Md.

COOPER, W. W., EASTMAN, C., JOHNSON, N., and KORTANEK, K. O. (1971) "Systems Approaches to Urban Planning: Mixed Conditional, Adaptive and Other Alternatives", *Policy Sciences*, **1**, 4:511–29.

CURRIE, L. (1975) "The Interrelation of Urban and National Economic Planning", *Urban Studies*, **12**:37–46.

CURRY, L., and MACKINNON, R. D. (1974) "Aggregative Dynamic Urban Models Oriented Towards Policy", Report to the Ministry of State for Urban Affairs by the Centre for Urban and Community Studies, University of Toronto, reprinted as Report C-75-12 (External), May, 1975.

*Daedalus* (1973) Journal of the American Academy of Arts and Sciences, "The No-Growth Society", special issue, **102**, 4, Fall.

DAKIN, J. (1972) *Telecommunications in the Urban and Regional Planning Process*, University of Toronto Press, Toronto.

—— (1973) *Telecommunications and the Planning of Greater Metropolitan Regions*, University of Toronto Press, Toronto.

DARWENT, D. F. (1969) "Growth Poles and Growth Centres in Regional Planning—A Review", *Environment and Planning*, **1**:5–32.

DAVIS, K. (1972) *World Urbanization 1950–1970*, Vol. 2, Institute of Governmental Studies, University of California, Berkeley.

DERTHICK, M. (1972) *New Towns In-Town: Why a Federal Program Failed*, The Urban Institute, Washington.

DÖKMECI, V. F. (1973) "An Optimization Model for a Hierarchical Spatial System", *Journal of Regional Science*, **13**:439–52.

DOMANSKI, R. (1973) "Structure, Law of Motion and Optimal Path of Growth of Complex Urban Systems", *Economic Geography*, **49**:37–46.

DOXIADIS, C. A. (1967) "Developments Toward Ecumenopolis—The Great Lakes Megalopolis", *Ekistics*, **22**, 128:14–31.

DUNN, E. S. (1971) *Economic and Social Development: A Process of Social Learning*, Johns Hopkins University Press, Baltimore, Md.

DYE, T. R. (1972) *Understanding Public Policy*, Prentice-Hall, Englewood Cliffs, N.J.

DZIEWONSKI, K. (1971) "General Theory of Rank-Size Distributions in Regional Settlement Systems; ReAppraisal and Reformulation", *Papers of the Regional Science Association*, **29**:73–86.

ELKINS, T. H. (1973) *The Urban Explosion*, MacMillan, London.

EMERY, F. E., and TRIST, E. L. (1972) *Towards a Social Ecology: Contextual Appreciations of the Future in the Present*, Plenum Press, New York and London.

EUROPEAN CULTURAL FOUNDATION (1972) *Europa 2000: Fears and Hopes for European Civilization*, Vol. 1, Martinus Nijhoff, The Hague.

—— (1973) *The Unknown Urban Realm*, Martinus Nijhoff, The Hague.

EUROPEAN FREE TRADE ASSOCIATION (1968) *Regional Policy in E.F.T.A.: An Examination of the Growth Centre Idea*, University of Glasgow, Social and

Economic Studies, Occasional Paper No. 10, Oliver and Boyd, Edinburgh.

—— (1973) *National Settlement Strategies: A Framework for Regional Development*, E.F.T.A., Geneva.

EVANS, A. W. (1972) "The Pure Theory of City Size in an Industrial Economy", *Urban Studies*, 9: 49–77.

FLAX, M. J. (1972) *A Study in Comparative Urban Indicators*, The Urban Institute, Washington.

FORRESTER, J. N. (1969) *Urban Dynamics*, M.I.T. Press, Cambridge, Mass.

FRIEDEN, B. J., and MORRIS, R. (1968) *Urban Planning and Social Policy*, Basic Books, New York.

FRIEDMANN, J. (1966) *Regional Development Policy*, M.I.T. Press, Cambridge, Mass.

—— (1968a) "An Information Model of Urbanization", *Urban Affairs Quarterly*, 4, 2: 235–44.

—— (1968b) "The Strategy of Deliberate Urbanization", *Journal of the American Institute of Planners*, 34, 6: 364–73.

—— (1971) "Implementation of Urban-Regional Development Policies", University of California, School of Architecture and Urban Planning, Los Angeles (mimeo).

—— (1972a) "A General Theory of Polarized Development", in N. M. Hansen, ed., *Growth Centres in Regional Economic Development*, The Free Press, New York.

—— (1972b) "The Spatial Organization of Power and the Development of Urban Systems", University of California, School of Architecture and Urban Planning, Los Angeles (mimeo).

—— (1973) *Urbanization, Planning and National Development*, Sage Publications, Beverly Hills and London.

—— and MILLER, J. (1965) "The Urban Field", *Journal of the American Institute of Planners*, 31: 312–20.

GALBRAITH, J. K. (1973) *Economics and the Public Purpose*, Houghton Mifflin, Boston, Mass.

GARN, H. A. (1970) *New Cities, New Communities and Growth Centres*, The Urban Institute, Washington.

—— and WILSON, R. H. (1970) *A Critical Look at Urban Dynamics*, The Urban Institute, Washington.

GODSCHALK, D. R. ed., (1974) *Planning in America: Learning from Turbulence*, American Institute of Planners, Washington, D.C.

GOTTMANN, J. (1961) *Megalopolis*, Twentieth Century Fund, New York.

HÄGERSTRAND, T. (1972) "An Equitable Urban Structure", Report to the E.F.T.A. Working Party on New Patterns of Settlement, Geneva (mimeo).

—— and KUKLINSKI, A., eds. (1971) *Information Systems for Regional Development*, Lund Studies in Geography, Series B, No. 37, Gleerup, Lund, Sweden.

HANSEN, N. M. (1968) *French Regional Planning*, Edinburgh University Press, Edinburgh.

—— (1970) *Rural Poverty and the Urban Crisis: A Strategy for Regional Development*, Indiana University Press, Bloomington.

—— (1971) "A Growth Centre Strategy for the United States", *Review of Regional Studies*, **5**:161–73.

—— ed. (1972) *Growth Centres in Regional Economic Development*, The Free Press, New York.

—— (1973) *Location Preferences, Migration and Regional Growth*, Praeger, New York.

HARRIS, C. D. (1970) *Cities of the Soviet Union*, University of Chicago Press, Chicago.

HARVEY, D. (1971) "Social Processes, Spatial Form and the Redistribution of Real Income in an Urban System", in M. Chisholm, *et al.*, eds., *Regional Forecasting*, Butterworths, London, 270–300.

—— (1973) *Social Justice in the City*, Edward Arnold, London.

HARVEY, S. (1974) "A Dualistic Model of Urban Growth", *Annals of Regional Science*, **8**, 1:58–69.

HAWLEY, W., and ROGERS, D. (1974) *Improving the Quality of Urban Management*, Sage Publications, Beverly Hills, Calif.

HIRSCHMAN, A. O. (1968) *The Strategy of Economic Development*, Yale University Press, New Haven, Conn.

HOCH, I. (1972) "Income and City Size", *Urban Studies*, **9**: 299–328.

HOCHMAN, H. M., and PATERSON, G. E., eds. (1974) *Redistribution through Public Choice*, Columbia University Press, Irvington, New York.

HOROWITZ, I. L., ed. (1971) *The Use and Abuse of Social Science and Behavioral Science in National Policy-Making*, Transactions, New Brunswick, N.J.

—— (1971) "A Growth Center Strategy for the United States", *Review of Regional Studies*, **1**:161–73.

HUGHES, J. W. (1972) *Urban Indicators, Metropolitan Evolution and Public Policy*, Center for Urban Policy Research, Rutgers University, New Brunswick, N.J.

HUTTMAN, J. P. and E. D. (1973) "Dutch and British New Towns: Self-Containment and Socio-Economic Balance", *Growth and Change*, **4**, L:30–7.

INTERNATIONAL COLLOQUIUM (1971) *The Mastery of Urban Growth*, Meus en Ruinte, Brussels.

ISARD, W. (1970) *General Theory: Social, Political, Economic and Regional*, M.I.T. Press, Cambridge, Mass.

JAKOBSON, L. and PRAKASH, V., eds. (1971) *Urbanization and Economic Development*, Sage Publications, Beverly Hills, Calif.

JANTSCH, E., ed. (1969) *Perspectives of Planning*, O.E.C.D., Paris.

—— (1972) "Forecasting and the Systems Approach: A Critical Survey", *Policy Sciences*, **3**:475–98.

JEFFREY, D. (1974) "Regional Fluctuations in Unemployment within the U.S. Urban Economic System: A Study of the Spatial Interaction of Short Term Economic Change", *Economic Geography*, **50**, 2:111–23.

JOHNSTON, R. J., ed. (1972) *Urbanization in New Zealand: Geographical Essays*, A. H. and A. W. Reed, Wellington.

—— (1974) *Spatial Structures*, Methuen, London.

KAIN, J. F. (1966) "Urban Form and the Cost of Urban Services", *Discussion Paper 6*, Harvard Program on Regional and Urban Economics, Cambridge, Mass.

KHOREV, B. S. and KHODZHAYEV, D. G. (1972) "The Conception of a Unified System of Settlement and the Planned Regulation of City Growth in the USSR", *Soviet Geography*, **8**:90–8.

KING, L., CASETTI, E., and JEFFREY, D. (1969) "Economic Impulses in a Regional System of Cities: A Study of Spatial Interaction", *Regional Studies*, **3**:213–18.

KLAASSEN, L. (1968) *Social Amenities in Economic Growth*, O.E.C.D., Paris.

KONRAD, G., and SZELÉNYI, I. (1969) *Sociological Aspects of the Allocation of Housing: Experiences from a Socialist non-Market Economy*, Hungarian Academy of Sciences, Budapest.

KUKLINSKI, A. R., ed. (1972) *Growth Poles and Growth Centres in Regional Planning*, Mouton, The Hague.

—— and PETRELLA, R., eds. (1972) *Growth Poles and Regional Policy*, Mouton, The Hague.

LASUÉN, J. R. (1971) "Multi-Regional Economic Development: An Open-System Approach", in Hägerstrand and Kuklinski, eds., *Information Systems for Regional Development*, 160–211.

—— (1973) "Urbanization and Development: The Temporal Interaction Between Geographical Clusters", *Urban Studies*, **10**:163–88.

LAWTON, R. (1972) "An Age of Great Cities", *Town Planning Review*, **43**:199–224.

MAASS, A., ed. (1959) *Area and Power*, The Free Press, Glencoe, Ill.

MAUCH, S. P. (1973) "A Hierarchical Model of the Planning Process", *Town Planning Review*, **44**, 2:147–66.

MEADOWS, D. L., *et al.* (1972) *The Limits to Growth: A Report for the Club of Rome*, Universe, New York.

MEADOWS, P., and MIZRUCHI, E. H., eds. (1969) *Urbanism, Urbanization and Change: Comparative Perspectives*, Addison-Wesley, Reading, Mass.

MERA, K. (1973) "On Urban Agglomeration and Economic Efficiency", *Economic Development and Cultural Change*, **21**, 2:309–37.

MERLIN, P. (1971) *New Towns: Regional Planning and Development*, Methuen, London (translated by Margaret Sparks).

MESAROVIC, M. D., and REISMAN, A., eds. (1972) *Systems Approach and the City*, North Holland, Amsterdam.

MILLS, E. (1972) *Studies in the Structure of the Urban Economy*, Johns Hopkins University Press, Baltimore, Md.

MIRRLESS, J. A. (1972) "The Optimum Town", *Swedish Journal of Economics*, **74**: 114–35.

MORRISON, P. A. (1972) *Population Movements and the Shape of Urban Growth: Implications for Public Policy*, Rand Corporation, Santa Monica, Calif.

MOYNIHAN, D. P., ed. (1970) *Toward a National Urban Policy*, Basic Books, New York.

MYRDAL, G. (1967) *Economic Theory and Under-Developed Regions*, Duckworth and Co., London.

—— (1971) "National Planning for Healthy Cities", in S. B. Warner, ed., *Planning for a Nation of Cities*, 13–32. M.I.T. Press, Cambridge, Mass.

ODLUND, J., CASETTI, E., and KING, L. J. (1973) "Testing Hypotheses of Polarized Growth within a Central Place Hierarchy", *Economic Geography*, **49**: 74–9.

O.E.C.D. (1973a) *Main Economic Indicators*, O.E.C.D. Publications, Paris.

—— (1973b) *Regional Policy in Member Countries*, Report of the Industrial Committee, O.E.C.D., Paris.

—— (1973c) *National Urban Growth Policies and Strategies: Evaluation of Implementation Experience and Innovation*, O.E.C.D., Environmental Directorate, Paris (prepared by P. H. Friedly).

—— (1973d) *Social Concerns Common to Most O.E.C.D. Countries*, Manpower and Social Affairs Directorate, Paris.

OSBURN, F. J., and WHITTICK, A. (1963) *The New Towns: The Answer to Megalopolis*, L. Hill, London.

OZBEKHAM, H. (1969) "Toward a General Theory of Planning", in E. Jantsch, ed., *Perspectives of Planning*, O.E.C.D., Paris.

PAHL, R. (1971) "Poverty and the Urban System", in M. Chisholm and G. Manners, eds., *Spatial Policy Problems in the British Economy*, 126–45.

PARR, J. B. (1970) "Models of City Size in an Urban System", *Papers of the Regional Science Association*, **25**: 221–53.

—— (1973) "Structure and Size in the Urban System of Lösch", *Economic Geography*, **49**: 185–212.

—— and SUZUKI, K. (1973) "Settlement Populations and the Lognormal Distribution", *Urban Studies*, **10**: 335–52.

PEDERSEN, P. O. (1970) "Innovation Diffusion within and between National Urban Systems", *Geographical Analysis*, **2**: 223.

PERLOFF, H. S., et al. (1960) *Regions, Resources and Economic Growth*, Johns Hopkins University Press, Baltimore, Md.

—— and SANDBERG, N. C. (1973) *New Towns: Why and For Whom?*, Praeger, New York.

PERROUX, F. (1950) "Economic Space: Theory and Applications", *Quarterly Journal of Economics*, **64**:89–104.

PRED, A. R. (1966) *The Spatial Dynamics of U.S. Urban Industrial Growth 1800–1914*, M.I.T. Press, Cambridge, Mass.

—— (1971) "Large City Interdependence and the Pre-Electronic Diffusion of Innovations in the U.S.", *Geographical Analysis*, **3**:165–81.

—— (1973a) *Urban Growth and the Circulation of Information: The United States System of Cities, 1790–1840*, Harvard University Press, Cambridge, Mass.

—— (1973b) "The Growth and Development of Systems of Cities in Advanced Economies", in A. R. Pred and G. Törnqvist, *Systems of Cities and Information Flows. Two Essays*, Lund Studies in Geography, Series B No. 38, Gleerup, Lund, Sweden, 9–82.

—— (1974) *Major Job-Providing Organizations and Systems of Cities*, Commission on College Geography, Resource Paper No. 27, A.A.G. Washington, D.C.

RICHARDSON, H. W. (1969) *Regional Economics*, Praeger, New York.

—— (1971) *Urban Economics*, Penguin Educational, London.

—— (1972) "Optimality in City Size, Systems of Cities and Urban Policy: A Sceptic's View", *Urban Studies*, **9**:29–48.

—— (1973a) "Theory of the Distribution of City Sizes: Review and Prospects", *Regional Studies*, **7**:239–51.

—— (1973b) *The Economics of Urban Size*, D. C. Heath, London.

—— (1973c) *Regional Growth Theory*, MacMillan, London.

—— (1973d) "The Effectiveness of Policy Instruments to Encourage the Growth of Small and Medium Sized Cities", Centre for Research in the Social Sciences, University of Canterbury (mimeo).

ROBINSON, E. A. G., ed. (1969) *Backward Areas in Advanced Countries*, MacMillan, London.

—— (1969) "Location Theory, Regional Economics and Backward Areas", in E. A. G. Robinson, ed., *Backward Areas in Advanced Countries*, 3–20.

ROBINSON, I. M., ed. (1972) *Decision-Making in Urban Planning*, Sage Publications, Beverly Hills, Calif.

RODWIN, L. (1970) *Nations and Cities: A Comparison of Strategies for Urban Growth*, Houghton Mifflin, Boston, Mass.

—— and Associates (1969) *Planning Urban Growth and Regional Development*, M.I.T. Press, Cambridge, Mass.

ROSE, RICHARD, ed. (1974) *The Management of Urban Change in Britain and Germany*, Sage Publications, Beverly Hills, Calif.

ROTHBLATT, D. N., ed. (1974) *National Policy for Urban and Regional Development*, Lexington Books, D. C. Heath, London.

SCHACHER, A. S. (1971) "Israel's Development Towns: Evaluation of a National

Urbanization Policy", *Journal of the American Institute of Planners*, **37**: 362–72.

SCHILLER, R. K. (1971) "Location Trends of Specialist Services", *Regional Studies*, **5**: 1–10.

SCHWIND, P. J. (1971) *Migration and Regional Development in the United States 1950–1960*, Department of Geography Research Paper 133, University of Chicago, Chicago.

SCOTT, R. W., ed. (1974) *Management and Control of Growth: Issues, Techniques, Problems, Trends*, Vol. 1, Urban Land Institute, Washington.

SIEGEL, J. and WOODYARD, M. (1974) "Position in the Urban Hierarchy as a Determinant of In-Migration", *Land Economics*, **50**, 1: 75–82.

SMITH, D. M. (1973) *The Geography of Social Well-Being in the United States. An Introduction to Territorial Social Indicators*, McGraw-Hill, New York.

STEIN, C. S. (1957) *Toward New Towns for America*, Reinhold, New York.

STEINITZ, C. and ROGERS, P. (1970) *A Systems Model of Urbanization and Change*, M.I.T. Press, London.

STEWART, M., ed. (1972) *The City: Problems of Planning*, Penguin, London.

STILWELL, F. J. B. (1972) *Regional Economic Policy*, MacMillan, London.

STOHR, W. (1974) *Interurban Systems and Regional Economic Development*, Commission on College Geography, Resource Paper No. 26, A.A.G. Washington, D.C.

STOLPER, W. F. (1965) "Spatial Order and the Economic Growth of Cities", *Economic Development and Cultural Change*, **3**: 137–46.

STONE, P. A. (1974) *The Structure, Size and Costs of Urban Settlements*, Cambridge University Press, Cambridge.

STRONG, A. L. (1971) *Planned Urban Environments*, John Hopkins University Press, Baltimore, Md.

THIRWALL, A. P. (1974) "Regional Economic Disparities and Regional Policy in the Common Market", *Urban Studies*, **11**, 1: 1–12.

THOMAS, M. D. (1972) "The Regional Problem, Structural Change and Growth Pole Theory", in A. Kuklinski, ed., *Growth Poles and Growth Centres in Regional Planning*, 69–102.

THOMPSON, W. R. (1965) *Preface to Urban Economies*, Johns Hopkins University Press, Baltimore, Md.

—— (1972) "The National System of Cities as an Object of Public Policy", *Urban Studies*, **9**: 99–116.

UNITED NATIONS, RESEARCH INSTITUTE FOR SOCIAL DEVELOPMENT (U.N.R.I.S.D.) (1973) *Regional Disaggregation of National Policies and Plans*, Mouton, The Hague.

—— CENTRE FOR HOUSING, BUILDING AND PLANNING (1973), "Interregional Seminar on New Towns", *Human Settlements*, **3**, 4: 1–26.

—— ECONOMIC COMMISSION FOR EUROPE (1973) *Urban and Regional*

*Research in E.C.E. Countries*, Svensk Byggtjanst, Stockholm.

*Urban Studies* (1972) "Special Issue on National Urban Policy", **9**, 1, Oliver and Boyd, Edinburgh (see Cameron and Wingo, 1973).

U.S. COMMISSION ON POPULATION AND THE AMERICAN FUTURE (1972) *Population and the American Future*, U.S. Government Printing Office, Washington.

U.S. DOMESTIC COUNCIL COMMITTEE (1972) *Report on National Growth, 1972*, U.S. Government Printing Office, Washington.

U.S. NATIONAL ACADEMY OF SCIENCES (1971) *Rapid Population Growth: Consequences and Policy Implications*, Johns Hopkins University Press, Baltimore, Md.

—— (1972) *Geographical Perspectives on Urban Problems*, A Symposium, The Academy, Washington.

U.S. NATIONAL ADVISORY COMMISSION ON RURAL POVERTY (1967) *The People Left Behind*, U.S. Government Printing Office, Washington.

U.S. NATIONAL GOALS STAFF (1970) *Toward Balanced Growth: Quantity and Quality*, U.S. Government Printing Office, Washington.

VANCE, J. E., Jr. (1970) *The Merchants World. The Geography of Wholesaling*, Prentice-Hall, Englewood Cliffs, N.J.

VICKERS, Sir G. (1971) *Freedom in a Rocking Boat: Changing Values in an Instable Society*, Basic Books, New York.

—— (1973) "Values, Norms and Policies", *Policy Sciences*, **4**: 103–11.

—— (1974) "Forecasting and Planning", *Journal of the Town Planning Institute*, April 1974.

VÖN BOVENTER, E. (1973) "City-Size Systems: Theoretical Issues, Empirical Regularities and Planning Guides", *Urban Studies*, 10: 145–62.

WÄRNERYD, O. (1968) *Interdependence in Urban Systems*, Regionkonsult Akticholag, Göteborg.

WEBBER, M. J. (1972) *Impact of Uncertainty on Location*, M.I.T. Press, Cambridge, Mass.

WEBBER, M. M. (1973) "Urbanization and Communications", in G. Gerbner, *et al.*, eds., *Communications Technology and Social Policy*, Wiley, New York, 293–304.

WEBER, A. F. (1899) *The Growth of Cities in the Nineteenth Century*, MacMillan, New York.

WENDT, P. F. (1962) *Housing Policy—The Search for Solutions: A Comparison of the United Kingdom, Sweden, West Germany and the United States*, University of California Press, Berkeley.

WHOLEY, J. S., *et al.*, eds. (1970) *Federal Evaluation Policy: Analyzing the Effects of Public Programs*, The Urban Institute, Washington.

WIDMAIER, H. P. (1970) *Infrastructure Planning for the Decades Ahead*, Council of Europe, Strasburg.

WILLIAMSON, J. G. (1965) "Regional Inequality and the Process of National

Development: A Description of the Patterns", *Economic Development and Cultural Change*, **13**: 3–45.

WILSON, A. G. (1970) *Entropy in Urban and Regional Modelling*, Pion, London.

—— ed. (1972) *Patterns and Processes in Urban and Regional Systems*, London Papers in Regional Science, 3, Pion, London.

WINGO, L. (1972) "Issues in a National Urban Development Strategy for the United States", *Urban Studies*, **9**: 3–27.

—— (1973a) "The Quality of Life: Toward a Micro-economic Definition", *Urban Studies*, **10**: 3–18.

—— ed. (1973b) *Metropolitanization and Public Services*, No. 3 in the Governance of Metropolitan Regions Series, Johns Hopkins University Press, Baltimore, Md., and London.

WINNICK, L. (1966) "Place Prosperity vs. People Prosperity: Welfare Considerations in the Geographic Redistribution of Economic Activity", in *Essays in Urban Land Economics*, University of California Press, Los Angeles.

WORLD BANK (1972) *Urbanization*, I.B.R.D., Washington.

WULFF, R. M. (1973) "Resources in the Comparative Study of Urbanization: Annotated Guide, Bibliography and Directory", *Comparative Urbanization Studies*, School of Architecture and Urban Planning, University of California, Los Angeles.

YOUNG, M. E., ed. (1968) *Forecasting and the Social Sciences*, Heinemann, London.

## B. URBAN BRITAIN

ABERCROMBIE, P. (1945) *Greater London Plan 1944*, H.M.S.O., London.

ADAMS, J. (1970) "Westminster: The Fourth London Airport", *Area*, **2**: 1–9.

ARMEN, G. (1972) "A Classification of Cities and City Regions in England and Wales, 1966", *Regional Studies*, **6**: 149–82.

ASHWORTH, W. (1964) *The Genesis of Modern British Town Planning*, Routledge and Kegan Paul, London.

BARBER, JOHN (1973) "New Towns in the United Kingdom: Administrative, Social and Financial Aspects". Paper presented to the U.N. International Seminar on New Towns, London, 4–19 June, 1973.

BARLOW REPORT (1940) *Report of the Royal Commission on the Distribution of Industrial Population*, Cmd. 6153, H.M.S.O., London.

BASSETT, K., and HAGGETT, P. (1971) "Towards Short-Term Forecasting for Cyclic Behaviour in a Regional System of Cities", in M. Chisholm *et al.*, eds., *Regional Forecasting*, Butterworths, London, 389–413.

BEST, R. H., and ROGERS, A. N. (1973) *The Urban Countryside*, Faber and Faber, London.

BRIGGS, A. (1963) *Victorian Cities*, Odhams, London.

BROWN, A. J. (1972) *The Framework of Regional Economics in Britain,* Cambridge University Press, Cambridge.

BUCHANAN, C. (1972) *The State of Britain,* Faber and Faber, London.

BURNS, W. (1973) "National Policies for Urban Development in the United Kingdom". Paper presented to the U.N. International Seminar on New Towns, London, 4–19 June, 1973.

CAMERON, G. C. (1970) "Growth Areas, Growth Centres and Regional Conversion", *Scottish Journal of Political Economy,* 21: 19–38.

—— and EVANS, A. W. (1973) "The British Conurbation Centres", *Regional Studies,* 7: 47–55.

CENTRE FOR ENVIRONMENTAL STUDIES (1973) "Urban and Regional Research in the U.K. 1972–3: An Annotated List", *Information Paper 28,* London.

CHERRY, G. E. (1972) *Urban Change and Planning: A History of Urban Development in Britain since 1750,* International Scholarly Books Services, Portland, Oregon.

CHISHOLM, M. (1970) "On the Making of a Myth? How Capital Intensive is Industry Investing in the Development Areas", *Urban Studies,* 7, 3: 289–93.

—— ed. (1972) *Resources for Britain's Future,* Barnes and Noble, New York.

—— and Manners, G., eds. (1971) *Spatial Policy Problems of the British Economy,* Cambridge University Press, Cambridge.

—— —— (1971) "Geographical Space: A New Dimension of Public Concern and Policy" in Chisholm and Manners, eds., *Spatial Policy Problems of the British Economy,* 1–23.

CLAWSON, M., and HALL, P. (1973) *Planning and Urban Growth: An Anglo-American Comparison,* Johns Hopkins University Press, Baltimore, Md.

COATES, B. G., and RAWSTRON, E. M. (1971) *Regional Variations in Britain,* Batsford, London.

CORDEY-HAYES, M., and GLEAVE, D. (1973) "Migration Movements and the Differential Growth of City Regions in England and Wales", Centre for Environmental Studies, *Research Paper 1,* London.

COWAN, P. (1969) *The Office: A Facet of Urban Growth,* Heinemann, London.

—— et al. (1969) *Developing Patterns of Urbanization,* Sage Publications, Beverley Hills, Calif.

—— ed. (1973) *The Future of Planning,* Heinemann, London.

CRIPPS, E. L., and FOOT, D. H. S. (1970) "The Urbanization Effects of a Third London Airport", *Environment and Planning,* 2: 153–92.

CULLINGWORTH, J. B. (1972) *Town and Country Planning in Britain,* Allen and Unwin, London.

—— (1973a) *The Social Framework of Planning,* Vol. 1 of Problems of an Urban Society, Allen and Unwin, London.

—— (1973b) *The Social Content of Planning,* Vol. 2 of Problems of an Urban Society, Allen and Unwin, London.

—— ed. (1973c) *Planning for Change*, Vol. 3 of Problems of an Urban Society, Allen and Unwin, London.

DEPARTMENT OF ECONOMIC AFFAIRS (1967) *The Development Areas: A Proposal for Regional Employment Premiums*, H.M.S.O., London.

DEPARTMENT OF THE ENVIRONMENT (1971) *Long Term Population Distribution in Great Britain*. Report of an Interdepartmental Study Group, H.M.S.O., London.

DEPARTMENT OF GEOGRAPHY (1974) "Urban Change in Britain: 1966–1971", *Working Report No. 1*, London School of Economics and Political Science, London.

DERBYSHIRE, A., *et al.* (1973) "Planning Methodology for Urban Development and New Towns". Paper presented to the U.N. International Seminar on New Towns, London, 4–19 June, 1973.

DEVELOPMENT COMMISSIONERS (1974) *Change and Development in Rural Areas*, Thirty-third report, for the eight years ending 31 March 1973, H.M.S.O., London.

DIAMOND, D. (1972) "New Towns in Their Regional Context", in Town and Country Planning Association, *New Towns The British Experience*, 54–65.

—— and MCLOUGHLIN, J. B., eds. (1973) *Progress in Planning*, Vol. 1, Pergamon, Oxford.

DONNISON, D., and EVERSLEY, D. E. C., eds. (1973) *London: Urban Patterns, Problems and Policies*, Heinemann Educational, London.

*The Economist* (1973) "The Community View of the Folk Beyond the Fringe", Vol. 247, 3 February 1973.

EUROPEAN FREE TRADE ASSOCIATION (1973) *Toward a National Settlement Strategy: A Framework for Regional Development*, EFTA, Geneva.

EVERSLEY, D. E. C. (1972) "Rising Costs and Static Incomes", *Urban Studies*, **9**, 3:347–68.

—— *et al.* (1965) *Population Growth and Planning Policy*, University of Birmingham, Birmingham.

FOLEY, D. L. (1963) *Controlling London's Growth*, University of California Press, Berkeley.

—— (1972) *Governing the London Region*, University of California Press, Berkeley.

FORBES, J., ed. (1974) *Studies in Social Science and Planning*, Scottish Academic Press, Edinburgh.

FOSTER, C. D., and SMITH, J. F. (1970) "Allocation of Central Government Budgets over City Regions", *Urban Studies*, **6**, 2:210–26.

GEDDES, P. (1949 rev. ed.) *Cities in Evolution*, Williams and Norgate, London.

GODDARD, J. (1973) "Information Flows and the Development of the Urban System, Theoretical Considerations and Policy Implications". Paper presented to the Urban Economics Conference, University of Keele, July.

—— (1974) "The National System of Cities as Framework for Urban and

Regional Policy", in M. Sant, ed. *Regional Policy and Planning for Europe*, Saxon House, London, 101–127.

GREGORY, D. (1970) *Green Belts and Development Control*, University of Birmingham, Centre for Urban and Regional Research, Birmingham.

HALL, P. (1968) "Land Use—the Spread of Towns into the Countryside", in M. E. Young, ed., *Forecasting and the Social Sciences*, Heinemann, London, 95–117.

—— (1969 rev.) *London 2000*, Faber and Faber, London.

—— (1971) "Spatial Structure of Metropolitan England and Wales", in M. Chisholm and G. Manners, eds., *Spatial Policy Problems of the British Economy*, 96–125.

——, GRACEY, H., DREWETT, R., and THOMAS, R. (1973) *The Containment of Urban England*, Vol. 1: *Urban and Metropolitan Growth Processes* (or Megalopolis Denied); Vol. 2: *The Planning System: Objectives, Operations, Impacts*, Allen and Unwin, London.

HARDMAN, Sir H. (1973) *A Review of the Possibility of Dispersing More Government Work from London*, Cmnd. 5322, H.M.S.O., London.

HART, R. A. (1972) "Regional Growth in Employment in the Manufacturing and Service Sectors, 1960 to 1965. The U.K. Experience and Expectation", *Tijdschrift voor Economische en Sociale Geographie*, **63**, 2: 88–93.

HOLMANS, A. E. (1964) "Industrial Development Certificates and Control of the Growth of Employment in South-East England", *Urban Studies*, **1**, 2: 144–7.

HOWARD, E. (1898) *A Peaceful Path to Real Reform.* Reprinted as *Garden Cities of Tomorrow*, 1965, ed. F. J. Osborn, Faber and Faber, London.

INSTITUTE OF ECONOMIC AFFAIRS (1973) *Regional Policy Forever*, The Institute, London.

JACKSON, J. N. (1972) *The Urban Future. A Choice Between Alternatives*, Allen and Unwin, London.

KIVELL, P. T. (1972) "A Note on Metropolitan Areas, 1961–71", *Area*, **4**, 3: 179–84.

LEE, C. H. (1971) *Regional Economic Growth in the United Kingdom Since the 1880's*, McGraw-Hill, New York.

LEVER, W. F. (1973) "A Markov Approach to the Optimal Size of Cities in England and Wales", *Urban Studies*, **10**: 353–65.

LOCATION OF OFFICES BUREAU (1969) *Offices in a Regional Setting*, LOB, London.

—— (1972) *Annual Report 1971–2*, LOB, London.

MANNERS, G., ed. (1972) *Regional Development in Britain*, Wiley, New York.

MCCRONE G. (1969) *Regional Policy in Britain*, Allen and Unwin, London.

McLOUGHLIN, J. B., and THORNEY, J. (1972), "Some Problems in Structure Planning: A Literature Review", Centre for Environmental Studies, *Information Paper 27*, London.

—— —— (1973) "Structure Planning: A Preliminary Testing of Some Research Hypotheses in Relation to Current Practice", Centre for Environmental Studies, *Working Paper 79*, London.

*Monthly Magazine* (1811), Vol. 31, 1, February, reprinted as "Economic Base and City Size", *Land Economics*, **50**, 2, 1974: 202–5.

NEEDLEMAN, L., and SCOTT, B. (1964) "Regional Problems and the Location of Industry Policy in Britain", *Urban Studies*, **1**, 2: 159–72.

ORGANIZATION FOR ECONOMIC CO-OPERATION AND DEVELOPMENT (1970) *The Regional Factor in Economic Development*, OECD, Paris.

OSBURN, F. J., and WHITTICK, A. (1969 rev.) *The New Towns: The Answer to Megalopolis*, Leonard Hill, London.

PERRATON, J. (1970) "Urban Systems: Data Collection and Management for a Complex Model", *Working Paper No. 46*, Land Use and Built Form Studies, Cambridge.

RHODES, J., and KAN, A. (1972) *Office Dispersal and Regional Policy*, Cambridge University Press, Cambridge.

ROBSON, B. (1973) *Urban Growth: An Approach*, Methuen, London.

RODWIN, L. (1956) *The British New Towns Policy*, Harvard University Press, Cambridge, Mass.

SCHAFFER, F. (1972a) *The New Town Story*, Granada, London.

—— (1972b) "The New Town Movement", in *New Towns: The British Experience*, Charles Knight, London, 11–21.

SELF, P. (1971) *Metropolitan Planning: The Planning System of Greater London*, Greater London Papers, No. 14, London.

—— (1972) "Introduction", in *New Towns: The British Experience*, Charles Knight, London.

SENIOR, D. (1973) "Planning and the Public", in P. Cowan, ed., *The Future of Planning*, 113–31.

SMITH, R. D. P. (1968) "The Changing Urban Hierarchy", *Regional Studies*, **2**: 1–19.

SOUTH EAST JOINT PLANNING TEAM (1970) *Strategy Plan for the South East*, H.M.S.O., London.

STONE, P. A. (1970) *Urban Development in Britain: Standards, Costs and Resources*, Vol. 1, Cambridge University Press, Cambridge.

TANNER, M. F., and WILLIAMS, A. F. (1967) "Port Development and National Planning Strategy", *Journal of Transport Economics and Policy*, **1**, 3: 1–10.

THOMAS, D. (1970) *London's Green Belt*, Faber and Faber, London.

THOMAS, R. (1969) *London's New Towns*. Political and Economic Planning, Broadsheet 510, PEP, London.

TOWN AND COUNTRY PLANNING ASSOCIATION (1972) *New Towns: The British Experience*, Charles Knight, London.

U.K. OFFICE OF INFORMATION (1964) *The New Towns in Britain*, British Information Services, London.

—— (1968) *Regional Development in Britain*, H.M.S.O., London.
VAUGHAN, R. (1843) *The Age of Great Cities*, Jackson and Walford, London.
WESTAWAY, J. (1973) "The Spatial Hierarchy of Business Organizations and Its Implications for the British Urban System", *Discussion Paper No. 46*, Department of Geography, London School of Economics and Political Science.
YANNOPOULOS, G. (1973) "Local Income Effects of Office Relocation", *Regional Studies*, 7: 33–46.

C. URBAN SWEDEN

ADAMS, C. (1973) "Stockholm's Success: Political Accommodation in the Metropolis", *Growth and Change*, 4, 3: 212–32.
ANDERSSON, A. E. (1973) "Regional Economic Policy—the Swedish Experience", Economic Institute, Göteborg (mimeo).
—— and JUNGEN, R. (1968) "Metropolitan Growth and Unbalanced Economic Development", *Plan*, 22: 12–23.
ÅSTRÖM, K. (1967) *City Planning in Sweden*, The Swedish Institute, Stockholm.
BYLUND, E. (1969) "Industrial Location Policy and the Problems of Sparsely Populated Areas in Sweden", in E. A. G. Robinson, ed., *Backward Areas in Advanced Countries*, MacMillan, London, 196–209.
—— (1972) "The Central-Place Structure and Accessibility to Services in Northern and Western Sweden", *Plan International*, 26: 31–35.
CARLESTAM, G., and LUNDAHL, I. (1972) "Environmental and Planning Research in Sweden", *Plan International*, 26: 2–4.
DEPARTMENT OF THE INTERIOR, ERU (1970) *Balanced Regional Development*, Report of the Expert Group for Regional Studies (ERU), Stockholm.
DEPARTMENT OF THE INTERIOR, MINISTRY OF LABOUR AND HOUSING (1973) "Report on Regional Policy in Sweden", Stockholm, 3 March 1973.
*The Economist* (1974) "Sweden: Which Way Now? A Survey", 13 April 1974.
EFTA (European Free Trade Association) Economic Development Committee (1973) *Swedish Government Relocation Policy in Norrköping*, Report of the Working Party on New Patterns of Settlement, Stockholm.
EMMELIN, LARS (1973) "Environmental Planning in Sweden", Royal Ministry for Foreign Affairs, Stockholm (mimeo).
GODLUND, S., and WÄRNERYD, O. (1968) "Applied Studies of the Urbanization Process", *Plan*, 22: 31–40.
GUTELAND, G. (1972) "Regional Policy Research in Sweden", *Plan International*, 26: 5–9.
HÄGERSTRAND, T. (1965) "Aspects of the Spatial Structure of Social Communication and the Diffusion of Information", *Papers of the Regional Science Association*, 16: 28–42.

—— (1970) *Urbaniseringen*, Gleerup, Lund.

—— (1972) "An Equitable Urban Structure", Report to EFTA, Economic Development Committee, Working Party on New Patterns of Settlement, Geneva (mimeo).

—— and KUKLINSKI, A. R., eds. (1971) *Information Systems for Regional Development*, Lund Studies in Geography, Series B, Human Geography, No. 37, Gleerup, Lund.

HANCOCK, M. D. (1972) *Sweden: The Politics of Post-Industrial Change*, Dryden Press, Hinsdale, Ill.

HANNERBERG, D. D., *et al.*, eds. (1957) *Migration in Sweden: A Symposium*, Lund Studies in Geography, Series B, Human Geography, No. 13, Gleerup, Lund.

HOLM, PER (1957) *Swedish Housing*, The Swedish Institute, Stockholm.

INRIKESDEPARTEMENT (1972) *Regionalpolitiskt handlingsprogram*, Proposition 1972: 111, Bilaga 1, Ministry of Labour, Stockholm.

—— (1973) "Report on Regional Policy in Sweden", Stockholm (mimeo).

JUNGEN, R., and LÖNNROTH, J. (1972) "Relations between Physical and Economic Planning", *Plan*, 26: 55–64.

KRISTENSSON, F. (1967) *People, Firms and Regions: A Structural Analysis*, Stockholm School of Economics, Stockholm.

LUNDKVIST, S. (1973) "Management of Land and Water Resources in Sweden", Royal Ministry for Physical Planning and Local Environment, Stockholm (mimeo).

ÖDMANN, E. (1973) "Some Views on Land Ownership in Urban Planning and Housing Production in Sweden", *Geoforum*, 13: 31–41.

—— and DAHLBERG, G.-B. (1970) *Urbanization in Sweden: Means and Methods of Planning*, National Institute of Building Research, Stockholm.

OLSSON, G., and PERSSON, A. (1963) "The Spacing of Central Places in Sweden", *Papers of the Regional Science Association*, 12: 87–93.

ORGANIZATION FOR ECONOMIC CO-OPERATION AND DEVELOPMENT (1972) *Sweden*, OECD Publications, Paris.

PETERS, B. G. (1973) "Income Inequalities in Sweden and the United Kingdom: A Longitudinal Analysis", *Acta Sociologica*, 16: 108–20.

*Plan* (1972) Special Issue, Vol. 26, Swedish Society for Town and Country Planning.

PRED, A. R. (1973c) "Urbanization, Domestic Planning Problems and Swedish Geographical Research", *Progress in Geography*, Vol. 5, Edward Arnold, London, 1–76.

ROYAL MINISTRY FOR FOREIGN AFFAIRS, ROYAL MINISTRY OF AGRICULTURE (1971a), *The Human Work Environment: Swedish Experiences, Trends and Future Problems*, Report to the U.N. Conference on the Human Environment, Stockholm.

—— (1971b) *Urban Conglomerates as Psycho-social Human Stressors.*

*General Aspects, Swedish Trends and Psychological and Medical Implications*, Report to the U.N. Conference on the Human Environment, Stockholm.

—— (1972) *Urbanization and Planning in Sweden*, Report to the U.N. Conference on the Human Environment, Stockholm.

ROYAL MINISTRY FOR FOREIGN AFFAIRS, AGRICULTURE, PHYSICAL PLANNING AND LOCAL GOVERNMENT (1972) *Management of Land and Water Resources*, Report to the U.N. Conference on the Human Environment, Stockholm.

ROYAL MINISTRY OF LABOUR AND HOUSING AND THE MINISTRY OF PHYSICAL PLANNING AND LOCAL GOVERNMENT (1973) *Planning Sweden. Regional Development Planning and Management of Land and Water Resources*, Report on Regional Policy in Sweden, March 3, 1973, Allmänna forlaget, Stockholm.

STRONG, A. L. (1971) *Planned Urban Environments*, Johns Hopkins University Press, Baltimore, Md.

SWEDISH COUNCIL FOR BUILDING RESEARCH (1972) *Urban Planning Research: A Problem Analysis*, Stockholm.

THORNGREN, B. (1970) "How do Contact Systems Affect Regional Development?", *Environment and Planning*, 2: 409–27.

THUFVESSON, B. (1973) "Sweden's New Regional Planning Legislation", Department of the Interior, Stockholm (mimeo).

TÖRNQVIST, G. (1970) *Contact Systems and Regional Development*, Lund Studies in Geography, Series B, Human Geography, No. 35, Gleerup, Lund.

—— et al. (1971) *Multiple Location Analysis*, Lund Studies in Geography, Series C. General, Gleerup, Lund.

VINDE, P. (1971) *Swedish Government Administration*, The Swedish Institute, Stockholm.

WÄRNERYD, O. (1968) *Interdependence in Urban Systems*, Göteborgs Universitets, Geografiska Institutionen, Series B, Göteborg.

—— (1971) "An Operational Model for Regional Planning and Development Control", in T. Hägerstrand and A. R. Kuklinski, eds., *Information Systems for Regional Development*, 230–45.

WENDEL, B. (1957), "Regional Aspects of Internal Migration and Mobility in Sweden", in D. Hannerberg et al., eds., *Migration in Sweden: A Symposium*, 7–26.


D. URBAN AUSTRALIA

ABBOT, C. J., and NAIRN, C., eds. (1969) *Economic Growth of Australia*, Melbourne University Press, Melbourne.

ARNOT, R. H. (1973) "Regionalism and Possibilities for Dispersal of Urban

Settlement in Australia", *Royal Australian Planning Institute Journal*, 11, 3:77–85.

AUSTRALIAN INSTITUTE OF POLITICAL SCIENCE (1966) *Australian Cities: Chaos or Planned Growth*, Angus and Robertson, Melbourne.

AUSTRALIAN INSTITUTE OF URBAN STUDIES (1972a) *The Price of Land, Second Report of the Task Force on the Price of Land*, The Institute, Canberra.

—— (1972b) *New Cities for Australia, First Report of the Task Force on New Cities for Australia*, The Institute, Canberra.

—— (1972c) *Proceedings of the Annual Meeting of the Australian Institute of Urban Affairs*, October 1972, The Institute, Canberra.

AUSTRALIAN LABOUR PARTY (1971) *Federal Platform and Policy*, Sydney, May 1971.

AUSTRALIAN NATIONAL LIBRARY (1971) *Bibliography of Urban Studies in Australia*, First Edition 1966–8, Canberra.

BLAINEY, G. (1966) *The Tyranny of Distance*, Sun Books, Melbourne.

BOURNE, L. S. (1974b) "Urban Systems in Australia and Canada: Comparative Notes and Research Questions", *Australian Geographical Studies*, 12:152–72.

BROTCHIE, J. F. (1971) *Systems and Urban Development*, Report SR5, Division of Building Research, CSIRO, Melbourne.

BURNLEY, I. H., ed. (1974) *Urbanization in Australia—The Post War Experience*, Cambridge University Press, Cambridge.

CAMERON, B. (1971) *Australia's Economic Policies*, Cheshire, Melbourne.

CLARKE, G. (1970) "Urban Australia", in A. F. Davies and S. Encel, eds., *Australian Society*, Cheshire, Melbourne, 31–83.

CLARKE, N., ed. (1970) *Analysis of Urban Development*, University of Melbourne Press, Melbourne.

COMMITTEE OF COMMONWEALTH/STATE OFFICIALS (1972) *Report of the Committee of Commonwealth/State Officials on Decentralization*, AGPS, Canberra.

COMMONWEALTH BUREAU OF ROADS (1972) *Population Estimates for Australian Cities 1970–2010*, AGPS, Canberra.

COMMONWEALTH MINISTRY OF POST-WAR RECONSTRUCTION (1949) *Regional Planning in Australia*, AGPS, Canberra.

DAY, P. D. (1972) "The Economic and Sociological Case for Decentralization", paper preseented to the 44th ANZAAS Congress, 17 August.

DEPARTMENT OF URBAN AND REGIONAL DEVELOPMENT (1973) *First Annual Report 1972–3*, AGPS, Canberra.

DOWNING, R. I. (1973) *The Australian Economy*, Weidenfeld and Nicolson, London.

FOSTER, C., ed. (1970) *Australian Economic Development*, Allen and Unwin, London.

GEISSMAN, J. R., and WOOLMINGTON, E. R. (1971) "A Theoretical Location Concept for Decentralization in Southeastern Australia", *New Zealand Geographer*, **27**:69–78.

GREENWOOD, G., ed. (1965) *Australia—A Social and Political History*, Angus and Robertson, Sydney.

HARRISON, P. (1966) "City Planning in Australia: What Went Wrong?", in AIPS, *Australian Cities: Chaos or Planned Growth*, 60–87.

—— (1971) "Planning the Metropolis—A Case Study", in R. S. Parker and P. N. Troy, eds., *The Politics of Urban Growth*, 61–99.

—— (1973) *Population Objectives for Australian Cities*, National Population Enquiry, Commissioned Paper No. 10, Canberra.

HARVEY, R. O., and CLARK, W. A. V. (1964) "Controlling Urban Growth: The New Zealand and Australian Experience", *The Appraisal Journal*, **32**, 4:551–8.

HOLMES, J. H. (1973) "Population Concentration and Dispersion in Australian States: A Macrogeographic Study", *Australian Geographical Studies*, **11**:150–70.

JAMES, C. (1971) *Agricultural Policy in Wealthy Countries*, Angus and Robertson, Sydney.

JEFFERY, D., and WEBB, D. J. (1972) "Economic Fluctuations in the Australian Regional System", *Australian Geographical Studies*, **10**:141–60.

JOHNSTON, R. J. (1966) "Commercial Leadership in Australia", *Australian Geographer*, **10**:49–52.

—— (1967) "Population Growth and Urbanization in Australia, 1961–66", *Geography*, **52**:199–202.

JONES, M. A. (1972) *Housing and Poverty in Australia*, Melbourne University Press, Melbourne.

KAN, A., and RHODES, J. (1972) "British Regional Policy: Some Implications for Australia", *Australian Economic Papers*, **1**, 19:163–79.

KERR, A. (1970) "Urban Industrial Change in Australia, 1954 to 1966", *The Economic Record*, **46**:355–67.

LANSDOWN, R. B. (1966) "Some Financial Aspects of an Australian New Town", *Australian Planning Institute Journal*, **4**:174–80.

—— (1971) "Canberra: An Exemplar For Many Decentralized Australian Cities", paper presented to the 43rd ANZAAS Congress, Brisbane, May 1971.

LINGE, G. J. R., and RIMMER, P. J., eds. (1970) *Government Influence and the Location of Economic Activity*, Australian National University Press, Canberra.

LOGAN, M. I. (1966) "Capital City Manufacturing in Australia", *Economic Geography*, **42**:139–51.

—— and WILMOTH, D. (1974) "Australian Initiatives in Urban and Regional Development", IIASA, Vienna (mimeo).

LONSDALE, R. (1972) "Manufacturing Decentralization: The Discouraging

Record of Australia", *Land Economics*, **48,** 4: 321–8.

MELBOURNE AND METROPOLITAN BOARD OF WORKS (1971) *Planning Policies for the Melbourne Metropolitan Region,* The Board of Works, Melbourne.

NATIONAL CAPITAL DEVELOPMENT COMMISSION (1972) *Development of the New Towns of Canberra—A Case Study,* report prepared for the U.N. Conference on the Human Environment, Stockholm.

NEILSON, L. (1974) "The New Cities Programme", *Royal Australian Planning Institute Journal,* **12,** 1: 14–20.

NEUTZE, M. (1965) *Economic Policy and the Size of Cities,* Australian National University Press, Canberra.

—— (1971) "The Growth of Cities", in J. Wilkes, ed., *How Many Australians?,* Angus and Robertson, Sydney, 61–74.

—— (1973) *The Case for New Cities,* National Population Enquiry Commissioned Paper No. 11, Canberra.

NEW SOUTH WALES, STATE PLANNING AUTHORITY (1967) *Sydney Region Growth and Change: Prelude to a Plan,* GPS, Sydney.

—— DEVELOPMENT CORPORATION (1969) *Report on Selective Decentralization,* GPS, Sydney.

—— DEPARTMENT OF DECENTRALIZATION AND DEVELOPMENT (1970) *Report on Public Capital Costs Associated with Selective Decentralization,* GPS, Sydney.

PARKER, R. S., and TROY, P. N., eds. (1972) *The Politics of Urban Growth,* Australian National University Press, Canberra.

PATERSON, J. (1971) *A Study of the Comparative Costs of Providing Public Utilities and Services in Melbourne and Selected Victorian Centres,* Report to the Division of State Development, Victoria.

PAYNE, M., and MILLS, G. (1972) "The Case for New Cities in Australia", *Royal Australian Planning Institute Journal,* October 1972.

PERKINS, J. O. N. (1972) *Macro Economic Policy: A Comparative Study,* Allen and Unwin, London.

POWELL, T. (1974) "National Urban Strategy", *Royal Australian Planning Institute Journal,* **12,** 1: 8–10.

PRESTON, R., ed. (1969) *Contemporary Australia: Studies in History, Politics and Economics,* Duke University Press, Durham, N.C.

RIMMER, P. J. (1967) "The Search for Spatial Regularities in the Development of Australian Seaports", *Geog. Annalar,* **49B,** reprinted in B. S. Hoyle, ed. (1973) *Transportation and Development,* MacMillan, London, 63–86.

—— (1974) *Economics and New Towns,* Praeger, New York.

ROBINSON, A. J. (1963) "Regionalism and Urbanization in Australia: A Note on Locational Emphasis in the Australian Economy", *Economic Geography,* **39,** 2: 149–55.

—— (1972) "New Towns in Australia", unpublished manuscript, York University, Toronto.

—— (1973) "A Planned New Town: The Canberra Experience", *Land Economics*, **49**, 3: 361–4.

ROBINSON, K. W. (1962) "Processes and Patterns of Urbanization in Australia and New Zealand", *New Zealand Geographer*, **18**, 1, 32–49.

ROSE, A. J. (1966) "Dissent from Down Under: Metropolitan Primacy as the Normal State", *Pacific Viewpoint*, **7**: 1–27.

—— (1967) *Patterns of Cities*, Nelson, Melbourne.

—— (1971) "The Future Pattern of Cities", in G. J. R. Linge and P. J. Rimmer, eds., *Government Influence and the Location of Economic Activity*, 421–38.

—— (1972) "Urbanization in Australia", Paper submitted to the IGU Commission on Patterns of Urbanization, Montreal.

RYAN, B. (1969) "Metropolitan Growth", in R. Preston, ed., *Contemporary Australia*, Duke University Press, Durham, N.C., 196–225.

SCOTT, P. (1968) "Population and Land Use in Australia: An Analysis of Metropolitan Dominance", *Tijdschrift voor Economische en Sociale Geografie*, **59**: 237–44.

SEBEL, R. (1969) "Some Cost Factors in Decentralized Industries", *Australian Quarterly*, **41**: 52–62.

SHERIDAN, K. (1968) "An Estimate of Business Concentration in Australian Manufacturing Industries", *Economic Record*, **44**: 26–41.

SMAILES, P. R. (1969) "Some Aspects of the South Australian Urban System", *Australian Geographer*, **11**: 29–51.

—— (1971) "Potential Roles of Tertiary Industry in Future Extra-Metropolitan Development: The South Australian Case", *Proceedings of the Institute of Australian Geographers*, Ninth Meeting February, 1971.

SMITH, R. H. T. (1965) "The Functions of Australian Towns", *Tijdschrift voor Economische en Sociale Geografie*, **56**: 81–92.

STILWELL, F. J. B. (1972) "Metropolitan Primacy: Economics and Welfare", paper presented to the 44th ANZAAS Congress, Sydney, August 1972.

—— (1974) *Australian Urban and Regional Development*, Sydney.

—— and HARDWICK, J. M. (1973) *Regional Development in Australia*, University of Sydney, Planning Research Centre, Sydney (mimeo).

STRETTON, H. (1970) *Ideas for Australian Cities*, Orphan Books, Melbourne.

TROY, P. (1974) "The Role of the Land Commissions", *Royal Australian Planning Institute Journal*, **12**, 1: 10–13.

UREN, T. (1973) "Policy Statement by the Minister of Urban and Regional Development", Canberra, 27 February 1973 (mimeo).

VICTORIA, DEPARTMENT OF STATE DEVELOPMENT (1967) *Report to the Decentralization Advisory Committee on the Selection of Places Outside the Melagopolis of Melbourne for Accelerated Development*, Division of Industrial Development, Melbourne.

WILKES, J., ed. (1971) *How Many Australians?*, Australian Institute of Political

Science, Angus and Robertson, Sydney.

WINSTON, D. (1966) "The Urban Explosion: The Nature of the Australian Problem", in D. Winston *et al.*, eds., Australian Cities: Chaos or Planned Growth, Angus and Robertson, Melbourne, 3–33.

WOOLMINGTON, E. R. (1970), "Government Policy and Decentralization", in G. J. R. Linge and P. J. Rimmer, eds., *Government Influence and the Location of Economic Activity*, Canberra.

—— PIGRAM, J. J. J., and HOBBS, J. E. (1971) "Attitudes Towards Decentralization", paper presented to the 43rd ANZAAS Congress, Brisbane, May 1971.

E. URBAN CANADA

ACRES RESEARCH AND PLANNING (1969) *Mid-Canada Development Corridor: A Concept*, Acres Research, Toronto.

ATLANTIC PROVINCES ECONOMIC COUNCIL (1971) *Fifth Annual Review: The Atlantic Economy*, APEC, Halifax.

AXWORTHY, L., and GILLIES, J., eds. (1973) *The City: Canada's Prospects, Canada's Problems*, Butterworths, Toronto.

BARBER, G. (1972) "Growth Determinants in the Central Canada Urban System", in L. S. Bourne *et al.*, eds., *Urban Systems Development in Central Canada: Selected Papers*, 147–61.

BLUMENFELD, H. (1966) "The Role of the Federal Government in Urban Affairs", *Journal of Liberal Thought*, **2**, 2.

—— (1974) "The Effects of Public Policy on the Urban System", in L. S. Bourne *et al.*, eds., *Urban Futures for Central Canada: Perspectives on Forecasting Urban Growth and Form*, University of Toronto Press, Toronto, 194–208.

BOOTHROYD, P., and MARLYN, F. (1972) "National Urban Policy: A Phrase in Search of a Meaning", *Plan Canada*, **12**, 1:4–11.

BOURNE, L. S., and GAD, G. (1972) "Urbanization and Urban Growth in Ontario and Quebec: An Overview", in L. S. Bourne and R. D. MacKinnon, eds., *Urban Systems Development in Central Canada: Selected Papers*, 7–35.

—— and MACKINNON, R. D., eds. (1972) *Urban Systems Development in Central Canada: Selected Papers*, University of Toronto Press, Toronto.

—— —— and SIMMONS, J. W., eds. (1973) *The Form of Cities in Central Canada: Selected Papers*, University of Toronto Press, Toronto.

—— ——, SIEGEL, J., and SIMMONS, J. W., eds. (1974) *Urban Futures for Central Canada: Perspectives on Forecasting Urban Growth and Form*, University of Toronto Press, Toronto.

BREWIS, T. N. (1968) *Growth and the Canadian Economy*, McClelland and Stewart, Toronto.

—— (1969) *Regional Economic Policies in Canada*, MacMillan, Toronto.

—— (1970) "Regional Economic Disparities and Policies", in L. H. Officer and L. B. Smith, eds., *Canadian Economic Problems and Policies*, McGraw-Hill, Toronto, 335–51.

BUCKLEY, H., and TIHANYI, E. (1967) *Canadian Policies for Rural Adjustment*, Economic Council of Canada Special Study No. 7, Queen's Printer, Ottawa.

CAMERON, K. D., ed. (1972) "Special Issue: National Urban Policy", *Plan Canada*, **12**, 1.

CAVES, R. E., and REUBER, G. L. (1969) *Canadian Economic Policy and the Impact of International Monetary Flows*, University of Toronto Press, Toronto.

COMEAU, R. (1969) *Économique québécoise*, Les Presses de l'Université du Québec, Québec(ville).

CROWLEY, R. W. (1971) "Labour Force Growth and Specialization in Canadian Cities", *Working Paper, A.71.1*, Ministry of State for Urban Affairs, Ottawa.

DAVIES, I. (1973) "The Development of Canada's North", *Scottish Geographical Magazine*, **89**, 1:36–43.

DAVIES, J. B. (1972) "Behaviour of the Ontario–Quebec Urban System by Size Distribution", in L. S. Bourne and R. D. MacKinnon, eds., *Urban Systems Development in Central Canada: Selected Papers*, 35–51.

DENNIS, M., and FISH, S. (1972) *Programs in Search of a Policy: Low Income Housing in Canada*, Hakkert, Toronto.

DEPARTMENT OF FORESTRY AND RURAL DEVELOPMENT (1966) *Social and Economic Disadvantages in Canada: Some Graphic Indicators of Location and Degree*, Queen's Printer, Ottawa.

DEPARTMENT OF REGIONAL ECONOMIC EXPANSION (1973) *Report on Regional Development Incentives*, DREE, Ottawa.

DRUMMOND, I. M. (1972) *The Canadian Economy*, Irwin-Dorsey, Georgetown.

ECONOMIC COUNCIL OF CANADA (1964) *First Annual Review: Economic Goals for Canada to 1970*, Queen's Printer, Ottawa.

—— (1968) *Fifth Annual Review*, "The Problem of Poverty", Chap. 6, Queen's Printer, Ottawa.

—— (1971) *Eighth Annual Review. Design for Decision-Making*, Queen's Printer, Ottawa.

—— (1973) *Tenth Annual Review*, Queen's Printer, Ottawa.

ENGLISH, H. E., WILKINSON, B. W., and EASTMAN, H. C. (1972) *Canada in a Wider Economic Community*, University of Toronto Press, Toronto.

FELDMAN, L., and GOLDRICK, M. D., eds. (1969) *Politics and Government of Urban Canada*, Methuen, Toronto.

—— and ASSOCIATES (1971) *A Survey of Alternative Urban Policies*, Research Monograph No. 6, Central Mortgage and Housing Corporation, Ottawa.

FIRESTONE, O. J., ed. (1974) *Regional Economic Development*, University of Ottawa Press, Ottawa.

GERTLER, L. O., ed. (1968) *Planning the Canadian Environment*, Harvest House, Montreal.

—— (1972) *Regional Planning in Canada: A Planner's Testament*, Harvest House, Montreal.

GOVERNMENT OF ONTARIO (1970) *Design for Development: The Toronto-Centred Region*, Toronto, May 1970.

GREEN, A. G. (1971) *Regional Aspects of Canada's Economic Growth*, University of Toronto Press, Toronto.

HARTWICK, J. M., and CROWLEY, R. W. (1973) "Urban Economic Growth: The Canadian Case", *Working Paper A.73.5*, Ministry of State for Urban Affairs, Ottawa.

HELLYER, P., et al. (1969) *Report of the Federal Government Task Force on Housing and Urban Development*, Queen's Printer, Ottawa.

HIGGINS, B. (1972) "Growth Pole Policy in Canada", in N. Hansen, ed., *Growth Centres in Regional Economic Development*, Free Press, New York.

HODGE, G. (1971) "Comparisons of Urban Structure in Canada, the United States and Great Britain", *Geographical Analysis*, **3**, 1:83–90.

—— (1974) "The City in the Periphery", in L. S. Bourne et al., eds., *Urban Futures for Central Canada: Perspectives on Forecasting Urban Growth and Form*, 281–301.

HUGO-BRANT, M. (1972) *The History of City Planning: A Survey*, Harvest House, Montreal.

JACKSON, C. I. (1971) *The Spatial Dimensions of Environmental Management in Canada*, Geographical Paper No. 46, Information Canada, Ottawa.

JACKSON, J. N. (1974) "The Relevance to Canada of British Policies for Controlling Urban Growth", paper presented to a Conference on The Management of Land for Urban Development, Toronto, 5–6 April 1974.

KAPLAN, H. (1972) "Controlling Urban Growth", *Discussion Paper B.72.20*, Ministry of State for Urban Affairs, Ottawa.

KERR, D. (1968) "Metropolitan Dominance in Canada", in J. Warkentin, ed., *Canada: A Geographical Interpretation*, Methuen, Toronto, 551–5.

KING, L. J. (1966) "Cross-Sectional Analyses of Canadian Urban Dimensions, 1951 and 1961", *Canadian Geographer*, **10**, 4:205–24.

LANG, R. (1972) "Oh Canada, A National Urban Policy", *Plan Canada*, **12**, 1:15–32.

LITHWICK, N. H. and PAQUET, G. (1968) "Urban Growth and Regional Contagion", in *idem*, eds., *Urban Studies: A Canadian Perspective*, Methuen, Toronto, 18–29.

—— (1970) *Urban Canada: Problems and Prospects*, Report prepared for the Central Mortgage and Housing Corporation, Ottawa.

—— (1970) "The City: Problems and Policies", in L. H. Officer and L. B. Smith, eds., *Canadian Economic Problems and Policies*, McGraw-Hill, Toronto, 258–74.

—— (1972a) "Urban Policy-Making: Shortcomings in Political Technology", *Canadian Public Administration*, **15,** 4:571–84.

—— (1972b) "Towards a New Urban Politics", *Community Planning Review*, **22,** 3:3–8.

—— (1972c) "Policy Planning for Urban Affairs", in A. Powell, ed., *The City: Attacking Modern Myths*, McClelland and Stewart, Toronto, 200–9.

—— (1972d) "Political Innovation, a Case Study", *Plan Canada*, **12,** 1:45–56.

—— (1972e) "An Economic Interpretation of the Urban Crisis", *Journal of Canadian Studies*, **7,** 3:36–49.

MACNEILL, J. W. (1972) *Environmental Management*, Constitutional Study prepared for the Government of Canada, Information Canada, Ottawa.

MAJOR, T. S. (1972) "Feasibility Studies of Large Scale Systems Models", *Discussion Paper B.72.11*, Ministry of State for Urban Affairs, Ottawa.

MARSHALL, J. (1972) "The Urban Network", in L. Gentilcore, ed., *Ontario: Studies in Canadian Geography*, University of Toronto Press, Toronto, 64–82.

MATHIAS, P. (1971) *Forced Growth: Five Studies of Government Involvement in Canada*, James, Lewis and Samuel, Toronto.

MAXWELL, J. W. (1967) "The Functional Structure of Canadian Cities: A Classification of Cities", *Geographical Bulletin*, **9**:61–87.

MEEKISON, J. P., ed. (1971) *Canadian Federalism: Myth or Reality*, Second Edition, Methuen, Toronto.

MILES, S. (1972) "Developing a Canadian Urban Policy: Lessons from Abroad", *Plan Canada*, **12,** 1:88–106.

—— COHEN, S., and DE KONING, G. (1973) *Developing a Canadian Policy*, Intermet, Toronto.

OFFICER, L. H., and SMITH, L. B., eds. (1970) *Canadian Economic Problems and Policies*, McGraw-Hill, Toronto.

ONTARIO ECONOMIC COUNCIL (1972) *Ontario: Society in Transition*, The Council, Toronto.

PODOLUK, J. R. (1968) *Incomes of Canadians*, Census Monograph, Queen's Printer, Ottawa.

POLESE, M., and THIBODEAU, J. C. (1973) *Localization et développement régional*, INRS—Urbanization, Montréal.

PRICE, T., ed. (1971) *Regional Government in Ontario*, University of Windsor Press, Windsor.

RAY, D. M. (1969) "The Spatial Structure of Economic and Cultural Differences: A Factorial Ecology of Canada", *Papers of the Regional Science Association*, **23**:7–23.

—— (1971) *Dimensions of Canadian Regionalism*, Information Canada, Ottawa.

—— (1972a) "The Location of United States Manufacturing Subsidiaries in Canada", *Economic Geography*, **47**: 389–400.

—— (1972b) "The Allometry of Urban and Regional Growth", *Discussion Paper B.72.10*, Ministry of State for Urban Affairs, Ottawa.

—— (1974) "Canada: The Urban Challenge of Growth and Change", *Working Paper B.74.3*, Ministry of State for Urban Affairs, Ottawa.

—— and MURDIE, R. A. (1972) "Comparative Dimensions of Canadian and American Urban Systems", in B. J. L. Berry, ed., *City Classification Handbook*, Wiley, New York.

—— and VILLENEUVE, P. Y. (1964) "Population Growth and Distribution in Canada: Problems, Processes and Policies", paper delivered to a Conference on the Management of Land for Urban Development, Toronto, 8 April 1974.

RAYNAULD, A. (1971) *Croissance et structure économiques de la province de Québec*, Ministère de l'Industrie et du Commerce, Québec(ville).

—— MARTIN, F., and HIGGINS, B. (1970) *Les Orientations du développement économique régional dans la province du Québec*, Ministère de l'Expansion Économique Régional, Ottawa.

RITCHIE, R. S. (1971) *An Institute for Research on Public Policy*, Information Canada, Ottawa.

ROBINSON, I. (1963) *New Towns on Canada's Resource Frontier*, Department of Geography Research Paper 73, University of Chicago, Chicago.

ROTSTEIN, A., and LAX, G., eds. (1972) *Independence: The Canadian Challenge*, Committee for an Independent Canada, Toronto.

RUSSWURM, L. H. (1970) *Development of an Urban Corridor System: Toronto to Stratford Area 1941–66*, Government of Ontario, Toronto.

SAYEED, K. B. (1973) "Public Policy Analysis in Washington and Ottawa", *Policy Sciences*, **4**: 85–101.

SCIENCE COUNCIL OF CANADA (1971) *Cities for Tomorrow: Some Applications of Science and Technology to Urban Development*.

SHAPIRO, H. T. (1970) "Poverty—A Bourgeois Economist's View", in L. H. Officer and L. B. Smith, eds., *Canadian Economic Problems and Policies*, 223–41.

SIMMONS, J. W. (1970) "Inter-provincial Interaction Patterns", *Canadian Geographer*, **14**, 4: 372–6.

—— (1972) "Interaction Among the Cities in Ontario and Quebec", in L. S. Bourne and R. D. MacKinnon, eds., *Urban Systems Development in Central Canada: Selected Papers*, 198–219.

—— (1974) "The Canadian Urban System", unpublished manuscript, Department of Geography, University of Toronto, Toronto.

—— and SIMMONS, R. (1969; rev. 1974) *Urban Canada*, Copp Clark, Toronto.

—— and BOURNE, L. S. (1974) "Defining the Future Urban System", in L. S. Bourne *et al.*, eds., *Urban Futures for Central Canada: Perspectives on Forecasting Urban Growth and Form*, 25–34.

SPELT, J. (1955) *Urban Development in South-Central Ontario*, Van Gorcum, Assen, Holland.

STONE, L. O. (1967) *Urban Development in Canada*, 1961 Census Monograph, Dominion Bureau of Statistics, Ottawa.

SWAIN, H. (1972) "Research for the Urban Future", *Working Paper B.72.13*, Ministry of State for Urban Affairs, Ottawa.

SWAN, N. M. (1972) "Differences in the Response of the Demand for Labour to Changes in Output Among Canadian Regions", *Canadian Journal of Economics*, **5**: 373–86.

SYSTEMS RESEARCH GROUP (1970) *Urban Canada 2000*, Population Projections, SRG, Toronto.

THOMAN, R. S. (1971) *Design for Development in Ontario: The Initiation of a Regional Planning Program*, Allister Typesetting, Toronto.

TINDALL, C. R. (1973) "Regional Development in Ontario", *Canadian Public Administration*, **16**, 1: 110–22.

ULRICH, M. (1972) "Macro-Urban Program Impact Model: Use Possibilities", *Discussion Paper B.72.12*, Ministry of State for Urban Affairs, Ottawa.

U.S. ADVISORY COMMISSION ON INTERGOVERNMENTAL RELATIONS (1974) *A Look to the North: Canadian Regional Experiences*, U.S. Government Printing Office, Washington.

WADE, M., ed. (1960) *Canadian Dualism*, University of Toronto Press, Toronto.

—— (1969) *The International Megalopolis*, Eighth Annual Seminar on Canadian-American Relations, University of Toronto Press, Toronto.

WARKENTIN, J., ed. (1968) *Canada: A Geographical Interpretation*, Methuen, Toronto.

WHEBELL, C. F. J. (1969) "Corridors: A Theory of Urban Systems", *Annals, Association of American Geographers*, **59**: 1–26.

WOLFE, R. (1968) "Economic Development", in J. Warkentin, ed., *Canada: A Geographical Interpretation*, 187–227.

WONNACOTT, R. J., and WONNACOTT, P. (1967) *Free Trade Between the United States and Canada*, Harvard University Press, Cambridge, Mass.

YEATES, M. (1974) *The Windsor to Quebec Axis in a Post Industrial Age*, McGill-Queens University Press (forthcoming), Montreal and Kingston.

—— and LLOYD, P. E. (1970) *Impact of Industrial Incentives: Southern Georgian Bay Region, Ontario*, Geographical Paper No. 44, Department of Energy, Mines and Resources, Ottawa.

# Index